H.L.A. Hart

Key Contemporary Thinkers series includes:

Jeremy Ahearne, *Michel de Certeau*
Lee Braver, *Heidegger*
John Burgess, *Kripke*
Claire Colebrook, *Agamben*
Jean-Pierre Couture, *Sloterdijk*
Colin Davis, *Levinas*
Oliver Davis, *Jacques Rancière*
Reidar Andreas Due, *Deleuze*
Edward Fullbrook and Kate Fullbrook, *Simone de Beauvoir*
Nigel Gibson, *Fanon*
Graeme Gilloch, *Siegfried Kracauer*
Christina Howells, *Derrida*
Simon Jarvis, *Adorno*
Rachel Jones, *Irigaray*
Sarah Kay, *Žižek*
S. K. Keltner, *Kristeva*
Matthew H. Kramer, *H.L.A. Hart*
Moya Lloyd, *Judith Butler*
James McGilvray, *Chomsky, 2nd edn*
Lois McNay, *Foucault*
Marie-Eve Morin, *Jean-Luc Nancy*
Timothy Murphy, *Antonio Negri*
Ed Pluth, *Badiou*
John Preston, *Feyerabend*
Severin Schroeder, *Wittgenstein*
Susan Sellers, *Hélène Cixous*
Anthony Paul Smith, *Laruelle*
Dennis Smith, *Zygmunt Bauman*
James Smith, *Terry Eagleton*
James Williams, *Lyotard*
Christopher Zurn, *Axel Honneth*

H.L.A. Hart
The Nature of Law

Matthew H. Kramer

polity

Copyright © Matthew H. Kramer 2018

The right of Matthew H. Kramer to be identified as Author of this Work has been asserted in accordance with the UK Copyright, Designs and Patents Act 1988.

First published in 2018 by Polity Press

Polity Press
65 Bridge Street
Cambridge CB2 1UR, UK

Polity Press
101 Station Landing
Suite 300
Medford, MA 02155, USA

All rights reserved. Except for the quotation of short passages for the purpose of criticism and review, no part of this publication may be reproduced, stored in a retrieval system or transmitted, in any form or by any means, electronic, mechanical, photocopying, recording or otherwise, without the prior permission of the publisher.

ISBN-13: 978-1-5095-2072-5
ISBN-13: 978-1-5095-2073-2 (pb)

A catalogue record for this book is available from the British Library.

Library of Congress Cataloging-in-Publication Data

Names: Kramer, Matthew H., 1959- author.
Title: H.L.A. Hart : the nature of law / Matthew H. Kramer.
Description: Medford, MA : Polity, 2018. | Series: Key contemporary thinkers | Includes bibliographical references and index.
Identifiers: LCCN 2018012974 (print) | LCCN 2018026770 (ebook) | ISBN 9781509520763 (Epub) | ISBN 9781509520725 (hardback) | ISBN 9781509520732 (pbk.)
Subjects: LCSH: Hart, H. L. A. (Herbert Lionel Adolphus), 1907-1992. | Law–Philosophy. | Jurisprudence. | Law–Interpretation and construction. | Law–Methodology. | Law–Moral and ethical aspects.
Classification: LCC K231 (ebook) | LCC K231 .K73 2018 (print) | DDC 340/.1–dc23
LC record available at https://lccn.loc.gov/2018012974

Typeset in 10.5 on 12 pt Palatino
by Toppan Best-set Premedia Limited
Printed and bound in the UK by CPI Group (UK) Ltd, Croydon

The publisher has used its best endeavours to ensure that the URLs for external websites referred to in this book are correct and active at the time of going to press. However, the publisher has no responsibility for the websites and can make no guarantee that a site will remain live or that the content is or will remain appropriate.

Every effort has been made to trace all copyright holders, but if any have been inadvertently overlooked the publisher will be pleased to include any necessary credits in any subsequent reprint or edition.

For further information on Polity, visit our website: politybooks.com

Contents

Preface	*vii*

1	A Discourse on Method	1
	1 Posing the questions	2
	2 Elucidation of a concept	4
	3 A method of central instances	5
	4 A philosophical scope	8
	5 Variations across societies	11
	6 A descriptive-explanatory methodology	12
	7 A reductionist ambition?	23
	8 A naturalistic ambition?	28
2	Hart on Legal Powers and Law's Normativity	32
	1 The Austinian model of law	33
	2 Power-conferring laws	36
	3 Legislators bound	52
	4 Custom-derived laws	53
	5 Limits on sovereignty	56
3	The Components of Hart's Jurisprudential Theory	60
	1 The internal/external distinction	61
	2 The simulative point of view	65
	3 The blurring of distinctions between viewpoints	68
	4 Primary norms and secondary norms: the general distinction	70

	5 Primary norms and secondary norms: Hart's thought-experiment	74
	6 The Rule of Recognition: to whom is it addressed?	78
	7 The Rule of Recognition: power-conferring and duty-imposing	81
	8 The unity of the Rule of Recognition: disagreements over details	84
	9 The unity of the Rule of Recognition: multiple criteria	85
	10 The unity of the Rule of Recognition: institutional hierarchies	88
	11 The ultimacy of the Rule of Recognition	91
	12 The Rule of Recognition: the foundational level and the codified level	92
	13 The intertwining of the Rule of Recognition and other secondary norms	97
	14 Interdependent but distinct: a riposte to Shapiro	99
	15 Interdependent but distinct: a riposte to Waldron	101
	16 Interdependent but distinct: a riposte to MacCormick	103
	17 The problem of circularity	105
	18 Necessary and sufficient conditions	107
4	Hart on Legal Interpretation and Legal Reasoning	110
	1 Crucial distinctions	112
	2 Hart on formalism and rule-skepticism	133
5	Law and Morality	148
	1 Separability theses	149
	2 Hart on the minimum content of natural law	164
	3 Inclusive versus Exclusive Positivism	173
	4 Hart as an expressivist?	180
6	Conclusion	204
Notes		207
References		215
Index		222

Preface

A few points of terminology should be highlighted here. First, whereas H.L.A. Hart persistently used the terms "rule" and "rules" in his writings, I much more often instead use the terms "norm" and "norms." My reason for doing so is that Hart's employment of the former terms led Ronald Dworkin (in his early critiques of legal positivism) to infer mistakenly that Hart was differentiating rules from principles. Dworkin concluded that the jurisprudential model expounded in *The Concept of Law* would not encompass principles. To avoid the confusion engendered by Dworkin on that point, I will usually employ the word "norm" to denote a standard that is endowed with any degree of abstraction or specificity and with any degree of vagueness or precision. Still, I will sometimes use the word "rule" (or "rules") as a synonym for "norm" (or "norms").

Second, some of the occasions on which I do use the term "rule" in that manner are any junctures at which I am discussing Hart's notion of the rule of recognition. Because the phrase "rule of recognition" is such a specialized and well-known item of Hart's parlance, any substitution of "norm" for "rule" in that bit of his wording would be unhelpful. However, in order to signal the specialized character of his phrase, I have departed from Hart by using uppercase letters; in this book, as in quite a few of my other writings, I employ the label "Rule of Recognition" (rather than "rule of recognition") to designate the fundamental standards for identifying the legal norms in any jurisdiction.

Third, in my penultimate chapter I also use upper-case letters to distinguish between the Rule of Law and the rule of law.[1] Whereas the Rule of Law is a moral ideal that comprises the formal and procedural aspects of a liberal-democratic system of governance, the rule of law obtains whenever a legal system of governance exists (regardless of whether the system is liberal-democratic or authoritarian). Unlike the Rule of Law, the rule of law is not an inherently moral ideal.

Fourth, I use the terms "legitimate" and "permissible" – and "legitimacy" and "permissibility" – interchangeably throughout the book. Hence, a course of conduct CC is morally legitimate if and only if it is not in contravention of any moral duties. An ascription of moral legitimacy to CC does not per se indicate whether CC is also morally obligatory, nor does it per se indicate whether the adoption of CC will impose some moral obligations on anyone. All that can be inferred from such an ascription is that CC is morally not wrong.

Fifth, I employ the word "citizens" in this book to denote private individuals (including public officials in their capacities as private individuals). That word is not limited to the individuals in any jurisdiction who are full members of the polity there. It extends also to residents who are not such members. The operative contrast is not between citizens and other residents, but is instead between citizens and people who are acting in their capacities as officials.

Sixth, I use the following terms and phrases interchangeably: "viewpoint," "point of view," "perspective," "standpoint," "vantage point."

Seventh, I use the term "valid" (or "validity" or "validly") in two main ways. When I refer to the validity of norms as laws in a jurisdiction, I am following Hart in talking about the inclusion of those norms in the array of laws comprised by a system of governance. When I refer to the validity of an argument or an inference, I am talking about validity in the ordinary logical sense. That is, an argument is valid if and only if it cannot be the case that all the premises of the argument are true and its conclusion is false.

Any citations consisting solely of page numbers are citations to the second edition (1994) of *The Concept of Law*. Every citation to some other work – whether the work is by Hart or by anyone else – includes the year of publication. Each such citation also includes

---

[1] As is evident, the word "rule" in the phrase "the rule of law" is not being used as a synonym of "norm."

the author's surname if the identity of the author has not been clearly specified in the text.

I thank George Owers at Polity Press for commissioning this book in 2016, and I thank Julia Davies and Rachel Moore and Sarah Dancy at Polity Press for helping to steer the book through the process of production. I am also grateful to the two anonymous readers of the book proposal which I submitted in response to the commissioning invitation. Their comments were very helpful. Extremely helpful as well was an anonymous assessment of the antepenultimate version of the book. Equally valuable have been a number of conversations with one of my current PhD students, Jyr-Jong Lin. My reflections on the import of power-conferring norms and on Hart's intermittent neglect of that import have been greatly sharpened by my discussions with Jyr-Jong, whose own approach to such matters is interestingly different from mine.

Cambridge, England
November 2017

1
A Discourse on Method

A full exposition of the philosophy of H.L.A. Hart would cover five main areas: (1) legal positivism and the general nature of law; (2) causation in the law; (3) responsibility and punishment; (4) the nature of rights; and (5) liberal political philosophy and civil liberties. His writings in each of those categories will continue to influence philosophical debates for many generations to come, but there is little doubt that the magnitude of his achievement is greatest in the first category. *The Concept of Law* will continue to be read – in its original language or in any of the myriad of languages into which it has been translated – until human beings altogether cease to be interested in the philosophy of law. It has rightly attained a place among the foremost classics in that area of philosophy. Hence, given that the limit on the length of each volume in the Key Contemporary Thinkers series will require selectivity in my engagement with Hart's *oeuvre*, the appropriate focus for that engagement is quite straightforward. Although the present book will occasionally refer to Hart's work on some of the other topics listed above, it will concentrate chiefly on *The Concept of Law* and on several of his main essays that likewise explore the fundaments of legal systems.

My principal aim in this book is to expound Hart's arguments and to assess their philosophical merits. Matters of intellectual history will enter into this volume only insofar as they help to shed light on the substance or quality of Hart's lines of reasoning. This rigorously philosophical orientation tallies nicely with his own objectives in writing *The Concept of Law*. As Hart stated at the outset of his classic text (vii), he sought to contribute to the philosophy of law rather than to the history of ideas.

Before we examine Hart's philosophical thinking, however, we should glance at his life.[1] Herbert Lionel Adolphus Hart was born into a Jewish family in Yorkshire, England in 1907. He pursued his undergraduate education at New College, Oxford, where he obtained a degree in 1929 in Literae Humaniores (a mixture of classical languages, ancient history, and philosophy). After completing his undergraduate endeavors, he undertook private studies in law that led to his qualifying as a barrister in the English legal profession. Having practiced law in London for several years during the 1930s, he worked for the British intelligence service MI5 during World War II. When the war ended, Hart returned to Oxford to take up a fellowship in philosophy at New College. In 1952, he was elected to Oxford's Professorship of Jurisprudence and to a concomitant fellowship of University College. Through his publications and his training of students, he made Oxford into the world's pre-eminent center of jurisprudential scholarship. A few years after stepping down from the Professorship of Jurisprudence in 1968, he became Principal of Brasenose College, Oxford. During the closing years of his career as an active scholar, he devoted much of his time to editing and interpreting the works of Jeremy Bentham. Hart died at the age of 85 in 1992. Many former students of his, including Joseph Raz, John Finnis, Neil MacCormick, Herbert Morris, and Wilfrid Waluchow, have been among the most prominent legal philosophers of the next generation.

1 Posing the questions

The opening chapter of *The Concept of Law* is a discourse on method. That is, Hart there broached the questions which he would address and the general approach which he would adopt for coming up with answers to those questions. His overarching concern was to delineate the general characteristics of law or of legal systems. However, instead of directly tackling that concern as a single question – the question "What is law?" – he differentiated among three main avenues of investigation that could together yield an answer to the overarching inquiry.

First, Hart proposed to ferret out the similarities and dissimilarities between the mandates introduced by a legal system and the orders uttered by a gunman. To what extent are the operations of a legal system analogous to the issuance of dictates that are backed by threats of force? In other words, to what extent are the multifarious legal relations in any society analogous to an array of starkly coercive relations? Hart addressed this question predominantly in the first half of his book, though naturally he drew upon his responses to it – implicitly or explicitly – throughout the rest of the volume.

Second, Hart sought to pin down the differences and affinities between legal requirements and moral requirements. Law shares with morality a repertoire of key notions. Both in legal systems and in the domain of morality, we encounter duties and rights and liberties and powers and immunities and so forth. Both legal norms and moral norms are authoritative standards by reference to which the normative import of anyone's conduct can be gauged. Are legal obligations, then, a subset of moral obligations? Is there always a moral obligation to comply with legal requirements? These and other questions pertaining to the relationships between law and morality were addressed by Hart primarily in the eighth and ninth chapters of *The Concept of Law* (and in some of his concomitant essays), but he touched upon them in virtually every other chapter as well.

Third, Hart endeavored to explain what norms are, as he pondered the extent to which any legal system operates as a system of norms. When we ask what norms are, we are asking about the difference that is made by the presence of any norms. What is the difference between behavioral regularities that occur through the guiding sway of some norms and behavioral regularities that are not similarly oriented toward any such guiding sway? What is the difference between an adjudicative or administrative decision that implements some pre-existent norm(s) and an adjudicative or administrative decision that is not similarly an application of any such norm(s)? To what extent do the decisions by adjudicators and administrators in a legal system give effect to laws that prescribe determinately correct outcomes, and to what extent do those decisions amplify or modify the existing law through discretionary choices? Hart came to grips with these questions in the early chapters of *The Concept of Law* and in the pivotal seventh chapter. Given his commitment to the proposition that legal systems are systems of norms, and given the centrality of that proposition in his efforts to differentiate his own theorizing from that of his great legal-positivist predecessors Jeremy Bentham and John Austin, the success of his jurisprudential project hinged in no small part on the adequacy of his answers to these questions.

2 Elucidation of a concept

Together, the three foregoing lines of enquiry can lead to a distillation of the fundamental properties of legal systems. In setting out to pursue those lines of enquiry, Hart aspired to elucidate the prevailing concept of law. Such a characterization of his project is easily misunderstood, however. As will be emphasized shortly, he was not engaging in a lexicographical enterprise whereby he would try to formulate necessary and sufficient conditions for the applicability of the term "law" or of the phrase "legal system." On the contrary, he repeatedly indicated that he regarded any such definitional endeavor as futile and misguided. Thus, although concepts undoubtedly correspond to general terms that are associated with them, the concept of law which Hart sought to elucidate is not a matter of linguistic usage. Rather, it is a way of understanding or apprehending some phenomenon. It is an understanding of law (or of legal systems) that informs everyday discourse and reflections.

Hart sketched that understanding of legal systems in some very early pages of *The Concept of Law* that are frequently overlooked or forgotten. Near the outset of his introductory chapter, he attributed to "[m]ost educated people" – or to "[a]ny educated man" – a general awareness of the structures of legal systems and a general familiarity with various types and instances of the laws that emanate from those systems (2–3). Such awareness and familiarity are components of the common-sense knowledge acquired by any reasonably well-educated person as a result of growing up in a society with a functional system of governance. That common-sense understanding is what Hart ventured to illuminate through his philosophical ruminations.

When Hart maintained that he was endeavoring to elucidate that everyday understanding of law – the concept of law – he meant that he was clarifying and refining it by expounding its presuppositions and entailments. In other words, he was attempting to show both what is taken for granted by that understanding and what follows from it. With his exposition of the nature of law, he was of course trying to shed light on an array of major institutions that profoundly affect the lives of people wherever those institutions operate, but he was also trying to acquaint his readers better with themselves. By gaining a more sophisticated comprehension of the workings of legal systems, Hart's readers can likewise gain a more sophisticated grasp of their own outlooks and assumptions.

Hence, the title of Hart's classic text denotes both the starting point and the destination of his enquiry. Hart embarked on his jurisprudential reflections by adumbrating a simple understanding of law that is serviceable for nearly all ordinary purposes. He then parlayed that elementary understanding into a philosophically rigorous theory, by elaborating its underpinnings and corollaries. Having begun with a relatively superficial concept of law, he finished with a greatly deepened concept.

What should be noted here is that the quotidian understanding of legal institutions that serves as the point of departure in *The Concept of Law* is indispensable for the very intelligibility of the book's theorizing. Hart relied throughout on the familiarity of his readers with the notions which he needed to invoke in order to develop a philosophical account of law. Had he and his readers not already been possessed of a pre-theoretical comprehension of law, he could not have arrived at a refined theoretical comprehension – because the transition from the former to the latter requires the building blocks which the former provides. Neither a philosophical theory nor any other theory can arise from nowhere; some propositions have to be treated as givens if a theory is to have any basis for its conclusions and any material for reaching those conclusions. In *The Concept of Law*, the paramount givens are the common-sense items of knowledge which Hart imputed to most educated people near the beginning of his book.

3 A method of central instances

Having framed the questions which he would tackle, and having recounted the elementary understanding of legal systems that would be his point of departure, Hart concluded the opening chapter of *The Concept of Law* by mulling over the method through which he would answer those questions. As has already been observed, he firmly eschewed any aspiration to supply a definition of the term "law" or of the phrase "legal system." As he wrote, "it seems clear, when we recall the character of the three main issues which we have identified as underlying the recurrent question 'What is law?', that nothing concise enough to be recognized as a definition could provide a satisfactory answer to it" (16). Believing that a definitional approach would consist in distilling the individually necessary and jointly sufficient conditions for the applicability of the term "law" or of the phrase "legal system," Hart was concerned that any such approach would be fruitless and inordinately rigid. It would oblige him to resolve certain matters straightaway – matters relating to marginal or borderline types of legal systems – which he wished to defer to the end of his investigation. Had he shaped the key elements of his theory to take account of those marginal matters *ab initio*, he would have been allowing the tail to wag the dog. He would have been skewing the central portions of his theory by adjusting their contours to fit the peripheral portions. Or so Hart contended, as he remarked that peripheral instances of legal systems would be "only a secondary concern of the book. For its purpose is not to provide a definition of law, in the sense of a rule by reference to which the correctness of the use of the word can be tested."[2]

This relegation of the borderline types of legal systems to the end of Hart's enquiry is indicative of the method at the heart of the enquiry. Hart embraced that method through his rejection of the cardinal assumption that underlies a definitional approach: namely, the assumption that the sundry phenomena covered by the concept of law are related to one another through their sharing of some distinctive set of properties. Hart did not deny that the phenomena grouped together by some other concept could be related to one another in such a fashion, but he maintained that the concept of law is different. He submitted that, when we contemplate the multifarious arrangements or institutions to which the concept of a legal system can correctly be applied, we will not find any set of distinctive characteristics common to every one of them.[3] Instead of searching quixotically for such a set, Hart trained his focus on central or standard instances of legal systems. With the aim of developing a jurisprudential theory that would encompass all of those central instances by specifying the key features which they share, he would then be in a position to judge whether the theory also encompasses any number of marginal instances of legal systems.

Central or standard instances of legal systems are central in two closely connected ways. First, the classification of any such instance as a legal system is clear-cut. Each such instance is a paradigm, in that its status as a legal system would be unproblematically recognized by anyone who can competently differentiate between things that are legal systems and things that are not. In this first sense, then, the centrality of an instance of a legal system resides in the straightforwardness of its status as such.

Second, central or standard instances of legal systems are central in that any marginal instances of such systems are comprehended under the concept of law (or the concept of a legal system) by virtue of their relations to the central or standard instances. Hart adverted to a number of different types of relations that can obtain between central and peripheral instances of various phenomena, but he contended that the most important such relations for the concept of law are resemblances of function and content. He affirmed that marginal instances of legal systems – for example, international law and the rudimentary systems of governance in very small and simple societies – are included within the scope of the concept of law because their functions and contents resemble those of the national legal systems which are straightforwardly within that scope. In Hart's view, resemblances of function and content are the cement that holds together the extension of the concept of law as they compensate for the absence of any distinctive set of properties that could correctly be ascribed to absolutely everything comprised by that extension.[4] Because the resemblances are to the central or standard instances of legal systems, those instances are collectively the pivot on which the complex unity of the concept of law depends.

Until the final chapter of *The Concept of Law*, Hart concentrated on the features of the central instances of legal systems. Until that closing chapter, he touched only occasionally upon the marginal instances of such systems. As has already been suggested, he shaped the main components of his theory to fit the central instances of legal systems without trying to ensure (or deny) that those components would also fit the marginal instances. Thus, when he presented the fundamental tenets of his theory, he did so with reference to paradigmatic legal systems rather than with reference to all legal systems. Readers who keep this point in mind can thereby avoid confusion at certain junctures as they peruse Hart's text. Most notably, this point should be kept in mind by anyone when reading the sixth chapter of that text. There, as we shall see later, Hart formulated "two minimum conditions necessary and sufficient for the existence of a legal system" (116). Rather perplexingly, the quoted wording appears to smack of the definitional approach which Hart disparaged in his opening chapter and in subsequent portions of his book. However, if we recognize that he was specifying necessary and sufficient conditions for the existence of a central or standard instance of a legal system – rather than for the existence of absolutely anything that would count as a legal system – we can grasp that the quoted wording is fully reconcilable with his shunning of a definitional approach. Even where Hart neglected to make explicit his employment of a central-instance method, that method suffuses *The Concept of Law*.

4 A philosophical scope

Although Hart put together the constituents of his jurisprudential theory to fit the central instances of legal systems (while only later determining whether those constituents also encompass the marginal instances), his theory is in another respect sweepingly broad. It comprehends all central instances of legal systems rather than only the legal system of this or that particular jurisdiction, and indeed it comprehends all central instances of legal systems that could credibly exist rather than only those that do exist. It is a philosophical theory that covers not only all actualities but also all credible possibilities.

By devising a theory that transcends particular jurisdictions, Hart pursued a project that differed markedly from the theorizing which he associated with his nemesis Ronald Dworkin. Hart took Dworkin to be propounding a model of law (or a model of adjudication) focused solely on the American and English legal systems. Whatever may be the merits of Dworkin's model as an account of Anglo-American law and adjudication, Hart contended, it is jurisdiction-specific rather than jurisdiction-transcendent. Hart quoted Dworkin's assertion that a theory of law should be "addressed to a particular legal culture" (Dworkin 1986, 102, quoted in Hart 1994, 240). Such a theory is "interpretive of a particular stage of a historically developing practice" (Dworkin 1986, 102). Hart pointedly dissociated himself from the parochialism of Dworkin's jurisprudential approach, as he emphasized that his own theorizing was "not tied to any particular legal system or legal culture" (239).

In addition to transcending the boundaries among particular jurisdictions, Hart's exposition of the nature of law transcends the divide between the actual and the potential. With his delineation of the necessary and sufficient conditions for the existence of any central or standard instance of a legal system, Hart was not developing a theory that might somehow be falsified by the emergence of a new paradigmatic legal system in the future. If any system of governance SG arises without some feature identified by Hart as a necessary condition for the existence of a central instance of a legal system, and if Hart's theory is correct, then the conclusion follows that SG is not such an instance (though of course it might be a marginal instance). His account of law is insusceptible in this manner to empirical falsification, precisely because the properties encapsulated by that account are essential features in any central instances of legal systems that might exist henceforward as well as in any central instances that have existed heretofore. Hart propounded a philosophical theory rather than a social-scientific or historical theory.

To be sure, the distinction between philosophical enquiries and social-scientific enquiries is not always clear-cut. As John Gardner has warrantedly opined, the explorations of social institutions undertaken by philosophers are not radically different from the most abstract ruminations undertaken by sociologists such as Max Weber and Emile Durkheim (2012, 277–9). Still, although the division between social philosophy and social science is blurred at its edges, there remains on the whole a pregnant difference between the empirical generalizations of social-scientific investigation and the conceptual theses of philosophical contemplation and analysis. At a high level of abstraction, those latter theses delimit the boundaries for the classification of any empirical findings. Whereas empirical generalizations are always susceptible to falsification or circumscription by new findings that reveal those generalizations to be untenable or excessively sweeping, the conceptual theses propounded by philosophers are not similarly susceptible to empirical falsification or circumscription – though of course they are susceptible to falsification or circumscription by philosophical reasoning which exposes some missteps or other inadequacies in the arguments that undergird those theses. This insusceptibility to empirical falsification stems from the fact that a philosophical explication of some phenomenon specifies the conditions on the basis of which anything either does count or does not count as an instance of that phenomenon. If some new findings are not in accordance with those conditions, then *ipso facto* the findings have not unearthed any instances of the phenomenon in question and have thus not supplied any grounds for concluding that the philosophical explication of that phenomenon is fallacious or inordinately broad. (A caveat should be entered here. Philosophers do sometimes successfully argue against the theories of their opponents by adverting to empirical entities or occurrences that are at odds with those theories. However, such rebuttals would be just as effective if the entities or occurrences adduced against the impugned theories were merely thought-experiments rather than things that have emerged in the actual world. After all, the point of any such rebuttal is to establish that a targeted theory has overlooked or mishandled some credible possibility; quite irrelevant for that purpose is the question whether the credible possibility has materialized as an actuality in the world or not. Hence, notwithstanding that one's invocation of some empirical entity or occurrence in one's challenge to a philosophical theory may superficially appear to be an empirical refutation of the theory, it is in fact – if successful – a refutation through philosophical reasoning.)

Like Hart's central-instance method, the philosophical character of his theorizing should be kept persistently in mind by readers of *The Concept of Law*. During the several decades since the book was first published, quite a few readers have mistakenly presumed that Hart therein embarked upon an anthropological enquiry into the origins of legal systems. His fairly frequent comments about transitions from pre-legal societies to legal systems of governance have fostered this confusion about the orientation of his jurisprudential project. As we shall see later, his references to such transitions are especially misleading in the fifth chapter of his text. There Hart sought to illuminate the nature and significance of the legal norms which he (somewhat unhelpfully) designated as "secondary." For that purpose, as we shall see, he contrasted a situation marked by the absence of secondary laws and a situation marked by the presence of such laws. His drawing of that contrast has quite often been perceived as an excursion into anthropological speculation whereby he was advancing a hypothesis about the ways in which legal systems of governance have evolved from pre-legal beginnings. Were his critics correct in perceiving his project as anthropological, they would also be correct in condemning that project as dubiously conjectural – since Hart did not undertake any empirical studies that might substantiate the hypothesis just mentioned. In fact, however, the discussion of secondary legal norms in *The Concept of Law* is not an instance of anthropology or of any other social-scientific theorizing. Instead, Hart engaged there in a philosophical endeavor to highlight and elucidate the important functions performed by those secondary norms. He did so by prescinding from all the effects of secondary norms and by then pondering how the patterns of intercourse among human beings would falter without those effects. His prescinding from those effects was an abstract thought-experiment, rather than a depiction of a society that ever has existed or ever could exist. By imagining the absence of secondary norms, Hart rightly presumed, we can vividly grasp the far-reaching import of such norms in every credibly possible society. He undertook a philosophical quest for clarification, rather than an anthropological quest for origins or causes. We shall return to this point in Chapter 3.

5   Variations across societies

Although Hart strove to craft a theory that would embrace all central instances of legal systems (both the central instances that actually exist and those that could ever credibly exist), one conspicuous feature of his theorizing is an emphasis on the variations among legal systems across jurisdictions. That emphasis was perhaps most prominent in his legal-positivist insistence on the contingency of any substantive connections between law and morality. As will be explored in my penultimate chapter, Hart ventured to confute a multiplicity of claims by natural-law theorists about ostensibly necessary ties between law and morality. In so doing, he repeatedly drew attention to the divergences among legal systems in their moral worthiness or unworthiness – and in the degree to which moral considerations figure as bases for legal judgments and as factors that motivate officials and citizens to abide by legal norms. When legal positivists such as Hart affirm the separability of law and morality, they are affirming that the moral bearings of systems of law are variable in these sundry respects.

Another aspect (a partly related aspect) of Hart's emphasis on the diversity of the central instances of legal systems will become apparent in Chapter 4. Important though his reflections on legal reasoning and interpretation are, Hart did not provide any detailed guidance on how legal reasoning does proceed or on how it should proceed. Yet he did not thereby fail to accomplish something which he set out to achieve. On the contrary, his disinclination to furnish such detailed guidance was largely due to his recognition that the techniques of legal reasoning and interpretation vary significantly across jurisdictions. Notwithstanding some fundamental and crucial similarities among the techniques that prevail in different societies, their specifics often diverge markedly from one society to another. Hart was attuned to such divergences and was thus extremely doubtful that a jurisdiction-transcendent account of the nature of law can usefully supply a template of the ways in which laws are construed and applied by legal officials.[5] Largely because he distanced himself from Dworkin by holding that a theory of the nature of law can and should be jurisdiction-transcendent, he was loath to join Dworkin in unfolding an elaborate model of adjudication which might accurately encapsulate the practices in some jurisdictions but which would not capture well at all the practices in other jurisdictions.

Hart also accentuated the obvious variability of the contents of laws across societies. To be sure, as my penultimate chapter will recount, Hart in his meditations on the "minimum content of natural law" did maintain that some elementary prohibitions on very serious misconduct have to be included among the laws in every system of governance that is to endure for any extended period of time. However, as we shall behold, he left ample room for differences of substance across societies even in relation to the basic prohibitions that are highlighted by his minimum-content-of-natural-law argument. (Some of those differences of substance are morally potent.) *A fortiori*, he left ample room for differences of substance across societies in relation to countless laws other than those prohibitions. Indeed, the overwhelming likelihood that such differences will obtain is a corollary of the insistence by legal positivists that laws in any society exist as such only through the law-establishing activities of human beings. Because the activities that give rise to laws are themselves so heterogeneous across jurisdictions, the contents of the laws that eventuate from those activities are likewise highly variable from one jurisdiction to the next.

In sum, while Hart sought to limn the fundamental structures and procedures of any central instances of legal systems, he simultaneously laid stress on a welter of far-reaching dissimilarities among such systems. Indeed, the very features which he perspicaciously singled out as common to all central instances of legal systems are promotive of those dissimilarities, for the basic structures and procedures of legal systems can be instantiated in multitudinously diverse ways. The substance which fills their forms is inevitably shaped by the contingencies of history and geography and culture. Hart was not only cognizant of the diversity bred by those contingencies, but was furthermore insistent on it as he highlighted the dispositiveness of human actions and decisions and attitudes in determining what counts as the law in any particular society.

6 A descriptive-explanatory methodology

A key to understanding Hart's theory of law is to recognize that his objectives in designing the theory were descriptive-explanatory rather than moral. Unlike Dworkin, Hart did not set out to vindicate legal institutions morally by ascribing to them some especially worthy point or purpose which they subserve. He of course did not deny that legal institutions can perform morally worthy and vital roles, but his aim was to shed light on the workings and contours of those institutions rather than to justify them morally. Among the many junctures at which Hart articulated that aim clearly is the end of his opening chapter in *The Concept of Law*, where he stated that he was endeavoring to "advance legal theory by providing an improved analysis of the distinctive structure of a municipal legal system and a better understanding of the resemblances and differences between law, coercion, and morality, as types of social phenomena" (17). He echoed that sentiment throughout the text, as when he declared that he was concentrating on certain phenomena in his theory "because of their explanatory power in elucidating the concepts that constitute the framework of legal thought" (81). Similar pronouncements abound in *The Concept of Law*, not least in the book's Postscript where Hart sustainedly retorted to Dworkin. There Hart affirmed that he sought "to give an explanatory and clarifying account of law as a complex social and political institution" (239). He pointedly added: "My account is *descriptive* in that it is morally neutral and has no justificatory aims: it does not seek to justify or commend on moral or other grounds the forms and structures which appear in my general account of law, though a clear understanding of these is, I think, an important preliminary to any useful moral criticism of law" (240, emphasis in original). Thus, Hart parted ways with Dworkin not only on the matter of the suitable scope of jurisprudential theorizing, but also on the question whether such theorizing is endowed with a moral mission or not.

6.1 *Theoretical-explanatory virtues*

For an account of law that is directed at elucidation and explanation rather than at commendation or censure, the strengths and shortcomings of the account are to be gauged by reference to theoretical-explanatory values rather than by reference to moral values. Among the main theoretical-explanatory virtues for which philosophers strive are clarity, precision, parsimony, adequacy, consilience, breadth, and depth. (Parsimony consists in the avoidance of superfluous hypotheses. Adequacy consists in covering all or nearly all the phenomena which a theory aspires to explain, instead of omitting or distorting substantial swaths of those phenomena. Consilience consists in the reinforcement of one's conclusions through one's reaching them from a number of different angles or via a number of different methods.)

Hart commended each of these theoretical-explanatory virtues, and he essayed to achieve them in his own work. For example, he famously wrote that the American jurist Oliver Wendell Holmes "was sometimes clearly wrong; but ... when this was so he was always wrong clearly. This surely is a sovereign virtue in jurisprudence." Hart continued: "Clarity I know is said not to be enough; this may be true, but there are still questions in jurisprudence where the issues are confused because they are discussed in a style which Holmes would have spurned for its obscurity" (1983, 49). In light of his high esteem for the clarity of Holmes's prose and analyses, it is not surprising that Hart strove for clarity in his own philosophizing. Throughout *The Concept of Law*, Hart characterized his project as an effort to elucidate the properties of legal systems and the concepts of legal thought. At the outset of his book, he indicated the obscurity which he was trying to overcome. That obscurity had arisen from the exaggeratedness and tendentiousness of the theses propounded by many of his predecessors in legal philosophy, including Holmes. As Hart commented on the endeavors of those predecessors, which were at once illuminating and obfuscatory: "They throw a light which makes us see much in law that lay hidden; but the light is so bright that it blinds us to the remainder and so leaves us still without a clear view of the whole" (2).

Hart similarly pursued the other cardinal theoretical-explanatory virtues in his ruminations on law. Let us consider one further instance: the virtue of adequacy. As will be seen in my next chapter, Hart forcefully complained that John Austin's model of law omits or grossly distorts most of the phenomena which any adequate account of law would encompass accurately in its explanatory schema. Austin's theory altogether disregards power-conferring laws, for example, and it egregiously distorts the bearings of sundry other phenomena such as custom-derived laws. Because of the numerous lacunae and misrepresentations in Austin's theory, its attempt to expound the fundaments of legal systems with "the simple idea[s] of orders, habits, and obedience, cannot be adequate for the analysis of law" (77). Hart allowed that Austin's writings generally partake of the virtue of clarity to a high degree, but he persuasively contended that they fall woefully short in the extent to which they partake of some of the other theoretical-explanatory virtues such as adequacy.

6.2 Centrality and morality

Dworkin has of course not been the only philosopher to assail Hart's methodological austerity. An equally prominent critic of Hart's methodology is John Finnis – one of Hart's erstwhile students – who has addressed this matter in the opening chapter of his book *Natural Law and Natural Rights* (1980). Finnis there applauds Hart for adopting a central-instance approach in his philosophizing about legal institutions, and further applauds him for differentiating between the internal perspective of any participants in those institutions and the external perspective of any observers thereof. Finnis submits that Hart was quite right to hold that the internal viewpoint of participants is pivotal for the very existence of any system of law.

Having extolled Hart for coming up with the insights just mentioned, Finnis then reproaches him for not taking those insights far enough. Specifically, Finnis chides Hart for not applying the central-instance method in his exposition of the internal point of view. Finnis maintains that Hart should have distinguished between central instances and marginal or deviant instances of the internal perspective, and he declares that the relevant distinction is to be drawn along moral lines (1980, 11–16; 2013, 234–5). That is, any central instance of the internal viewpoint adopted by legal officials is the perspective of an official who acts on the basis of morally worthy considerations – with a concern for the common good – in the application of legal norms and in the operation of legal institutions. A deviant instance of the internal point of view is the perspective of an official who acts on the basis of self-interested considerations or iniquitous considerations; such an official either is utterly unconcerned with the common good or is guided by a hideously mistaken understanding of it. If the prevailing legal-governmental institutions in some jurisdiction are run by officials whose viewpoints as officials are predominantly deviant in these ways, then those institutions are a marginal or deviant instance of a legal system. Or so Finnis contends, as he upbraids Hart for declining to embrace a morally laden methodology that would classify legal systems (as central instances or marginal instances) on moral grounds.

I have elsewhere written at length to rebut Finnis's critique of Hart.[6] Here we should simply take note of one consideration that might erroneously be perceived as supportive of Finnis's position. Every theory of law – indeed, every theory of anything – is evaluative. Every such theory rests on judgments concerning what is important and what is unimportant in relation to the topic of the theory. Judgments about importance and unimportance are evaluative judgments, and thus every theory is evaluative. Finnis is on perfectly solid ground in asserting as much. However, as has been observed, Hart formed his judgments about importance by reference to theoretical-explanatory values rather than by reference to moral values. He picked out certain phenomena as especially important because of their roles in the major institutions on which he was seeking to shed light. Having affirmed that his concentration on those phenomena would best serve his theoretical-explanatory aims, Hart proclaimed: "It is for this reason that they are treated as the central elements in the concept of law and of prime importance in its elucidation" (17).

Hence, although Hart's philosophy of law is like every other theory in being underpinned by evaluative judgments, the evaluations do not pertain to the moral bearings of law or of any legal systems. Just as an exposition of quantum physics is not turned into a moral doctrine by the sheer fact that it rests on evaluations about explanatory importance, so too Hart's theory of law has not become endowed with a moral orientation through the sheer fact that it rests on such evaluations. By Hart's reckoning, the distinction between the central instances and the marginal instances of legal systems – along with the distinction between the central instances and the marginal instances of the internal viewpoint of the officials who run such systems – is not morally laden. It is centered not on the moral propriety of officials' outlooks or on other moral qualities, but instead on the extent of each system's compliance with rule-of-law requirements which are themselves formal and procedural rather than moral. Systems of governance that largely abide by those requirements are central instances of legal systems, regardless of their moral worthiness or unworthiness. We shall return to this matter in Chapters 3 and 5.

6.3 *An ostensible departure*

Some critics of Hart have alleged that he forsook his strictly descriptive-explanatory methodology at key junctures in his theorizing. Most such allegations are misdirected, especially insofar as they relate to his highlighting of the normativity of law. As will be seen in my next chapter, Hart condemned Austin's jurisprudential model as inadequate largely because of that model's wholesale unattunedness to the normativity of legal institutions. Normativity consists in an orientation toward what ought to be or what ought to occur. Thus, if the only type of normativity were moral normativity

– an orientation toward what morally ought to be or what morally ought to occur – Hart might seem to be presuming that the adequacy of jurisprudential theories is partly a moral property.

However, any such queries about Hart's animadversions on Austin are flawed in two chief respects. First, as my penultimate chapter will emphasize, moral normativity is not the only type of normativity. Hart discerned that the normative considerations which guide the actions and decisions of the officials in any particular legal system might be focused predominantly or exclusively on the interests of the officials themselves rather than predominantly or exclusively on the interests of other people. Insofar as such a possibility is an actuality in some system of law, the normativity of the institutions in that system is prudential rather than moral. Someone who underscores the normativity of law is hardly thereby committed to accepting that that normativity is always moral. Consequently, when Hart deplored Austin's theory as inadequate largely because of its neglect of law's normativity, he was not suggesting that Austin had overlooked an inherently moral property – and he was therefore not implying that the virtue of adequacy for a jurisprudential theory is itself a partly moral property.

Second, even if Hart had mistakenly presumed that the normativity of law is inherently moral and is thus never prudential, and even if (while taking such a view) he had continued to maintain that any adequate jurisprudential theory will acknowledge the normativity of law, he would not have been suggesting that jurisprudential theorizing is itself a moral endeavor. Nor would he have been suggesting that the virtue of adequacy for such theorizing is a partly moral virtue. Nonprudential adjurations by officials in the workings of legal systems would have to be taken into account by any adequate jurisprudential theory – if, contrary to fact, the occurrence of such adjurations were indeed indispensable in those workings – but they would get taken into account as something to be reported rather than as something to be endorsed. As Hart ringingly proclaimed in his retorts to Dworkin: "Description may still be description, even when what is described is [an array of nonprudential exhortations]" (244).

6.4 Another ostensible departure

We have already glanced at Hart's account of the putative transition from pre-legal societies to legal systems of governance in the fifth chapter of *The Concept of Law*. In addition to being derided as an instance of armchair anthropology, that account has been perceived by some critics as a deviation from the purely descriptive-explanatory methodology which Hart purported to be employing.[7] Those critics construe Hart's account as an effort to justify morally the role of legal institutions in various societies. They note that Hart characterized the secondary laws of legal systems as solutions to problems that would otherwise grievously afflict the endeavors of people to live alongside one another in large groupings, and they infer that he was commending the salutariness of the secondary laws instead of simply describing and explaining the functions which those laws perform.

Like the worries about Hart's supposed excursion into anthropology from his armchair, the worries about his supposed diversion from the austerity of his descriptive-explanatory method are to some degree understandable in light of his frequently careless wording. Nonetheless, like the former worries, the latter are unfounded. A full response to them will have to be deferred to my third and fifth chapters, but a laconic anticipation of that response is appropriate here. When commentators assert that Hart shifted from a descriptive-explanatory method to a method of moral justification in his meditations on the functions of secondary laws, they are guilty of the non sequitur which I have exposed during my brief discussion of Finnis in §6.2 above. That is, they are conflating importance with moral worthiness. Hart certainly regarded the roles of secondary laws as extremely important, and – as we shall see – he made clear that the presence of such laws is advantageous for coordinating people's behavior and for other reasons. However, as he also made clear at more than one juncture in *The Concept of Law*, the importance of those secondary legal norms does not translate into any inherent moral worthiness. Any advantages obtainable through such legal norms can be put to deeply immoral uses as well as to more benign uses. Hence, Hart's judgments about importance in his reflections on the functions of secondary laws were not moral judgments. Rather, they were theoretical-explanatory judgments concerning the extent to which certain phenomena have shaped the institutions and interaction of people in any society. We shall return to these points later.

6.5 *A genuine departure*

Heretofore, the claims about Hart's apparent departures from his descriptive-explanatory methodology have turned out to be unfounded when subjected to scrutiny. However, there is one genuine deviation by him from his normal methodological stance. At the close of the ninth chapter of *The Concept of Law*, he pondered the competing merits of a relatively expansive positivist understanding of legal norms and a relatively narrow natural-law understanding. Whereas the proponents of the former understanding deny that the moral decency of norms is perforce a necessary condition for the status of those norms as laws, the proponents of the latter understanding contend that norms are never genuinely classifiable as laws unless they meet or surpass some threshold of moral decency. Hart as a legal positivist naturally favored the relatively broad concept of law, and he therefore had to marshal some arguments in support of that concept.

Given the general character of the methodology in *The Concept of Law*, a reader might well have expected Hart to adduce purely theoretical-explanatory considerations that would vindicate his broader concept of law. Hart did adduce such considerations, but somewhat disconcertingly he also invoked certain moral considerations – and some large empirical conjectures – in his advocacy of that broader concept. Having aptly dismissed the idea that one's choice between the more expansive concept of law and the more restrictive concept should be oriented toward the proprieties of linguistic usage, Hart proceeded to outline his method for addressing that choice: "If we are to make a reasoned choice between these concepts, it must be because one is superior to the other in the way in which it will assist our theoretical inquiries, *or advance and clarify our moral deliberations*, or both" (209, emphasis added). As is evident from the wording which I have italicized, Hart believed that legal positivism might be defensible at least partly on moral grounds.

Hart went on to implement his announced method by initially appealing to some theoretical-explanatory considerations that militate in favor of the broader concept of law (209–10). His summation of those considerations, which we shall probe in my fifth chapter, is persuasive but extremely terse. By contrast, he then dilated rather lengthily on the moral factors that tell in favor of the stance of legal positivists. In his endeavor to buttress that stance morally, he developed two principal lines of thought.

First, with the aid of some empirical surmises which he made no effort to substantiate, Hart contended that the widespread acceptance of the relatively expansive concept of law among the members of a society would sharpen their acuity in reaching decisions about complying with legal requirements. He started quite modestly by averring that the widespread acceptance of the relatively narrow concept of law would not enhance the wisdom and fortitude of people in reaching such decisions. As he declared, "it scarcely seems that an effort to train and educate men in the use of a narrower concept of legal validity, in which there is no place for valid but morally iniquitous laws, is likely to lead to a stiffening of resistance to evil, in the face of threats of organized power, or a clearer realization of what is morally at stake when obedience is demanded" (210). However, Hart then more boldly submitted that the prevalence of the relatively expansive concept of law among the members of a society would salutarily disincline them to comply with odious legal requirements. As he mused: "What surely is most needed in order to make men clear-sighted in confronting the official abuse of power, is that they should preserve the sense that the certification of something as legally valid is not conclusive of the question of obedience, and that, however great the aura of majesty or authority which the official system may have, its demands must in the end be submitted to a moral scrutiny." He climaxed this first strand of moral argumentation with a ringing reaffirmation of the legal-positivist understanding of law: "This sense, that there is something outside the official system, by reference to which in the last resort the individual must solve his problem of obedience, is surely more likely to be kept alive among those who are accustomed to think that rules of law may be iniquitous, than among those who think that nothing iniquitous can anywhere have the status of law" (210).

Hart's first main moral consideration in favor of the broader concept of law is marred by two major shortcomings. One problem, as I have already observed, is that Hart relied on some far-reaching empirical speculations. The problem is not that his speculations are implausible; on the contrary, they are quite plausible. Rather, the problem is that Hart omitted to corroborate his empirical suppositions – his claims of social psychology – with any relevant data or studies. Credible though his suppositions are, their truth is not so obvious that it can be taken for granted.

Another problem, which also afflicts Hart's second line of moral argumentation, is even more profound. That is, his shift from a theoretical-explanatory method to a method of moral justification was curiously out of place in a project aimed at encapsulating the key features of institutions such as legal systems. After all, if his first moral consideration in favor of legal positivism is correct, then it simply establishes that certain morally benign consequences are likely to ensue from the widespread adoption of a positivist understanding of law. Had Hart's project been fundamentally prescriptive, with the aim of selecting among theories to bring about desirable social consequences – an aim connected only fortuitously if at all to theoretical-explanatory objectives – his reflections on the morally valuable upshot of the prevalence of a positivist outlook would have been highly germane. However, from his opening chapter onward in *The Concept of Law*, Hart stoutly adhered to a theoretical-explanatory methodology that was fundamentally descriptive rather than prescriptive. I have already quoted several passages in which he articulated the orientation of his methodology, and many further passages could have been cited. In light of his general methodological allegiance, his abrupt and temporary switch to a partly moralized methodology at the conclusion of his ninth chapter is puzzling.

Let us briefly examine Hart's second chief line of moral reasoning in support of the broader concept of law. This latter line of reasoning can be construed as independent of any large empirical conjectures. Hart maintained that the natural-law theorists' restrictive concept of legal validity, which holds that the status of norms as laws is always dependent on their moral decency, will oversimplify and obscure a medley of knotty moral issues that can arise from the existence of evil laws. Questions concerning whether such laws should be heeded by citizens are not the only pressing moral matters that call for attention. In addition, there are questions concerning whether officials should give effect to such laws, and questions concerning whether citizens should acquiesce in being punished for contraventions of such laws, and questions concerning whether courts can legitimately impose sanctions on people for performing wicked actions that were lawful at the time of the actions' occurrence. Hart believed that these and other cruxes would become submerged by any natural-law approach which denies that evil enactments are laws at all. As he asseverated: "These questions raise very different problems of morality and justice, which we need to consider independently of each other: they cannot be solved by a refusal, made once and for all, to recognize evil laws as valid for any purpose. This is too crude a way with delicate and complex moral issues" (211).

This second moral argument by Hart in favor of legal positivism is underdeveloped and is probably successful only against versions of natural-law thinking that are quite crude. Against the more sophisticated doctrines espoused by contemporary natural-law theorists such as Finnis, Hart's argument is far less telling. Still more damaging than these difficulties, however, is a point similar to that which

I have broached in the penultimate paragraph above. That is, Hart's presentation of a moral case for the positivist understanding of law was peculiarly out of place in his overall project. Though Hart did not rely on grand empirical surmises in his second line of moral reasoning, he did in effect contend that the positivist understanding of law reveals the moral intricacies of any number of situations much more astutely and subtly than does any natural-law understanding. Even if that contention were straightforwardly correct, it would simply alert us to the fact that we have a strong moral reason for embracing a positivist outlook. It would not per se indicate that such an outlook contributes valuably to a theoretical-explanatory endeavor of the kind which Hart declared himself to be pursuing. Hence, although Hart at the end of his ninth chapter implied that the proffered moral reasons for upholding the positivist concept of law could be sufficient to vindicate his adoption of that concept, those reasons are actually orthogonal to the purport of the theory which he was devising. They do not detract from that theory, of course, but they likewise do not bolster it as an analysis of the workings of some major societal institutions.

Leslie Green (2013, 203–6) has recently argued that Hart did not really deviate from his normal methodology in his championing of legal positivism. Green suggests that Hart was merely trying to outwit the crude natural-law theorists at their own game by showing that their very standards for selecting among theories would favor legal positivism over natural-law doctrines. According to Green, Hart "says not only is the [natural-law philosopher] wrong to think the positivist's theory is dangerous, it is actually morally *superior*!" Green concludes: "Like everyone else, Hart thinks a correct understanding of law is a better foundation for moral deliberation than a confused or mistaken one. But he does not think it correct *because* it is more useful to moral deliberation" (2013, 205, emphases in original). Had Hart confined himself to taking the positions which Green ascribes to him, then his discussion at the close of the ninth chapter in *The Concept of Law* would indeed not have constituted any departure from his descriptive-explanatory methodology. However, as is evidenced by the first sentence from Hart which I have quoted in this subsection, he did not in fact so confine himself. Instead of simply venturing to show that the natural-law thinkers' criterion for selecting among theories of legal institutions would pick out jurisprudential positivism as correct, Hart endorsed that criterion as one sufficient basis – albeit not the only sufficient basis – for choosing between the narrower concept and the wider concept of law. Hence, contrary to what Green asserts, Hart did thereby imply that the correctness of legal positivism as an account of law can be grounded on its moral salutariness. In so implying, he swerved quite dismayingly (though only passingly) from his usual methodology.

7 A reductionist ambition?

In recent years, some philosophers have supposed that Hart in *The Concept of Law* was engaged in a reductionist project. Such a view has been expressed most bluntly by Andrei Marmor, who proclaims that "Hart's main objective in *The Concept of Law* was not essentially different from that of Austin, namely, to provide a reductionist theory of law" (2013, 209). To assess this contention by Marmor, we shall obviously need to gain a clear sense of what he means by "reductionist."

Immediately after the sentence just quoted, Marmor supplies his initial gloss on his invocation of reductionism: "The main purpose of Hart's theory was to offer an explanation of law in terms of something more foundational in nature, that is, in terms of social facts, which, in turn, can be explained by reference to people's actual conduct, beliefs, and attitudes" (2013, 209). Given that Marmor is here elaborating on his characterization of Hart's theory as reductionist, he is presuming that the reduction of some phenomenon X to some other phenomenon Y consists in establishing the explanatory priority of Y over X. If a theory explains X fully by reference to Y and not vice versa, then the theory has reduced X to Y – or so this initial conception of reductionism suggests. Concomitant to that explanatory conception of reductionism is a metaphysical conception that is signaled by the wording about "something more foundational in nature." That is, Marmor here assumes that the reduction of X to Y consists in showing that Y is metaphysically deeper than X. Patently, anyone propounding such a conception of reductionism will need to elucidate the nature of the metaphysical priority of Y over X.

Both of these intimately related understandings of reductionism are operative in Marmor's essay as it unfolds. When Marmor embarks upon his principal discussion of the reductionist character of Hart's theorizing, he virtually echoes the statements that have been quoted above: "Hart clearly shared Austin's view that a theoretical explanation of the nature of law should explain what the law is in terms of social facts, facts that can be explained by more foundational truths about how people behave, the kind of beliefs they have about their conduct, and the kind of attitudes and dispositions that tend to accompany those shared beliefs." He continues: "In other words, the hallmark of Hart's theory is the idea that social rules are at the foundations of law, and that social rules, in turn, can be explained reductively in terms of people's actual conduct, beliefs, and attitudes" (2013, 214).

Still, none of these statements so far has shed much light on the specifics of the metaphysical priority which Marmor has in mind when he talks of reducing law to social facts about people's conduct and attitudes and beliefs. After wisely denying that Hart was pursuing a project of semantic reductionism – whereby all statements expressed in legal terms could be fully replaced with statements formulated in the terms of some other discipline such as social psychology – Marmor expands slightly, though only slightly, on the type of metaphysical priority that he envisages. He declares that the reductionism endorsed by Hart and other legal positivists is centered on "a metaphysical or constitutive form of reduction. The idea of a metaphysical reduction is to show that a distinct type of phenomenon is actually constituted by, and fully reducible to, some other, more foundational type of phenomenon." Having introduced the notion of a constitutive relationship that obtains between a metaphysically deep phenomenon and any phenomenon that is reducible to it, however, Marmor returns to his invocation of explanatory priority: "In [Hart's] case, the idea is to show that law is constituted by social practices that can be fully explained by the way people actually behave, the kind of beliefs they share about their behavior, and the attitudes and dispositions that they exhibit in the relevant contexts" (2013, 216). Marmor makes a few further such remarks, but none of them is more informative than those that have already been quoted. Hence, he has not specified what a constitutive relationship is, nor has he told us why a relationship of constitutive priority or explanatory priority between Y and X is suitably characterized as the reducibility of X to Y.

These lacunae in Marmor's discussion are significant, since we cannot assess his attribution of a reductionist methodology to Hart until we know the kind of reductionism that is being invoked. We know of course that Marmor is not contemplating any semantic reductionism, but quite unclear are the specifics of the metaphysical reductionism which he is contemplating. Let us, then, mull over a couple of possibilities.

Marmor almost certainly does not have in mind a merely causal relationship between Y and X, for causal relationships are ordinarily contrasted with constitutive relationships. Moreover, the sheer fact that Y causes X is hardly in itself a basis for the conclusion that X is reducible to Y (under any plausible conception of reducibility, and under any plausible conception of causation). Accordingly, much more likely is that Marmor is envisioning a constitutive relationship of the following type. X is fully constituted by Y if and only if (1) Y, in combination with all the prevailing circumstances other than any causal laws, logically entails X; and (2) without Y, the prevailing circumstances other than any causal laws would not logically entail X.

Suppose for example that John and Tony are the sole competitors in a two-mile race, and that John finishes the race ahead of Tony without having contravened any rules of the competition. His having finished ahead of Tony, in combination with all the prevailing circumstances other than any causal laws, logically entails his having won the race. Indeed, his having finished ahead of Tony – in combination with all the prevailing circumstances other than any causal laws – amounts to his having won the race. Among the prevailing circumstances, of course, are the rules of the race which specify the conditions for winning. Likewise among those prevailing circumstances is the fact that John has not contravened any of the applicable rules.

When Marmor asserts that the reducibility of X to Y involves a constitutive relationship between Y and X, he may well be invoking the notion of constitutiveness in the sense just outlined. If so, he is attributing to Hart the view that – in combination with the prevailing circumstances other than any causal laws – certain behavioral patterns and beliefs and dispositions on the part of legal officials and citizens logically entail the existence and operations and norms of a legal system. The attribution of such a view to Hart is well founded, but much more doubtful is whether that view is appositely classifiable as "reductionist." Of course, Marmor might simply stipulate that the term "reductionist" applies to any theory which postulates a constitutive relationship of the kind just indicated. Though Hart did indeed propound a model of law that is reductionist in the stipulated sense, the appropriateness of any such stipulation is precisely what is in question here. If a stipulation is highly misleading, it should be eschewed. Yet the application of the "reductionist" label to Hart's jurisprudential theory would indeed be highly misleading – since that label would strongly convey the impression that legal norms (as items supposedly reducible to some other set of phenomena) are not to be counted in an overall reckoning of entities that exist and events that occur.

I will here apply the designation "Not Counted Thesis" to the proposition that any phenomenon *constituted* by some other phenomenon or set of phenomena is not to be counted in any overall reckoning of entities that exist and events that occur. To understand the Not Counted Thesis and to see why it is inapposite in application to legal norms, we should first ponder a scenario to which that thesis is germanely applicable, and we should then ponder a different scenario to which the thesis does not pertinently apply. Each of those scenarios involves a constitutive relationship. While probing each of them, we shall in effect be inquiring whether a constitutive relationship is non-misleadingly classifiable as a relationship of reducibility.

The first scenario is the race between John and Tony broached in the antepenultimate paragraph above. Given the prevailing circumstances other than any causal laws, John's having finished the race ahead of Tony is constitutive of his having won the race. Now, when we bring to bear the Not Counted Thesis on John's accomplishment, it diagnoses the situation correctly. John's having finished the race ahead of Tony and his having won the race are not two separate events that are each to be counted in an overall reckoning of events that have occurred. Rather, they are one and the same event under two somewhat different descriptions. As I have said above, John's having finished the race ahead of Tony amounts to his having won the race. Hence, we would be guilty of double counting if we were to include both the winning and the finishing ahead of Tony as items in a register of events that have occurred. Only the latter item is to be included. In this situation, the constitutive relationship between John's finishing the race ahead of Tony and his winning the race is aptly classifiable as a relationship of reducibility.

Now let us think about a multitude of communicative actions over time that cumulatively constitute a natural language such as English. The communicative actions and dispositions of the users of the language (including their actions of compiling dictionaries and grammatical treatises, for example), in combination with the prevailing circumstances other than any causal laws, are collectively constitutive of the language and of its sundry syntactical and semantic rules. Should we conclude, then, that those rules of syntax and semantics are not to be counted in any overall reckoning of entities that exist and events that occur? Given that the multifarious communicative actions and dispositions of the users of the language are to be counted in such a reckoning, would we be guilty of double counting if we also included the syntactic and semantic rules that are constituted by those actions and dispositions? As should be evident, the answer to each of these questions is negative. Although the communicative actions and shared dispositions of the users of a language do constitute the language's semantic and syntactic rules in the sense that has been specified here, they are also oriented toward those rules – for the rules guide and structure the very actions and dispositions that sustain them.[8] We would be missing the reciprocality of this process of constitution and guidance if we declined to include the rules of syntax and semantics along with the communicative actions and dispositions in an overall reckoning of entities that exist and events that occur. Whereas John's winning the race and John's finishing ahead of Tony are one and the same event under slightly different descriptions, the communicative actions and dispositions of the users of a language are not exactly the same things as the rules of syntax and semantics that are constituted by those actions and dispositions. Hence, the constitutive relationship between the actions and dispositions on the one hand and the rules on the other hand is not aptly classifiable as a relationship of reducibility.

Of course, the rules of syntax and semantics are abstract normative entities rather than material entities. They are immanent in the communicative practices of which they are the normative structure and lodestars. They guide those practices not by serving as causal mechanisms, but instead by serving as foci for the exercise of people's linguistic competences. Still, in any satisfactory overall reckoning of entities that exist and events that occur, we have to take account of normative entities as well as of material entities.

Let us, then, turn to the norms of a legal system. As has been readily granted, Hart took the view that the norms of a legal system are constituted by certain beliefs and dispositions and behavioral patterns of officials and citizens (in combination with the prevailing circumstances other than any causal laws). Is that constitutive relationship relevantly similar to the relationship between John's finishing ahead of Tony and John's winning the race, or is it relevantly similar instead to the relationship between the communicative actions and dispositions on the one hand and the rules of syntax and semantics on the other hand? In other words, is it a relationship of reducibility or not? *Pace* Marmor, the answer to this question is that the constitutive relationship which Hart envisaged is not aptly classifiable as a relationship of reducibility. As will be emphasized in my next chapter – and as has already been briefly suggested in this chapter – Hart repeatedly assailed Austin for obfuscating the crucial role played by norms in undergirding and structuring the operations of any legal system.

Marmor persistently contends that "Hart's own theory of law is as reductionist as Austin's" (2013, 214). Such an assertion is true if the term "reductionist" simply denotes a theory which recounts a constitutive relationship between phenomena, but the assertion is false if Marmor is implying that Hart aligned himself with Austin by obscuring the reality and centrality of norms in the workings of legal systems. Far from obscuring the reality of the norms in such systems – that is, far from suggesting that those norms are not to be included in any overall reckoning of entities that exist – Hart again and again insisted that we shall not understand the nature of law unless we grasp that legal systems are systems of norms. Although those norms are constituted by the actions and beliefs and attitudes of officials and citizens, they are operative in guiding the very actions and beliefs and attitudes that sustain them, and they are operative in enabling the composition of legal institutions. Given that Hart laid stress on these guiding and enabling roles of norms (as we shall behold in some of my subsequent chapters), the epithet "reductionist" in application to his theorizing is highly misleading at best. Hart recognized that the constituting of legal norms by actions and beliefs and attitudes is fully consistent with the fact that the norms are not simply the actions and beliefs and attitudes under a different description.

8 A naturalistic ambition?

My response to Marmor might elicit dissatisfaction among some other legal philosophers, for in recent years some such philosophers have attributed to Hart a starkly naturalistic position. In other words, these philosophers have submitted that Hart denied the reality of any entities that are not causally efficacious. Since abstract normative entities are not causally efficacious, these philosophers are contending that Hart denied the reality of legal norms.

The ascription of such a view to Hart has been undertaken most assertively by Brian Leiter, though Leiter states the ascription principally with reference to moral norms. He writes that "Kelsen and Hart, as everyone knows, were both metaphysical anti-realists about moral norms: that is, they denied that such norms had any objective existence, they denied that the best metaphysical account of what the world contains would include facts about what is morally right and wrong" (2011, 671). Leiter subsequently refers to "an antirealism about *norms*, which Hart accepts" (2011, 671–2, emphasis in original). Stephen Perry similarly affirms that "[d]espite Hart's rejection of his predecessors' sanction- and prediction-based theories of law, he nonetheless shared their commitments to naturalism and empiricism" (2009, 311). Kevin Toh likewise claims that Hart strove for "an account of … legal discourse that is congruent with the naturalistic conception of the world," and Toh remarks that any partisan of the naturalistic conception is "loath to countenance properties that do not figure in our explanations in natural and social sciences" (2005, 84, 80). In much the same vein, Scott Shapiro declares that Hart harbored an "impulse to make room for law in the natural world. Hart, therefore, proposed an account of legal semantics that attempted to make legal language naturalistically reputable" (2006, 1168).

Before we can come to grips with these pronouncements, a bit of elucidation is necessary. When Leiter uses the phrase "objective existence," he appears to be referring specifically to strongly mind-independent existence. The occurrence of some event or the continued existence of some entity is strongly mind-independent if and only if it does not hinge on the mental functioning of any members of any group either individually or collectively (Kramer 2009a, 26).

Now, although we shall see in my fourth and fifth chapters that the bearings of Hart's views concerning the nature of morality were not as clear-cut as Leiter suggests with his phrase "as everyone knows," Hart did usually cleave to the notion that the correct principles of morality are not strongly mind-independent.[9] Much more clearly, he aptly held that the continued existence of legal norms is not strongly mind-independent; were all creatures with minds to go permanently out of existence, legal norms too would cease to exist. Instead of being strongly mind-independent, the continued existence of general legal norms is weakly mind-independent. That is, the continued existence of such norms is not dependent on the mental activity of any particular individual. Still, although the mind-independence of the continued existence of any general legal norms is weak rather than strong, there is no basis for the conclusion that such norms are to be omitted from an overall reckoning of entities that exist and events that occur (a reckoning which Leiter somewhat tendentiously labels as "the best metaphysical account of what the world contains"). Moreover, as I have already maintained, there is no basis for saddling Hart with such a conclusion.

Given that Leiter is talking about moral norms rather than about legal norms in my main quotation from him above, he might not seem to be saying anything that is inconsistent with what I have just said about legal norms. However, he appears there to be inferring the unreality of moral norms from the premise that their continued existence is not strongly mind-independent. Since the continued existence of *legal* norms is indeed not strongly mind-independent, Leiter would presumably draw a parallel inference about their unreality. Such an inference would be in keeping with the pugnaciously naturalistic outlook to which he subscribes throughout his writings, whereby he takes causal efficacy to be the hallmark of entities that are real.

Having elsewhere mounted quite a lengthy critique of Leiter's naturalism (2009a, 199–207) – with particular strictures on his failure to differentiate between supernatural entities such as gods and non-natural entities such as moral principles, and on his transmogrification of an apt scientific methodological precept into a nonscientific metaphysical dogma – I will not here recapitulate my objections to his general stance. Instead, the key point for my present purposes is that no sweepingly naturalistic outlook can credibly be imputed to Hart in connection with questions about the reality of legal norms. Hart repeatedly asserted the reality of such norms and repeatedly presupposed their reality. While he fully recognized that the continued existence of general legal norms is only weakly mind-independent and that those norms are constituted by the behavior and dispositions and attitudes of officials and citizens in the manner outlined in §7 above, he roundly affirmed that such norms guide and structure and enable the operations of any legal system. Legal norms can perform those guiding and structuring and enabling functions not by virtue of being endowed with causal efficacy, but instead by virtue of human capacities to reason about normative matters.

Hart undertook his jurisprudential ruminations in a period before minimalist theories of truth and reality had become as prominent as they are today, but he would very likely have been attracted to such theories if he had written in a later era.[10] In other words, he would – for example – have postulated the logical equivalence of (i) a proposition affirming that a legal prohibition on murder really does exist in some jurisdiction J and (ii) a proposition affirming that murder is legally proscribed in J. When the reality or existence of legal norms is understood in this minimalist fashion, which obviously extends *mutatis mutandis* to laws with any contents, there are no grounds whatsoever for doubting that such norms can and do really exist. One's recognition of their reality is not "unscientific" in any way. Hart was right to insist that such norms are to be included in any overall reckoning of entities that exist, and he was therefore right to espouse a position that is not pertinently classifiable as "reductionist."

2
Hart on Legal Powers and Law's Normativity

In much of the opening half of *The Concept of Law*, Hart set the stage for the elaboration of his own jurisprudential theory as he first dissected the model of law that had been propounded by the nineteenth-century jurist John Austin. Though Hart at some junctures amplified or amended Austin's model for the purpose of highlighting its strengths in order to reveal ultimately the profundity of its failings, the command theory of law which he recounted and then attacked is closely similar to the theory championed by Austin. On the one hand, while Hart impeached Austin's understanding of law in many far-reaching respects, he did not seek to demolish it altogether. He esteemed Austin and Jeremy Bentham as his two greatest predecessors in the tradition of legal positivism, and he repeatedly applauded their emphasis on the distinction between what the law is and what the law ought to be. On the other hand, notwithstanding his admiration for Austin's positivism and for the perspicuity of Austin's prose and analyses, Hart felt that the command theory of law is overall an impediment to a clear-sighted apprehension of the nature of legal systems. In particular, as I have already suggested in my opening chapter, he objected to the ways in which the command theory obscures the normativity of law. His sundry criticisms of Austin were all aimed at demonstrating the inadequacy of a theory that is so unattuned to the operativeness of norms in legal systems.

Although Austin's presentation of the command theory of law was especially influential during the second half of the nineteenth century and the first few decades of the twentieth century, and although it has remained prominent because of Hart's engagement with it, it is not the sole version of that theory. As Hart remarked more than once in essays written after *The Concept of Law* (1982, 108–9, 201, 225–7), Bentham had produced a far more sophisticated version of the command theory wherein he had avoided some of the shortcomings which Hart exposed in Austin's subsequent elaboration of the theory. Nevertheless, ingenious and perceptive though Bentham's theory often is, it does not escape the chief vice of Austin's account; that is, it obfuscates rather than illuminates the normativity of law, and it therefore distorts virtually every major aspect of law of which it treats. Hence, had Hart in *The Concept of Law* come to grips with Bentham's jurisprudential doctrines rather than with Austin's, his general conclusions and quite a few of his specific conclusions would have been essentially the same as those which he reached in response to Austin.

Notwithstanding the superiority of Bentham's version of the command theory, Austin's version of that theory of law is itself somewhat stronger and more resourceful than Hart allowed. I have elsewhere defended Austin against a few of Hart's strictures (1991, 106–12), and I have occasionally sought to highlight some of the virtues of Austin's writings (2013a, 117–19). Nonetheless, I have always readily affirmed the soundness of most of Hart's specific objections along with the general point of those objections – concerning the normativity of law – and indeed I have added some queries of my own about certain facets of Austin's legal philosophy (1999, 98–101; 2013a, 104–17). Thus, although a defender of the command theory of law could successfully parry a few of Hart's specific lines of attack, the upshot of Hart's confrontation with Austin has clearly been the supersession of Austinian jurisprudence by Hartian jurisprudence. Accordingly, while some of my discussions in this chapter will be critical of Hart, they will not be supportive of Austin. This chapter will take as given that, on the whole, Hart vanquished his great legal-positivist forebear.

1 The Austinian model of law

Hart devoted the whole of his second chapter in *The Concept of Law* to a conspectus of the main elements of an Austinian approach to law, but here a terse sketch will suffice. Austin strove to portray the diverse relationships within any legal system as an array of coercive relationships. The dominant figure in those relationships is the Austinian sovereign, a person or body of people to whom everyone else in a society defers through habitual obedience. Obeyed habitually by everybody else in the jurisdiction, the sovereign does not obey anybody either within or beyond the jurisdiction. In the Austinian model, the relationships between the sovereign and the obedient citizens are akin to the relationships between a gunman and his victims. While the gunman will have issued some behests to his victims, the sovereign will have issued some behests to the citizens who are subject to the sovereign's sway. In each case, the behests are backed by threats of violent measures that will be undertaken against anyone who declines to comply with the directives that have been articulated. Hence, just as the relationships between a gunman and his victims are starkly coercive, so too are the relationships between a sovereign and the citizenry.

Though the Austinian sovereign is a gunman writ large in that all the sovereign's relationships with the citizenry are unalloyedly coercive, Austin recognized that the mandates enacted by a sovereign – that is, the mandates which are standing laws rather than situation-specific directives – characteristically differ quite conspicuously from any typical orders uttered by a gunman. When a gunman bids his victims to raise their hands, he is addressing some particular individuals, and he is directing them to engage in conduct of a highly specific type. Even if the gunman says "Raise your hands" rather than "Raise your hands here and now," everyone involved will recognize that (in the circumstances) the former formulation is to be construed as equivalent to the latter. Moreover, any typical order snarled by a gunman is only ephemerally in effect. If a gunman relieves his victims of their wallets and then flees – or if his effort to rob them is aborted, perhaps by the intervention of a third party such as a police officer – his injunction to the victims about raising their hands will cease to be operative.

By contrast, the mandates introduced by a legal sovereign as standing laws are typically general in two chief respects and are typically in effect for lengthy periods (years or decades or even longer). Their generality pertains both to the modes of conduct for which they call and to the range of people on whom they impose their requirements. Instead of calling for a situation-specific course of conduct with the place and time of performance specified to a high degree of precision – through implicit or explicit indexicals such as "here" and "now" – a standing law that imposes some requirement will typically call for a general type of conduct that could occur at any number of times and places. Likewise, instead of being addressed to particular individuals who are picked out by name or through second-person pronouns, a standing law is typically addressed to a general class of persons such as the class of all citizens.[1] Both in their manner of application and in their manner of address, then, most of the mandates enacted by a legal sovereign are general. Similarly, most such mandates are durable in that they retain their status as laws for years rather than merely for seconds or minutes. In their durability as well as in their generality, the laws of an Austinian sovereign differ from any typical orders uttered by a gunman.

Austin was aware of the foregoing dissimilarities between a sovereign's commands and a gunman's dictates, and he took account of them in his model of law. A further dissimilarity between the sway of a sovereign and the sway of a gunman is directly related to the durability of a sovereign's mandates. Whereas the dominion of a gunman over his victims is almost always highly transitory, the dominion of a legal sovereign over the citizenry in the sovereign's jurisdiction is longstanding. Consequently, whereas the submissiveness of the victims to the gunman is transient, the obedience of the citizenry to the sovereign is persistent. Austin characterized the citizens' obedience as habitual. Their obedience, like the submissiveness of the gunman's victims, is rendered in response to threats of the violence that will be wielded against them in the event of their noncompliance. Because those threats are protractedly in effect, the obedience elicited by them is commensurately protracted.

Typically, if not always, the number of people subject to the reign of a sovereign is far larger than the number of people subject to the dictates of a gunman. Accordingly, whereas the continuation of the dominance of a gunman over his victims will normally involve compliance by all of them with his orders (since recalcitrance on the part of the victims will normally result either in their being immediately shot or in the collapse of the gunman's sway), there is greater latitude for some noncompliance with the mandates of a sovereign. Although the habitual obedience of citizens to those mandates must be widespread, it need not be universal within the relevant jurisdiction. By Austin's reckoning, a sovereign can reign even if some citizens persistently manage to flout the sovereign's laws with impunity. Hence, the conditions for the existence of the dominion of an Austinian sovereign are somewhat vague, as Hart made clear: "The question how many people must obey how many [of the sovereign's] general orders, and for how long, if there is to be law, no more admits of definite answers than the question how few hairs must a man have to be bald" (24).

All these features of the Austinian model of law were pithily captured by Hart in his recapitulation at the close of the second chapter in *The Concept of Law* (25):

> On this simple [Austinian] account of the matter, ... there must, wherever there is a legal system, be some [person] or body of persons issuing general orders backed by threats which are generally obeyed, and it must be generally believed that these threats are likely to be implemented in the event of disobedience. This person or body must be internally supreme and externally independent. If, following Austin, we call such a supreme and independent person or body of persons the sovereign, the laws of any country will be the general orders backed by threats which are issued either by the sovereign or subordinates in obedience to the sovereign.

2 Power-conferring laws

Having synopsized the Austinian account of law, Hart proceeded to deliver a number of telling blows against it. Although a few of his specific criticisms underestimate the resilience of Austinian jurisprudence, most of them reveal how badly distortive and inadequate the Austinian approach to law is – and how the woes of that approach derive chiefly from its blindness to the normativity of law and of legal institutions. Hart assembled his objections into several categories: objections focused on Austin's preoccupation with duty-imposing laws to the neglect of power-conferring laws; objections focused on Austin's inability to explain how laws can place the members of a sovereign body under legal duties; objections focused on Austin's failure to accommodate any custom-derived laws within his model of legal systems; and objections focused on the shortcomings of Austin's account of sovereignty, especially in regard to limitations on the range of matters over which a sovereign can legislate. Instead of trying bootlessly to cover all of Hart's queries within the compass of this chapter, I will explore a few of them in depth. Let us begin with his complaints about Austin's disregard of power-conferring laws.

A preliminary bit of clarification is needed here, however. Hart in *The Concept of Law* did not specify very precisely what he took a legal power to be. According to the influential analysis propounded by the American jurist Wesley Hohfeld, a legal power consists in an ability to bring about some change(s) in legal relationships through the adoption of some course of conduct.[2] Under that broad conception of a legal power, somebody who contravenes a legal requirement has thereby exercised a power to alter her own legal positions and the legal positions of certain other people such as law-enforcement officers; she has made herself liable to undergo arrest or other measures of enforcement, and she has invested certain people with legal powers and legal liberties to resort to such measures. Now, although Hart was admiringly acquainted with Hohfeld's work, his own conception of legal powers was narrower than the Hohfeldian conception. He did not delimit the contours of his conception with any precision in *The Concept of Law*, but he appeared to confine the category of powers to Hohfeldian powers that are normally beneficial for the people who are endowed with them. In other words, being vested with a legal power (in the relevant sense) is normally better for a holder of it than is not being vested with it.[3] Like any Hohfeldian legal power, a legal power in this circumscribed sense is correlated with a liability on the part of the power-holder or of someone else. A liability is a position of susceptibility or exposure to the effects of the exercise of a power by oneself or by someone else. The existence of a legal power entails the existence of a legal liability with the same content, and vice versa. (Liabilities, in this Hohfeldian sense, are by no means always detrimental for the people who bear them. For example, being liable to undergo the effects of the exercise of a donative power by a munificent and wealthy cousin is typically beneficial rather than typically detrimental.)

Hart allowed that there is some resemblance between the mandates of an Austinian sovereign and the statutes of criminal law or tort law that impose legal duties on people. However, he submitted that there is no such resemblance between Austinian mandates and the sundry laws of any jurisdiction that confer legal powers on people. Among those latter laws are norms that enable people to carry out private transactions such as the formation of contracts or the conveyance of real estate or the donation of funds to charities. Also among the power-conferring laws are norms that authorize public officials to perform their functions of legislation or administration or adjudication. Such power-conferring laws are integral to the very existence and operativeness of any legal system, yet they find no place in Austin's model of law. In his model, all laws are commands that impose requirements which are supported by threats of violence for disobedience. As Hart proclaimed, "there is a radical difference between rules conferring and defining the manner of exercise of legislative powers and the rules of criminal law, which at least resemble orders backed by threats" (31). Austin, like Bentham, did leave room for liberty-conferring laws – as expressions of the sovereign's will that retract or modify the requirements imposed by previous commands – but the role of power-conferring laws is effaced by his theoretical schema. Hart, in his criticisms of Austin, showed time and again that the Austinian model of law presupposes the operativeness of power-conferring norms even while it fails to supply any account of their operativeness. (Worth noting here is that Hart should also have frowned upon Austin's disregard of immunity-conferring laws. An immunity, as explicated by Hohfeld, is a position of insusceptibility to the bringing about of some change in legal relations. For example, the First Amendment to the US Constitution confers upon everyone in the American populace an immunity against being deprived of certain legal liberties by Congressional enactments. An Austinian command theory cannot generate an adequate account of immunity-conferring laws any more than of power-conferring laws.)

Hart underscored the differences between duty-imposing laws and power-conferring laws in several ways. He observed for example that, whereas duty-imposing laws establish unconditional requirements, the requirements specified by a power-conferring law are conditional on someone's wishing to exercise the power that is conferred. While a duty-imposing law provides that some specified mode of conduct is "to be avoided or done by those to whom [the law] applies, irrespective of their wishes," a power-conferring law does "not require persons to act in certain ways whether they wish to or not" (27). To be sure, especially in the public sector, people are sometimes under legal duties to exercise legal powers with which they are endowed. In such circumstances, somebody who holds one of those powers is legally required to follow the specified procedure for exercising it – whether or not she wishes to do so. However, the categorical requirement is created not by the conferral of the power but instead by the imposition of the duty that accompanies the power. Even if the power and the duty are established by the same statute, the power-conferring component and the duty-imposing component of the statute are not equivalent.

A closely related way in which Hart marked the differences between duty-imposing laws and power-conferring laws is that, whereas the former laws normatively close off opportunities by prohibiting modes of conduct, the latter laws expand opportunities by presenting individuals with "facilities for realizing their wishes" (27, emphasis omitted). When drawing the contrast in this fashion, Hart particularly had in mind the opportunities presented to individuals to form private-law arrangements such as contracts and wills and trusts and marriages and corporations. He further noted that noncompliance with the procedures specified for the creation of some such arrangement will nullify an effort to create it but will not constitute "a 'breach' or 'violation' of any obligation or duty nor an 'offence' and it would be confusing to think of [the noncompliance] in such terms" (28).

Dissimilarities between duty-imposing norms and power-conferring norms are even more salient in public-law settings than in private-law settings. While recounting a host of laws that empower officials to engage in their legislative or administrative or adjudicative activities (28–32), Hart drew on a legislative example to accentuate vividly the divergences between such laws and duty-imposing mandates: "If a measure before a legislative body obtains the required majority of votes and is thus duly passed, the voters in favour of the measure have not 'obeyed' the law requiring a majority decision nor have those who voted against [the measure] either obeyed or disobeyed [that law]: the same is of course true if the measure fails to obtain the required majority and so no law is passed" (31–2). As Hart declared: "The radical difference in function between [a law that prescribes the majoritarian procedures and a law that imposes some duty] prevents the use here of the terminology appropriate to conduct in its relation to rules of the criminal law" (32).

2.1 Should power-conferring laws be reconstrued as duty-imposing laws?

A defender of Austin might retort to Hart by contending that power-conferring laws are in fact duty-imposing laws. A defender so inclined would submit that, when something which appears to be a legal arrangement of some kind is deemed to be null or invalid because it does not comply with the legally specified conditions for the effecting of such an arrangement, the nullity or invalidity is a sanction administered in response to a contravention of a legal requirement. Hence, the defender would maintain, any law that specifies the procedures for forming a contract or some other legal arrangement is a duty-imposing law that carries the threat of a sanction for nonconformity.

Hart posited and cogently countered a rejoinder along these lines. He began by observing that a law which specifies the conditions for the exercise of a power is thereby supplying the normative structure of a certain practice rather than laying down some duties with sanctions to be imposed on people who engage in activities or endeavors which differ from that practice. He compellingly substantiated this first point with reference to legislative and game-playing contexts (34):

> Even more absurd is it to regard as a sanction the fact that a legislative measure, if it does not obtain the required majority, fails to attain the status of a law. To assimilate this fact to the sanctions of the criminal law would be like thinking of the scoring rules of a game as designed to eliminate all moves except the kicking of goals or the making of runs. This, if successful, would be the end of all games; yet only if we think of power-conferring rules as designed to make people behave in certain ways and as adding "nullity" as a motive for obedience, can we assimilate such rules to orders backed by threats.

Persuasive though the examples from legislative and game-playing contexts are, Hart regrettably overstated this first point against the defenders of Austin. He should have acknowledged that nullity can sometimes aptly be construed as functionally equivalent to a sanction that is designed to steer people away from certain modes of behavior. After all, there are undoubtedly some power-conferring laws which specify conditions in order to deter people from adopting certain courses of conduct. For example, when a law provides that an agreement will be invalid as a contract unless each party to it is above a specified age and is of sound mind, those two conditions specified as necessary for the exercise of a contract-forming power are doubtless prescribed partly in order to deter people from engaging in some exploitative modes of behavior; and the nullity resulting from noncompliance with those conditions is functionally tantamount to a sanction. Hart could and should have granted as much, because all that he needed to maintain was that many power-exercising conditions – such as those that are operative in the legislative and game-playing contexts to which he referred – are markedly different from the conditions for the formation of contracts which I have broached here. Many power-exercising conditions are specified to supply the normative frameworks of various activities and enterprises, rather than to deter undesirable conduct.

At any rate, even more powerful is a second point advanced by Hart against the defenders of Austin. He noted that a duty-imposing mandate can intelligibly exist even if no sanctions are attached to it for noncompliance. Indeed, as I have discussed elsewhere (2001, 66–7, 69–73), legal mandates that are utterly unenforceable rather

Legal Powers and Law's Normativity   41

than merely unenforced can nonetheless perform important conduct-directing functions. By contrast, a power-conferring law without any specification of necessary conditions for the exercise of the conferred power would be unintelligibly vacuous, and therefore a power-conferring law that involves no prospect of nullity for noncompliance with conditions prescribed by that law would be unintelligibly vacuous – since one's noncompliance with necessary conditions for the exercise of a power entails the nullity of one's attempt to exert the power in question. As Hart declared (35, emphasis in original):

> [I]f failure to comply with [any] essential condition [for the exercise of a power] did not entail nullity, the [power-conferring] rule itself could not be intelligibly said to exist … even as a non-legal rule. The provision for nullity is *part* of this type of rule itself in a way which punishment attached to a rule imposing duties is not. If failure to get the ball between the posts did not mean the "nullity" of not scoring, the scoring rules [and the game for which they supply the normative structure] could not be said to exist.

2.2 Another reconstrual of power-conferring laws as duty-imposing laws

Neil MacCormick did not seek to uphold an Austinian command theory of law, nor did he rely at all on the thesis that nullity is tantamount to a sanction. Indeed, he robustly rejected that thesis (2008, 111). Nevertheless, through a different route, he reconstrued power-conferring norms as duty-imposing norms. Having recounted and amplified Hart's exposition of a moral norm that confers a power on each person to bind herself by satisfying the conditions for the making of a promise, MacCormick asserted that that norm "belongs to Hart's class of 'obligation-imposing rules.' It tells us what one 'is bound' to do." MacCormick added: "The obligation in question is, however, conditional. It is a condition of my coming under *that* [promissory] obligation to you that I have said the appropriate words in the appropriate circumstances, both of us being appropriate persons" (2008, 95, emphasis in original). Slightly later, MacCormick characterized the promissory power-conferring norm as "a fairly simple 'obligation-imposing rule'" (2008, 96). He reiterated that characterization several pages further on in his discussion, when he asserted that the promissory power-conferring norm is "an 'obligation-imposing rule'; the 'powers' [are] conferred by the rule because of the conditions set for determining when a person is 'bound' in virtue of the rule." MacCormick averred that "the rule in question does not solely confer power nor solely impose obligation. It does both. By imposing an obligation which is conditional on the performance of a 'rule-invoking' act, it also confers a power" (2008, 101).

As might be inferred from the flurry of cautionary quotation marks in these extracts – including the threefold instances of such quotation marks on the phrase "obligation-imposing rule" or "obligation-imposing rules" – MacCormick went astray in his conflation of power-conferring norms and duty-imposing norms. Contrary to what he presumed, the conditional obligation to which he referred is not an obligation at all. Rather, it is a Hohfeldian liability; specifically, it is a liability to incur an obligation. Let us recall that a legal or moral liability is a position of susceptibility to the effects of someone's exercise of a legal or moral power. In other words, a liability and a power are correlative positions, as the existence of either of them with a certain content entails the existence of the other with that same content. Thus the moral power of Jane to impose a promissory obligation on herself entails, and is entailed by, her moral liability to incur such an obligation through her exercise of that moral power. *Pace* MacCormick, the conditional obligation to which he referred is a liability of this very kind. Hence, *pace* MacCormick, the promissory norm which he recounted is not an obligation-imposing norm. Instead, it is a norm which confers a power (one's power to impose promissory obligations on oneself through a specified procedure) and which establishes a correlative liability (one's liability to incur promissory obligations through one's adoption of that specified procedure). It is, in short, a power-conferring norm – exactly as Hart contended.

Because the existence of any power with a certain content entails the existence of a liability with that same content and vice versa, every power-conferring norm is also a liability-establishing norm. A norm cannot confer a power without also establishing a liability. Utterly unsurprising, then, is that the promissory power-conferring norm expounded by Hart is also a norm that establishes a liability. Despite MacCormick's suggestions to the contrary, such a norm does not impose any obligations – though of course a successful exertion of the power conferred by it will impose a promissory obligation on the person who has performed that exertion.

A further reason for rejecting MacCormick's conflation of power-conferring norms and duty-imposing norms is that not all powers are powers to impose obligations. There can also be powers to create liberties or powers or immunities. A power to create a liberty is correlated not with a liability to incur an obligation but instead with a liability to acquire a liberty. Likewise, of course, a power to create a power is correlated with a liability to acquire a power, and a power to create an immunity is correlated with a liability to acquire an immunity. Hence, a norm that confers a power of any of these kinds will not be establishing a conditional obligation (that is, a liability to incur an obligation). For example, when a norm confers a power on a person to invest somebody else with a certain immunity through a specified procedure, the norm has thereby established a conditional immunity (that is, a liability to acquire an immunity). Consequently, even if somebody commits MacCormick's error of taking conditional obligations to be obligations, she should deny that all power-conferring norms are properly construable as obligation-imposing norms.

2.3 Should power-conferring laws be construed as elements of duty-imposing laws?

We have heretofore examined a couple of misconceived attempts to reduce power-conferring laws to duty-imposing laws. We should now ponder the following proposition, which I will designate as the "Subsumability Thesis":

> Instead of being reducible to duty-imposing laws, power-conferring laws are subsumable into duty-imposing laws as mere components or elements thereof.

In *The Concept of Law* Hart chiefly mulled over a version of this thesis that had been propounded by Hans Kelsen (35–42), whereas in some later essays he principally probed a milder version that had been developed by Bentham (1982, 118–22, 200–19).

The Subsumability Thesis does not run afoul of the errors exposed hitherto. It depends neither on the classification of nullity as a sanction nor on MacCormick's conflation of duties and conditional duties. Indeed, Hart did not object to the thesis on logical or formal grounds; instead, as we shall see, he objected to it on the ground that it obscures the distinctive functions or social roles of power-conferring laws.

Though Hart in *The Concept of Law* concentrated predominantly on the extreme version of the Subsumability Thesis which he associated with Kelsen, he did also recount there the moderate version developed by Bentham. According to the moderate version, duty-imposing mandates such as statutes that prohibit theft and arson are full-blown laws that are addressed to citizens, whereas ostensible power-conferring laws are not full-blown laws but are instead specifications of sufficient conditions for the applicability of certain duty-imposing laws. Proponents of the moderate version of the Subsumability Thesis thus understand power-conferring legal norms as parts or fragments of veritable laws, which impose duties. Advocates of the extreme version of the Subsumability Thesis agree that power-conferring legal norms are mere parts or fragments of complete laws, but they submit that the sole complete laws are addressed not to citizens but to officials. Those laws direct officials to apply sanctions under certain conditions. Power-conferring legal norms are themselves some of the conditions that are cumulatively sufficient to trigger sanctions, and they specify further such conditions. Duty-imposing legal norms addressed to citizens are likewise some of those conditions, according to the partisans of the extreme version of the Subsumability Thesis.

Hart convincingly argued that the extreme form of the Subsumability Thesis inverts the paramount aspects and the subordinate aspects of law. Paramount among the functions of a system of legal governance, through the promulgation of authoritative standards, are the provision of guidance to citizens and the coordination of citizens' doings and the preservation of public order and the establishment of the normative frameworks of sundry activities.[4] Crucial but ancillary to those main functions are mechanisms for the resolution of disputes and for the disciplining of malefactors. Hart again fruitfully analogized the norms of a legal system to the rules of a game such as baseball. He underscored the perversity of perceiving all such rules as instructions to umpires and scorers about the conditions under which they are to reach certain determinations and perform certain actions. Important though the rules addressed specifically to umpires and scorers are, most of the rules of a game such as baseball are addressed principally to the players. We would darken counsel if we were to construe all the rules as addressed primarily or exclusively to umpires and scorers, for we would be scanting the ways in which the rules furnish guidance to players and enable them to interact with one another concertedly. As Hart declared, "the uniformity imposed on the rules by this transformation of them conceals the ways in which the rules operate, and the manner in which the players use them in guiding purposive activities, and so obscures their function in the co-operative, though competitive, social enterprise which is the game" (40).

Although the moderate version of the Subsumability Thesis does not contend that all legal norms are addressed chiefly or exclusively to officials, it too purchases uniformity at the price of distortion and obfuscation. Hart encouraged his readers to contemplate power-conferring laws "from the point of view of those who exercise [the conferred powers]." When we attend to that internal point of view, we can grasp that the laws which bestow powers on private individuals are "an additional element introduced by the law into social life over and above that of coercive control." Hart elaborated: "This is so because possession of these legal powers makes of the private citizen, who, if there were no such rules, would be a mere duty-bearer, a private legislator. He is made competent to determine the course of the law within the sphere of his contracts, trusts, wills, and other structures of rights and duties which he is enabled to build." Hart drove home his point with a rhetorical question (41): "Why should rules which are used in this special way, and confer this huge and distinctive amenity, not be recognized as distinct from rules which impose duties, the incidence of which is indeed in part determined by the exercise of such powers?" (Note that Hart did not claim, and did not need to claim, that private powers are abundantly present in every legal system or even in every central instance of a legal system. In some rudimentary legal systems and in Communist legal systems, the presence of private powers is quite exiguous. Hart would readily have granted as much while maintaining that the Subsumability Thesis obscures the distinctiveness of the laws which confer private powers even in such systems – and while maintaining that the Subsumability Thesis is egregiously distortive in its obscuring of the distinctiveness of the laws which confer private powers in the many legal systems where those powers abound.)

Norms that confer public powers of law-ascertainment and legislation and adjudication and administration on officials are likewise misrepresented when they are treated as mere fragments of duty-imposing norms. As will become apparent in my next chapter, Hart discerned that such power-conferring norms are pivotal to the very existence and operativeness of any legal system. He therefore wrote: "To represent such rules as mere aspects or fragments of the rules of duty is, even more than in the private sphere, to obscure the distinctive characteristics of law and of the activities possible within its framework" (41). Here as elsewhere, Hart objected to the Subsumability Thesis not on logical or formal grounds but on the ground that any such understanding of power-conferring laws badly fails to capture the import of those laws in the structuring of social institutions and intercourse.

2.4 Hart's neglect of power-conferring norms: the internal point of view

Given the trenchancy of Hart's animadversions on Austin's disregard of power-conferring norms, it is surprising that Hart himself omitted to take account of such norms at some key junctures in his theorizing. Quite a few examples of his neglect of power-conferring norms could be adduced here, but – to keep this chapter to a manageable length – I will confine myself to two. (I present the first of those examples in this subsection and the second of them in my next subsection. A further example will appear at the end of my third chapter.)

In the penultimate paragraph of §2.3, I have referred to the internal point of view of power-holders. Hart invoked that internal viewpoint in his riposte to the moderate version of the Subsumability Thesis. Quite striking, then, is the fact that he never presented an account of the internal viewpoint of power-holders. His exposition of the internal point of view – one of his most important contributions to the philosophy of law – was focused squarely on duty-imposing norms and not on power-conferring norms (nor on immunity-conferring norms). With that exposition he purported to be recounting the perspective of anyone who accepts social norms, but in fact he was recounting only the perspective of anyone who accepts social *duty-imposing* norms.

In the fourth chapter of *The Concept of Law*, Hart delineated the critical reflective attitude that is the hallmark of the internal point of view (55–7). With that delineation, he was illuminating two distinctions that vitally informed his critique of Austin and his own alternative theory of law: the distinction between norm-guided behavior and merely habitual behavior, and the distinction between the characteristic perspective of a participant in a practice and the characteristic perspective of an observer of a practice. In my next chapter, we shall look at Hart's meditations on the external perspective of an observer (along with another important perspective that might be adopted by a nonparticipant). Here we should concentrate solely on the internal viewpoint, which involves acceptance of some norm or practice or institution by a participant.

Though the critical reflective attitude is an affect, it manifests itself as a trio of behavioral dispositions. (The internality of the internal point of view is internality to a norm or practice or institution in response to which those behavioral dispositions are elicited.) A person who evinces the critical reflective attitude in relation to some norm N is generally disposed to comply with N's requirements, and is also generally disposed to criticize any contraventions of those requirements by other people, and is likewise generally disposed to acknowledge the appropriateness of censure directed against her on any occasions when she herself has – perhaps unwittingly – contravened N. These dispositions can be underlain by various motivations, as Hart persistently emphasized (197, 231–2).

Now, in the present context, what is disconcerting about Hart's otherwise insightful analysis of the internal point of view is that the analysis applies only to duty-imposing norms and not to power-conferring norms.[5] Throughout his discussion of social norms and the internal point of view, Hart was envisaging the categorical requirements established by duty-imposing norms. As he wrote, "where there is [a social norm,] deviations are generally regarded as lapses or faults open to criticism, and threatened deviations meet with pressure for conformity" (55). In other words, the social norms contemplated at this juncture by Hart were markedly different from the power-conferring norms which he envisioned when he contended that the role of many of those latter norms is to provide the structures or frameworks of sundry legal arrangements rather than to deter people from engaging in modes of conduct that are perceived as wrongful. He did of course advert elsewhere in *The Concept of Law* to power-conferring social norms such as uncodified rules of games that specify how goals or runs are to be scored, but he omitted to cover such norms in his exposition of the critical reflective attitude. Similarly, although he invoked the viewpoint of power-holders in his endeavors to highlight the functional differences between power-conferring laws and duty-imposing laws, he did not elucidate that viewpoint with an analysis comparable to his analysis of the critical reflective attitude that is displayed by anyone who accepts a duty-imposing norm.

This lacuna in Hart's theory is significant not only because it aligns Hart *malgré lui* with the throng of other legal philosophers who have overlooked the roles of power-conferring norms in systems of law, but also because his account of the internal perspective that pertains to duty-imposing norms is not straightforwardly modifiable into an account of an internal perspective that pertains to power-conferring norms. Though there will be some clear parallels between the former account and any satisfactory account of the latter kind, there will also have to be some major dissimilarities between them. Let us, then, consider two pathways for an exposition of the internal perspective of a participant in relation to power-conferring norms. These pathways are not mutually exclusive, and will probably have to be combined in an appositely thorough approach to this matter.

First, we might hold that somebody has adopted the internal viewpoint of acceptance in relation to some power-conferring norm PN only if (1) she is generally disposed to recognize the effects produced by any acts of exercising the power(s) which PN has bestowed, and she is generally disposed to recognize the non-occurrence of such effects when any attempts to exercise the power(s) in question are unsuccessful; (2) she is generally disposed to criticize or correct other people who fail to recognize the occurrence or non-occurrence of the aforementioned effects; and (3) she is generally disposed to acknowledge the appropriateness of criticism directed at any failures of her own to recognize the occurrence or non-occurrence of those effects. These three elements are, patently, counterparts of the three elements in Hart's explication of the critical reflective attitude. However, instead of being oriented primarily toward PN itself, each element is oriented primarily toward acts of exercising the powers that have been conferred by PN. Recognizing the effects of any acts of exercising those powers is both a cognitive matter and a behavioral matter. One recognizes the effects by apprehending them whenever one has any occasion to apprehend them, and by adjusting one's conduct and decisions in response to them. Of course, the adjustments in one's conduct and decisions might be utterly routine and unreflective in many contexts. Still, insofar as one fails to undertake those adjustments when one has any occasion to undertake them, one is *pro tanto* failing to adopt the internal viewpoint of acceptance in relation to PN – unless one promptly corrects one's lapses either as a result of self-criticism or as a result of remonstrations from others.

Second, we might hold that someone has adopted the internal viewpoint of acceptance in relation to PN only if (1a) she is generally disposed to exercise some power bestowed on her by PN, in contexts where her exercising of that power will plainly be beneficial and legitimate; (2a) she is generally disposed to criticize other people who have persistently omitted to exercise some power bestowed on each of them by PN, in contexts where the exercising of that power would plainly have been beneficial and legitimate; and (3a) she is generally disposed to acknowledge the appropriateness of objections directed against her own persistent failures to exercise the aforementioned power in contexts where her exercising of it would plainly have been beneficial and legitimate. Again, of course, each element in this triadic distillation is a counterpart of an element in Hart's explication of the critical reflective attitude.

Somebody might worry that the foregoing two paragraphs have not expounded the internal point of view in relation to power-conferring norms, and that they have instead expounded the internal point of view in relation to certain duty-imposing norms. According to such a line of thought, the penultimate paragraph above has distilled the internal viewpoint of a person who accepts a norm that imposes a duty to recognize the effects of any acts of exercising some specified power, and the final paragraph above has distilled the internal viewpoint of a person who accepts a norm that imposes a duty to exercise some specified power in contexts where doing so will plainly be beneficial and legitimate. Readers inclined to raise this worry will thus presume that I have not managed to provide an account of an internal perspective that applies to power-conferring norms.

Two rejoinders to such a query are pertinent here. In the first place, even if we were to grant *arguendo* that each of my explications of the viewpoint internal to a power-conferring norm PN has specified the viewpoint internal to a certain duty-imposing norm, we should continue to maintain that those explications have together recounted the internal viewpoint of anyone who accepts PN. Given that the relevant duty-imposing norms pertain either to recognizing the effects of exercises of powers or to exercising those powers, the specifics of the critical reflective attitude in relation to each such norm will coincide with the specifics of the internal viewpoint in relation to PN. Someone who adopts the internal perspective that consists in accepting one of the relevant duty-imposing norms will *pro tanto* have adopted the internal perspective that consists in accepting PN.

Further militating against the worry outlined in the penultimate paragraph above is that my explications of the internal viewpoint of someone who accepts PN are more capacious than the worry implies. Each of those explications does recount a viewpoint internal to a certain duty-imposing norm, but each of them also ranges more widely. My first account also covers any situation in which the criticism to which the account adverts is concerned not with a breach of duty but with an instance of intellectual obtuseness. Similarly, my second account also covers any situation in which the criticism to which the account adverts is concerned not with a breach of duty but with an instance of imprudence. In other words, somebody can adopt the internal perspective of acceptance in relation to PN without being under a duty to recognize the effects of any acts of exercising the powers conferred by PN, and without being under a duty to exercise any of those powers in contexts where the exercising of them would plainly be beneficial. Hence, my distillation of the internal perspective of somebody who accepts PN is not reducible (in either of its two versions) to a distillation of the internal perspective of somebody who accepts a certain duty-imposing norm.

Now, although I have just sought to rebut a query about my two expositions of the perspective that is internal to power-conferring norms, I have not propounded either of those expositions as a definitive formulation. Rather, each of them is meant to be suggestive and to stimulate further thinking about this matter. As I have already mused, the two expositions will probably have to be combined in any full treatment of this problem; each of them articulates a necessary tripartite condition, rather than a sufficient tripartite condition, for the existence of an internal point of view in relation to PN. Of key importance for our present purposes is simply the fact that Hart neglected power-conferring norms (and immunity-conferring norms) in his analysis of the internal point of view. Quite remarkable is such an oversight by a philosopher who did so much to draw the attention of his fellow philosophers to the import of power-conferring norms.

2.5 Hart's neglect of power-conferring norms: self-imposed obligations

In the final chapter of *The Concept of Law*, Hart presented a largely commendable discussion of the limits on national sovereignty that are imposed by the constraints of international law. However, one brief portion of his discussion is disastrously confused – and the confusion stems from another instance of his neglect of power-conferring laws.[6] Hart there set out to refute voluntarist theories of international law, which purport to "reconcile the (absolute) sovereignty of states with the existence of binding rules of international law, by treating all international obligations as self-imposed like the obligation which arises from a promise" (224). In this characterization of the voluntarist theories, Hart correctly declared that the explanandum of any such theory is the existence of obligations incumbent on states under international law. A proponent of the voluntarist approach maintains that any such obligations have been activated through the acceptance of them by each nation-state that is now under them. Having opened his discussion of voluntarism correctly in this manner, however, Hart stumbled into confusion by resolving to demonstrate the incoherence of "the argument designed to show that states, because of their sovereignty, can only be subject to or bound by rules which they have imposed upon themselves" (224, emphasis omitted). Notwithstanding that he had begun by correctly attributing to the voluntarists a thesis about self-imposed *obligations*, Hart here incorrectly attributed to them a thesis about self-imposed *rules*. His blunder on that point permeated his whole attempt to expose the incoherence of voluntarism, as he argued that "the [voluntarist] view that a state may impose obligations on itself by promise, agreement, or treaty is not, however, consistent with the theory that states are subject only to rules which they have thus imposed on themselves." He elaborated (225, emphases in original):

> For, in order that words, spoken or written, should in certain circumstances function as a promise, agreement, or treaty, and so give rise to obligations and confer rights which others may claim, *rules* must already exist providing that a state is bound to do whatever it undertakes by appropriate words to do. Such rules obviously cannot derive *their* obligatory status from a self-imposed obligation to obey them.

Though Hart was correct in contending that any blanket denial of the possibility of acceptance-independent norms in the international arena would be incoherent if combined with the proposition that states can impose obligations on themselves, he was thereby attacking a straw man – because voluntarists deny not the possibility of acceptance-independent norms but instead the possibility of acceptance-independent obligations. Their denial of that latter possibility is consistent with an affirmation of the former possibility, since the norms applicable to states include power-conferring norms. Some of those power-conferring norms are acceptance-independent. Power-conferring norms are not in themselves obligatory; they do not *sans plus* impose any obligations on the states that are within their power-conferring sway. Hence, the acceptance-independence of some norms which confer powers in the international domain is consistent with the proposition that all obligations incumbent on states are self-imposed through acceptance.

When Hart wrote in the passage above that the norms under which a state imposes obligations on itself cannot derive their own obligatoriness from any self-imposed obligations to obey them, he was strangely failing to notice that those norms are power-conferring rather than duty-imposing. Like other power-conferring norms, they are not obligatory; and thus they do not need to derive obligatoriness from any source. Instead of imposing obligations on each state, they endow each state with powers to impose obligations on itself. What is so puzzling and dismaying is that I am here making points which Hart himself made *mutatis mutandis* in his own discussions of power-conferring norms in the third chapter of *The Concept of Law*. He there emphasized that power-conferring laws are not obligatory on anyone to whom they are addressed – "Such laws do not impose duties or obligations" (27) – and he rightly held that promissory norms which enable individuals to bind themselves through certain commitment-incurring procedures are paradigmatic instances of norms that confer powers (43). Given that those promissory norms which make possible the self-binding of individuals are the moral counterparts of the international-law norms which make possible the self-binding of states, the blindness of Hart to the power-conferring character of the latter norms is truly baffling.

3 Legislators bound

Hart's general strategy in his critique of the Austinian command theory of law, consisting in his efforts to show that any such theory will founder as it obfuscates law's normativity, is well exemplified in his complaint about the inability of the command theory to explain how the members of a sovereign legislative body can be bound by their own directives (42–4). Though the members of the supreme legislative body in virtually any society are exempt from some of the legal requirements that apply to most other people, they along with everyone else are subject to most ordinary legal requirements. Like everyone else, those members are not legally at liberty to engage in acts of arson or murder or fraud or rape. Yet, in this respect as in sundry other respects, the actualities of virtually every system of governance do not fit the Austinian model of a gunman writ large. When a gunman issues his behests to his victims, he is solely the addressor of those behests and not an addressee thereof. Austin's top-down model of law, with its portrayal of a sovereign whose mandates are imposed on citizens from a position of dominant ascendance, does not leave room for a sovereign body whose members are bound by those very mandates.

As Hart observed, the most enticing route of escape for a defender of Austin lies in differentiating between the capacity of each legislator as a private individual and the capacity of each legislator as a sovereign official. Legal requirements incumbent on each legislator have been imposed on her in her former capacity by the legislators collectively, each of whom has acted in his or her latter capacity as a member of a sovereign body. So a defender of Austin might be inclined to respond. A private/public distinction of this kind is irreproachable in itself, but, as Hart remarked, it is not available to a supporter of Austin. After all, any such private/public distinction presupposes the operativeness of power-conferring laws that invest some people with public powers as legislators – yet, as we have seen, power-conferring laws have no place in an Austinian command theory. When somebody invokes a private/public distinction to accommodate Hart's observation that ordinary legal requirements in any typical society apply to the members of the topmost legislative body therein, he or she has abandoned the Austinian understanding of law.

Thus, by advancing the observation just mentioned, as well as by advancing his volley of other objections, Hart revealed how the insuperable weaknesses of the Austinian command theory flow from that theory's unremitting disregard of the normativity of law. Time and again, a defender of Austin will find that the limitations of the command theory can be overcome only through the renunciation of that theory in favor of an approach which recognizes that any legal system operates as a matrix of complicatedly interrelated norms. That same basic point emerges in each of the remaining criticisms of Austin by Hart which I shall summarize in this chapter.

4 Custom-derived laws

In just about every legal system, laws derive not only from formal sources such as legislative enactments and adjudicative rulings and administrative regulations and constitutional provisions, but also from some customary practices. When practices in certain areas of life such as commerce are longstanding and prevalently observed and reasonable, the norms that inform those practices will typically be regarded by adjudicators or administrators as legally binding in some contexts. Though the import of custom as a provenance of laws has diminished over the centuries in most legal systems, it has not disappeared altogether. Any adequate account of the nature of law has to explain how customary norms can become legal norms.

Austin did indeed try to provide such an explanation. The problem which he faced, of course, is that the entry of customary norms into the law of a jurisdiction appears to be starkly irreconcilable with his top-down model of law-creation. Whereas the edicts of an Austinian sovereign emanate from a position of ascendance over the citizens who are subjected to those edicts, customary norms arise from patterns of interaction that gradually materialize among diffuse individuals or organizations. The emergence of such norms is a bottom-up crystallization rather than a top-down imposition.

Cognizant of the apparent inconsistency between his account of law-creation and the ways in which customary norms develop into standards that are sufficiently longstanding and widely practiced to become legally binding, Austin attempted to overcome this difficulty through a line of reasoning that comprised two main premises. He first maintained that customary norms never become laws in any particular jurisdiction until they are individually invoked and applied by adjudicators or administrators (the sovereign's functionaries). He then contended that the sovereign has tacitly endorsed any determinations by adjudicators and administrators wherein they invoke and apply customary norms as laws, since the sovereign could have intervened to countermand their decisions but has not done so. Austin thus took himself to have squared the status of some customary norms as laws with his thesis that all laws are grounded in the will of the sovereign as manifestations or expressions of that will.

Hart assailed each of the premises in Austin's argument (46–8). Responding to the first premise, Hart submitted that – at least with reference to the legal systems that are familiar to us – Austin had inverted the actual relationship between customary norms and adjudicative or administrative decision-making. Instead of its being the case that customary norms acquire the status of laws in virtue of their having been invoked and applied by adjudicative or administrative officials, customary norms are to be invoked and applied by adjudicative and administrative officials because those norms are laws which the officials are both legally obligated and legally empowered to recognize as such. Hart allowed that, as a matter of sheer possibility, there could exist a central instance of a legal system in which some customary norms acquire the status of laws in the manner described by Austin. However, in the central instances of legal systems with which we are acquainted, the processes through which such norms become laws are the inverse of what Austin recounted. At the very least, those familiar instances of legal systems are highly credible possibilities – which means that Austin's disregard of them, through his insistence that customary norms can never be laws until those norms are individually invoked and applied, is another manifestation of the fatal inadequacy of his theorizing about law.

In response to Austin's premise about tacit assent, Hart accepted that the factor behind a sovereign's not overturning a particular adjudicative or administrative decision might reside in implicit approval of what has been done. However, that reason for non-interference is by no means the only possible such reason and is very frequently not the consideration that most plausibly accounts for the sovereign's abstention from countermanding the determinations reached by adjudicative or administrative underlings. In a large national legal system, the factor that most likely underlies the non-interference of the sovereign on myriad occasions is the utter infeasibility of monitoring all the judgments that are rendered by the aforementioned underlings. A sovereign's non-interference is attributable more often to unavoidable ignorance than to approval. Moreover, even on the relatively few occasions when the members of a sovereign legislature are aware of invocations of customary norms by adjudicators or administrators, their acquiescence in those invocations might not stem from their agreeing with what has been done; instead, they might simply recognize that the authority of the adjudicators or administrators will be undermined if everyday judgments are continually being overturned. Hence, although the implicit endorsement of the sovereign might be correctly inferable in some contexts where customary norms are invoked and applied without any countermanding interventions by superiors, there are countless other contexts in which alternative considerations explain why no such interventions have occurred. Defenders of Austin cannot correctly presume that the sovereign tacitly concurs with every adjudicative or administrative determination that is left unimpugned. Consequently, the defenders of Austin cannot correctly insist that every such determination is discretely grounded in the will of the sovereign. Customary norms can enter into the law without being so grounded.

In short, an Austinian approach to the status of customary norms as laws is woefully inadequate. Hart's own account of the status of such norms as laws will become evident in my next chapter, but what should already be clear is that that status is itself a product of norms. As we shall see, the foundational norms that endow some customary norms with the status of laws – by specifying certain properties, such as longstandingness and widespread observance and reasonableness, which render that status applicable – are not properly analyzable as Austinian commands. Many of those foundational norms are power-conferring, and even the ones that are duty-imposing are not edicts that emanate from a locus of dominant ascendance. Thus, although the problem of accounting for the status of some customary norms as laws may initially seem to be rather esoteric, it has proved to be one of the wedges with which Hart was able to split open the Austinian model of law-creation. His alternative model, which we shall examine in my next chapter, derives its strength precisely from its avoidance of the irreparably distortive features of Austin's theory.

5 Limits on sovereignty

Let us close this chapter by pondering Austin's insistence on the legal illimitability of the prerogatives of any sovereign. Unlike Bentham, who grasped that the supreme law-making authority in a society can be limited and divided (Hart 1982, ch. 9), Austin proclaimed that the sway of a sovereign is never susceptible to any legal restrictions. Hart, in his ripostes to Austin on this point, allowed that there can exist a system of legal governance in which the prerogatives of the supreme ruler or body are indeed not subject to any legal curbs. However, Austin was not merely making a claim about the possibility or actuality of such a system; much more boldly, he was contending that the legal illimitability of a sovereign's prerogatives is a matter of conceptual necessity in every system of law. Hart rightly looked askance at that conceptual thesis, and he highlighted several potential sources of confusion that might beguile somebody into subscribing to such a thesis. We should particularly take note of two of his points here.

First, a potential source of confusion is the notion that any legal curbs on the sway of a sovereign must consist in legal duties. To be sure, even if that notion were correct, it would not exclude the possibility of such curbs – since, as Bentham discerned (Hart 1982, 108–9), the legal duties incumbent on a sovereign body could be given effect through mechanisms such as judicial review in any of its diverse forms. However, the possibility of legal limitations on the sway of a sovereign becomes even clearer when we recognize that such limitations usually consist in the withholding of legal powers rather than in the imposition of legal duties (69, 70). For example, the First Amendment to the US Constitution withholds from the US Congress the legal power to deprive Americans of various legal liberties. If the Congress enacts a putative law that purports to abridge one or more of the liberties protected by the First Amendment, any courts that rule upon the matter correctly will deem the putative law to be invalid as a result of its going beyond what the Congress is legally empowered to do. In line with what has been remarked in §2.1 of this chapter, the nullity of the Congressional enactment is not a sanction levied in response to a breach of a legal duty; rather, it is the upshot of an attempt to exercise a nonexistent legal power. Limitations on the law-making sway of a sovereign are frequently, indeed typically, of this kind.

Second, another potential source of confusion is the conflation of supremacy with unlimitedness (70–1). At the federal level of the system of governance that prevails in the United States, the topmost legislative body is the Congress; the topmost executive office is the Presidency; and the topmost adjudicative body is the US Supreme Court. Paramount though each body or office is within its branch of government, however, no body or office is unlimited in the scope of its legal powers. Anyone inclined to defend Austin should always strive to keep clearly in view this distinction between legal supremacy and legal unrestrictedness.

Austin himself scarcely failed to notice that the supreme legislative body in the American system of governance is limited in the range of matters over which it is legally empowered to enact laws. However, instead of concluding that the prerogatives of a legal sovereign are not necessarily unrestricted by law in any particular jurisdiction, Austin concluded that – despite appearances to the contrary – the US Congress, either on its own or in combination with the Presidency, is not the sovereign in the American system of governance. Rather, Austin affirmed, the real sovereign behind the ostensible sovereign in the American system is the electorate.

Hart delivered himself of a barrage of retorts to this maneuver by Austin (71–8), but the key point is that Austin again had to presuppose the operativeness of power-conferring laws even while he took no account of such laws in his command theory. Let us mull over the matter as follows. At present, the electorate in the USA comprises approximately 230 million people. If those people are to perform the role of an Austinian sovereign, they have to be able to reach decisions. Could they do so by arriving at informal consensuses, in the manner of a few friends who decide among themselves to eat lunch at a certain restaurant? One obstacle is that the adoption of such informal methods of decision-making would render outlandish the proposition that an Austinian sovereign acts as a commander in a top-down fashion. Friends do not command themselves to patronize a certain restaurant when they informally agree unanimously to go there for their lunch, and they do not obey themselves when they proceed to go there. Likewise the members of the American electorate will not be commanding themselves to abide by certain legal norms, if those norms are all established through informal and consensual modes of decision-making. Austin's whole model of command and obedience would lack any purchase on the situation of the electorate. An even more severe problem, however, is the sheer ludicrousness of the notion that 230 million people will be able to arrive at informal consensuses in the manner of a handful of friends. Even one such informal consensus on a narrowly focused matter would be utterly infeasible among so many people. Laughably preposterous is the prospect of numerous such consensuses on multitudes of large and complicated issues of public policy over extended periods of time.

In short, if the members of the American electorate are to act as a sovereign, their methods of decision-making cannot resemble the deliberations of a handful of friends. Unanimity reached informally is not even remotely credible as an objective. Instead, their methods of decision-making will have to be structured and guided by an array of rules and formal procedures. Complex arrangements will address matters such as the following: who is eligible to participate in the processes of decision-making; when and where and how can eligible people participate in those processes; how are issues to be identified and selected for resolution through the processes of decision-making; how are people's contributions to those processes best aggregated; what levels of support are needed for the success of proposals or the election of candidates; how are any decisions to be implemented? With a medley of rules and procedures in place to handle those questions and any number of other questions, an electorate of 230 million people can arrive at decisions collectively. If anyone hopes to defend the idea that the electorate of a large country (or even a small country) can perform the role of an Austinian sovereign, he or she will have to accept that the fulfillment of that role must involve such a medley of rules and procedures. What is so problematic for a supporter of Austin, however, is that the rules and procedures in question are established by power-conferring laws – precisely the laws for which the Austinian command theory leaves no room. Such laws enable the members of the electorate to reach authoritative decisions by conforming to specified procedures and arrangements for the bindingness of acts of participation in collective decision-making. Without such laws that prescribe those procedures and arrangements, any processes of collective decision-making would be amorphously futile. Thus, to vindicate Austin's relocation of sovereignty in the electorate, defenders of Austin will have to jettison his command model and replace it with a theory that adequately takes account of the full range of laws in any legal system.

Hence, by dissecting the Austinian account of sovereignty, Hart once again pressed home his central objection to Austin's whole jurisprudential theory. No jurisprudential approach that obscures the normativity of law can be satisfactory. As Hart declared in the peroration of his critique of Austin (77):

> These arguments against the [Austinian command] theory ... are fundamental in the sense that they amount to the contention that the theory is not merely mistaken in detail, but that the simple idea of orders, habits, and obedience, cannot be adequate for the analysis of law. What is required instead is the notion of a rule conferring powers, which may be limited or unlimited, on persons qualified in certain ways to legislate by complying with a certain procedure.

Hart also raised many ancillary objections to Austin's model of law, but the *fil conducteur* that ran throughout his ruminations on Austinian jurisprudence was his insistence that legal systems are fundamentally systems of norms. Of course, to insist as much is scarcely to deny that legal systems are vehicles for the exertion of coercive control and direction. Hart was acutely mindful of the ways – the potentially very dangerous ways – in which the operations of a legal system enhance the collective might of the people who run it. However, he blended his awareness of that crucial point with his equally firm recognition that those operations are essentially normative. As we turn now to investigate the main elements of Hart's own theory of law, we shall find his emphasis on the normativity of law everywhere.

3

The Components of Hart's Jurisprudential Theory

Having distanced himself from the Austinian command theory of law, Hart put together the components of his alternative approach. Though he remained firmly within the tradition of legal positivism to which the command theory in its several versions had also belonged, he set out to dissociate that tradition from the misrepresentations and distortions which he had exposed in the Austinian account of law. Instead of trying to tinker with the command theory to remedy its shortcomings while staying within its confines, he sought to displace that theory and to steer the tradition of positivism along a markedly different path. In so doing, he was aiming to supply satisfactory answers to the three main questions which he had broached at the outset of *The Concept of Law* (questions about the relationships between law and coercion, the relationships between law and morality, and the normative character of law). Most notably, in opposition to the Austinian command theory, he was endeavoring to give due salience to the normativity of legal institutions – while also emphasizing that the normativity of those institutions is not necessarily moral. As he proclaimed: "The root cause of failure [of the command theory] is that the elements out of which the theory was constructed, viz. the ideas of orders, obedience, habits, and threats, do not include, and cannot by their combination yield, the idea of a rule, without which we cannot hope to elucidate even the most elementary forms of law" (80).

Hart assembled most of the constituents of his own jurisprudential model after he had completed his critique of the command theory, but he introduced some of those constituents in the course of that

Components of Hart's Jurisprudential Theory

critique. In my second chapter, I have already touched upon his distinction (or set of distinctions) between the internal point of view and other points of view. Although he presented his chief discussion of the several points of view after he had finished his confrontation with Austin, he initially adverted to the internal viewpoint while he was still waging that confrontation. Partly for that reason, and partly because the distinctions among the various points of view are of such moment in Hart's legal philosophy, this chapter will commence with those distinctions.

A preliminary caveat is needed, however. In §2.4 of my second chapter, I have chided Hart for his having analyzed the internal point of view in a way that is applicable only to duty-imposing norms and not to power-conferring or immunity-conferring norms. I have there ventured two explications of a viewpoint that is internal to power-conferring norms. Any full account of the outlooks that sustain the operations of legal systems would have to incorporate those explications or some alternative explications in order to cover the outlooks of officials and citizens that are centered on power-conferring norms. However, because the continuation here of my effort to rectify Hart's oversight would lead my present discussion to become unmanageably lengthy, I will at this juncture follow his example by delineating the contours of the internal point of view only in application to duty-imposing norms. (In the final section of this chapter, I will reproach Hart afresh for his oversight.)

1 The internal/external distinction

As has been recounted in my second chapter, the internal point of view is that of a person who participates in some practice or activity or institution. Such a person seeks to uphold the duty-imposing norms of the practice or activity or institution, by adopting the critical reflective attitude in relation to them. As we have seen, the critical reflective attitude manifests itself as a triad of behavioral dispositions: a general disposition to comply with the requirements of some duty-imposing norm(s), a general disposition to object to contraventions of those requirements by other people, and a general disposition to acknowledge the appropriateness of censure that is directed against one's own contraventions of those requirements. Somebody who has adopted the critical reflective attitude in relation to some duty-imposing norm N is thereby accepting N and displaying a commitment to N. However, as will be stressed hereafter, and as I have fleetingly mentioned in §2.4 of Chapter 2, the stance of commitment need not be based on any perception of N as morally worthy. A person can adopt the critical reflective attitude toward N for moral reasons, of course, but her embrace of such a stance might alternatively be grounded on self-interested considerations or some other factors. Hart commented more than once that the motivations which impel citizens or officials to uphold legal norms can be quite diverse (197, 203, 231–2, 257). Still, whatever may be the considerations that prompt someone to assume a posture of commitment in relation to N, that posture is distinctive of the viewpoint of a participant. Anyone who occupies such a perspective – the internal perspective – maintains that the requirements established by N are binding on herself and on others.

As has been remarked in my second chapter, the internal standpoint of a participant in a practice is to be contrasted with the external standpoint of an observer. However, there are two varieties of the external perspective that should be taken into account here. Somewhat peculiarly, Hart in *The Concept of Law* devoted most of his attention to an implausibly extreme variety of the external perspective, and he devoted considerably less attention to a far more important variety.[1] An observer who adopts the extreme external viewpoint in relation to some practice or institution will regard that practice or institution as a configuration of regularities in the behavior of the people who participate therein. Such an observer makes no effort to understand people's actions in the ways in which they are understood by the people themselves. Instead, while charting the regularities in their conduct that involve their manifesting of the critical reflective attitude with reference to the practice or institution in which they are participants, she proceeds in much the same manner as a meteorologist who monitors the patterns of cloud-formation or who gauges the pressure of the atmosphere. Attending only to the surface of people's behavior, the extreme external observer relies on notions such as "cause," "effect," "regularity," "predictability," and "probability" as the key concepts for an account of an institution or practice. Though such an observer might not deny that people harbor outlooks and beliefs, she ignores such mental states in order to concentrate solely on visible instances of behavior (such as reprimands or commendations).

Quite different is the approach of someone who theorizes from a moderate external perspective. While such an observer certainly does not ignore the aspects of institutions and practices that are the preoccupation of an extreme external theorist, she attributes normative attitudes and beliefs and concerns to the people who participate in those institutions or practices. She takes account of the ways in which those people perceive their own conduct, and she incorporates their perceptions into her overall exposition of their institutions or practices. Although she of course detects the regularities of behavior in which those institutions or practices consist, she also recognizes that outlooks of acceptance or commitment or allegiance are operative in those patterns of behavior, and she ascribes such outlooks to the people involved. She herself, qua external observer, does not harbor those attitudes toward the institutions or practices which she studies – but she discerns that any adequate analysis of those institutions or practices will have to reveal how they are animated by those attitudes on the part of participants. Moreover, of course, she herself might be a participant in some of those institutions or practices as well as an observer of them; if so, then she too displays the attitudes which she imputes to the other participants. (Note that, because the outlooks of acceptance or commitment harbored by participants in institutions and practices do not necessarily derive from moral concerns, a moderate external observer of those institutions and practices should typically leave open the nature of the underlying considerations that prompt people to participate supportively in them. As has been mentioned above, Hart himself left open this very matter when he recounted the internal viewpoints of citizens and officials in relation to legal institutions.)

Now, although Hart in *The Concept of Law* treated of the moderate external viewpoint far more tersely than of the extreme external viewpoint, the former is in fact markedly more important for the philosophy of law than is the latter. It is the perspective adopted by Hart himself in his ruminations on legal systems, and it is the perspective adopted by virtually every contemporary legal positivist (and also by many contemporary legal philosophers who are not legal positivists). Even the contemporary philosophers of law who do not proceed from a moderate external point of view – such as the followers of Ronald Dworkin – are scarcely opting instead for the extreme external perspective. Rather, they present their accounts of law from the internal point of view of committed participants. Hence, the most significant perspectival division in the philosophy of law is not between the internal point of view and the external point of view *tout court*, but is instead between the internal point of view and the moderate external point of view. Whatever might be the import of the extreme external standpoint for some legal sociologists, that extreme perspective does not figure saliently in the philosophy of law.

Hart somewhat misled his readers about the extreme external viewpoint when he suggested that it is the perspective characteristically adopted by citizens who eschew the full critical reflective attitude toward the duty-imposing laws of their society and who comply with those laws solely in order to avoid the imposition of sanctions (90–1). Were Hart's suggestion true, the extreme external point of view would be of greater significance than I have contended. However, the viewpoint that is in fact characteristically adopted by citizens who concern themselves solely with the avoidance of sanctions is the moderate external perspective rather than the extreme external perspective. A disaffected citizen will generally understand the workings of a legal system far more insightfully – and will therefore be far more advantageously positioned to anticipate the outcomes of those workings in particular contexts – if he recognizes that such a system is run by people who harbor certain normative attitudes. A disgruntled citizen does not share those attitudes, of course, but he will be able to pursue his objectives more effectively if he is not blind to the fact that those attitudes are held by others in his society. In short, he will be able to pursue his objectives more effectively by proceeding from the moderate external viewpoint than by proceeding from the extreme external viewpoint. The former perspective, rather than the latter, is the characteristic posture of a citizen who wants to stay within the restrictions of the law in order to forestall the punitive measures (or other rectificatory measures) that would most likely follow as responses to any contraventions of those restrictions. Certainly, the former perspective rather than the latter is the characteristic posture of anyone with legal expertise who might advise such a citizen.

Hart further misled his readers when he submitted that the deontic terminology employed in ascriptions of legal duties is "required only by those who see their own and other persons' conduct from the internal point of view. What the external point of view, which limits itself to the observable regularities of behavior, cannot reproduce is the way in which the rules function as rules in the lives of those who normally are the majority of society" (90). Hart was here disregarding the moderate version of the external point of view altogether and was writing as if the extreme version of that point of view were the only version. A legal philosopher who adopts the moderate external perspective will have to avail herself of deontic terminology – the language of "obligation" or "duty" and associated concepts – as she comes to grips with the juridical institutions and practices which she is probing. Likewise, as she comes to grips with those institutions and practices, she will be endeavoring to recount the ways in which the norms that structure them are upheld as norms by the participants therein. Her task as a moderate external observer is to apprehend the normative attitudes of the participants, so that she can attribute to them those very attitudes. She cannot perform that task without fathoming the participants' perceptions of their own endeavors.

In sum, although Hart laconically adverted to the moderate external perspective when he drew the internal/external distinction in *The Concept of Law*, he thenceforward largely slighted it while he preoccupied himself with the failings of the extreme external perspective.[2] His slighting of the moderate external viewpoint occurred even though he occupied that very viewpoint throughout his theorizing about law. He was of course justified in marshaling his objections to the extreme external point of view, but at times he conveyed the impression that the lone alternative to the shortcomings of that point of view is the internal perspective. Readers can dispel such an impression by attending to the moderate external viewpoint from which he himself wrote.

2 The simulative point of view

Even when we have taken full account of the moderate external point of view as an alternative both to the extreme external viewpoint and to the internal viewpoint, we have yet to note another important perspective that can be occupied by people who are not participants in the practices or institutions to which their investigations pertain. Hart in *The Concept of Law* neglected this additional perspective almost entirely, though he drew attention to it in some of his later work (1982, 153–5; 1983, 14–15). It is what I have elsewhere designated as the "simulative" point of view (Kramer 1999, 165–6; 2013b, 38–40). Like a person who proceeds from a moderate external perspective, a person who proceeds from a simulative perspective will strive to apprehend the normative attitudes of the participants in some practice or institution. However, unlike an observer who occupies the moderate external point of view, somebody who occupies the simulative point of view does not merely impute normative attitudes and beliefs to the aforementioned participants; in addition, she articulates those attitudes and beliefs as if they were her own. She gives voice to the participants' internal point of view without thereby committing herself to it.

To some degree the epithet "recitative" would be suitable for this perspective, since a person engaged in simulation is doing something quite closely akin to a performance by a theatrical actor. For example, if an actor plays Iago in a production of *Othello*, he will recite Iago's lines and do his best to convey Iago's thoughts and emotions – Iago's outlook or viewpoint – to the audience. Even a superb rendition of the role, however, does not count at all as an endorsement of Iago's villainy. When an adept actor succeeds in fathoming Iago's point of view and consequently manages to deliver a riveting performance, he can nonetheless disapprove strongly (and almost certainly does disapprove strongly) of the knavery which he is feigning to carry out.

Yet, in one major respect, an analogy between the recitations of a thespian and the discourses of a simulative theorist breaks down. Though some productions of plays require or permit the improvisation of numerous lines, most do not; most productions involve the recitation of lines that have been written beforehand by dramatists. In a typical production of *Othello*, the man who performs the role of Iago will recite some or all of the lines written by Shakespeare for that character, and he will add few or no lines of his own making. By contrast, a theorist who adopts the simulative perspective will frequently elaborate the implications of the set of beliefs which he is articulating. He may well draw inferences or develop lines of argument or undertake extensions that have not thitherto occurred to anyone else. Even when his discourse is a straightforward recapitulation of thoughts and sentiments that have previously been expressed by other people, he does not usually confine himself to repeating lines verbatim that have already been written or uttered. Hence, a simulative discourse is both illuminatingly similar to recitation and importantly different from it. Either of those modes of communication can be serviceable for giving voice to a point of view that is not one's own, but – even if we allow for the creativity and ingenuity that enliven a deft theatrical performance – the simulative perspective leaves much more latitude for innovation than does the recitation of lines.

In *The Concept of Law* the simulative perspective surfaces only once, and quite inconspicuously. While discussing the assertions through which the officials of a legal system identify certain norms as laws that belong to the system, Hart maintained that those assertions – which are made from the internal point of view of the officials

Components of Hart's Jurisprudential Theory 67

– "presuppose the truth of the external statement of fact that the system is generally efficacious" (104, emphasis omitted). However, he cautioned against the notion that an affirmation of the general efficacy of the system is an element in the very meaning of each of the aforementioned assertions. He explained why any such notion would be too strong (104, emphasis in original):

> For though it is normally pointless or idle to talk of the validity of a rule of a system which has never established itself or has been discarded, none the less it is not meaningless nor is it always pointless. One vivid way of teaching Roman Law is to speak *as if* the system were efficacious still and to discuss the validity of particular rules and solve problems in their terms; and one way of nursing hopes for the restoration of an old social order destroyed by revolution, and rejecting the new, is to cling to the criteria of legal validity of the old regime. This is implicitly done by the White Russian who still claims property under some rule of descent which was a valid rule of Tsarist Russia.

In an endnote Hart added that his stance on this point in the quoted passage differentiated him from Hans Kelsen, whom he construed as claiming that an implicit affirmation of the general efficacy of a legal system is essential for the very meaningfulness of any statement that identifies a norm as an operative law of the system (295).

Though Hart did not make clear that he was here delineating a further point of view to be placed alongside the internal perspective and the two external perspectives, he was indeed gesturing toward a simulative standpoint from which law-ascertaining pronouncements or other pronouncements can be intoned. Unlike a jurist in the era of ancient Rome, a modern-day teacher of the law of that era does not presuppose the efficacy of the Roman legal system when she asserts that certain norms belong to that system as laws. Instead, she speaks *as if* that system were still efficacious. She simulates the utterances of the ancient jurists without actually subscribing to the presuppositions (about the efficacy of the Roman system of law) that would have been attached to their utterances.

Of course, some law-ascertaining statements enunciated from a simulative perspective do presuppose the efficacy of the particular legal system that is under consideration. Suppose for example that, instead of simulating the law-ascertaining pronouncements of the judges in ancient Rome, a teacher of law simulates the pronouncements of the judges in her present-day jurisdiction. She is thereby speaking from the simulative viewpoint, for she is giving voice to an internal perspective which she does not genuinely occupy. However, each of the laws identified as such in her simulative declarations is a product of a legal system that actually operates throughout the jurisdiction where she utters those declarations. Hence, unlike a teacher who simulates the law-ascertaining determinations of the officials in a legal system that long ago ceased to exist, the teacher who simulates the law-ascertaining determinations of the officials in her own society does presuppose the general efficacy of the system whose laws are identified as such in her simulative pronouncements. Indeed, precisely because she takes for granted that the prevailing system is generally efficacious, she is inclined to believe further that her students have an important stake in knowing what the laws of that system are. She adopts the simulative point of view as a vivid pedagogical technique with the aim of fulfilling their stake in the acquisition of such knowledge.

Still, although not every law-ascertaining utterance made from the simulative perspective will have suspended the normal presupposition about efficacy, some such utterances (like those made by the teacher of Roman Law or by the White Russian) do suspend that presupposition. Accordingly, the operativeness of such a presupposition can be specified as follows. Every law-ascertaining statement articulated from the internal point of view – the point of view characteristically adopted by legal officials in the course of their endeavors to ascertain the existence and contents of the laws in their system of governance – does carry a presupposition about the general efficacy of the system to which the identified laws belong. By contrast, not every law-ascertaining statement articulated from the simulative point of view is invested with such a presupposition. Sometimes in a statement of the latter type, the simulative aspect pertains not only to the role of an adjudicative or administrative official but also to the functionality of the legal system about which the statement is made.[3]

3 The blurring of distinctions between viewpoints

Distinct though the simulative point of view and the internal point of view are as an uncommitted stance and a committed stance respectively, the division between them is problematic in some contexts. Let us consider three main varieties of such contexts. An example of the first variety was adumbrated by Hart in his reference

Components of Hart's Jurisprudential Theory 69

to White Russians who expressed loyalty to the erstwhile tsarist regime during the Soviet era by continuing to claim the property that would have been inherited by them under the tsarist laws. On the one hand, if the White Russians had deludedly believed that the tsarist regime still operated as a generally efficacious system of governance, their claims of inheritance would have been straightforward instances of assertions uttered from the internal point of view rather than from the simulative point of view. Attached to those assertions would have been a presupposition about the efficacy of the system – a false presupposition, of course. On the other hand, Hart was clearly assuming that the White Russians were not deluded. Their claims of inheritance emanated from the simulative point of view, without carrying any presupposition about the efficacy of the tsarist system of governance. Yet the White Russians pressed those claims precisely in order to underscore their commitment to that system of governance. In relation to some or all of the laws of the tsarist era, they harbored the dispositions of the full critical reflective attitude. Thus, although their utterances were simulative in that they did not labor under any illusions about the current efficacy of the system whose laws they invoked, their utterances – like internal utterances – were committed rather than uncommitted. They straddled the divide between the internal perspective and the simulative perspective.

I have discussed elsewhere a second kind of context in which the internal/simulative distinction becomes blurred (Kramer 1999, 166 n19). Suppose that an official in some system of governance exhibits the full critical reflective attitude in relation to the duty-imposing laws of the system, and that he does so purely because he wishes to avoid the sanctions that are likely to be levied upon him if he declines to behave in such a fashion. His reasons for acting are centered entirely on the avoidance of sanctions, as he does not feel any independent ethical or prudential commitment to the laws which he invokes and applies. On the one hand, his utterances as an official are advanced from the internal viewpoint in that they are products of all the dispositions of the critical reflective attitude. Given that he is upholding the laws which he invokes and applies, he can accurately be said to display a commitment to those laws and to the system that comprises them. On the other hand, the display is only a display. He is simulating the sense of allegiance that is signaled by his actions of invoking and applying the laws of the system wherein he occupies his position as an official. Although his simulation of a sense of allegiance will be robustly persistent if his worries about sanctions for remissness are robustly persistent, it is indeed an instance of feigning. Hence, in application to his utterances, the distinction between the internal point of view and the simulative point of view has become effaced.

We should turn from the legal domain to the ethical domain for a third category of cases in which the internal/simulative distinction breaks down. Specifically, we should briefly ponder the mentality of psychopaths.[4] Most psychopaths are able to understand moral concepts, but many of them are completely unmoved emotionally or conatively by the applicability of such concepts, and others are moved in the wrong directions by the applicability of those concepts. That is, psychopaths of the latter kind derive intense gratification from the knowing perpetration of wickedness as such. They recognize that their acts are heinous, and they are impelled to perform those acts by precisely that recognition. Their awareness of the iniquity of their conduct is what drives them on with special delight. Now, when such a psychopath forms a judgment that a certain course of conduct is evil, he is indeed forming his own judgment rather than simulating or recapitulating the judgments reached by other people. He needs to apprehend what is morally right and obligatory – rather than merely what is thought by others to be morally right and obligatory. Only by descrying what is actually right and obligatory can he fulfill his objective of flouting what is right and obligatory. Consequently, his moral conclusions are not voiced from a simulative perspective. Yet, although he reaches his conclusions in the non-simulative manner of someone who proceeds from the internal point of view, he is not at all disposed to act in accordance with the terms of those conclusions. On the contrary, he is strongly disposed to act athwart their terms. Thus, his moral judgments straddle the internal/simulative division in a peculiarly unsettling fashion.

4 Primary norms and secondary norms: the general distinction

In addition to differentiating among the standpoints that people can adopt in relation to norms, Hart differentiated among types of norms. My second chapter has already scrutinized his distinction between duty-imposing norms and power-conferring norms. Let us now examine his related distinction between primary norms and secondary norms, which is central to his theory of law.

Hart went somewhat astray both with his "primary"/"secondary" terminology and with his way of introducing the distinction marked by that terminology. As has been discussed in my opening chapter, he misled his readers by declaring that the supplementation of primary norms with secondary norms is tantamount to a transition from a pre-legal society to a legal system of governance. Having characterized the matter in that vein, Hart conveyed the impression that he was indulging in anthropological surmises from his armchair. Readers should not succumb to such an impression, and should recognize that Hart was instead undertaking a thought-experiment to stimulate reflection on the crucial functions that are performed by secondary norms. If we reflect on an imaginary state of affairs from which those functions are absent, we can grasp vividly how far-reaching the roles of secondary norms in any society are.

What, then, is the distinction between primary norms and secondary norms? Hart did not fully succeed in providing a satisfactory general formulation of that distinction. His main effort to encapsulate it should be quoted at length here (81):

> Under rules of the one type, which may well be considered the basic or primary type, human beings are required to do or abstain from certain actions, whether they wish to or not. Rules of the other type are in a sense parasitic upon or secondary to the first; for they provide that human beings may by doing or saying certain things introduce new rules of the primary type, extinguish or modify old ones, or in various ways determine their incidence or control their operations. Rules of the first type impose duties; rules of the second type confer powers, public or private. Rules of the first type concern actions involving physical movement or changes; rules of the second type provide for operations which lead not merely to physical movement or change, but to the creation or variation of duties or obligations.

This oft-quoted passage abounds with shortcomings. One relatively minor weakness is that the passage twice intimates that all the powers established by secondary norms are abilities to alter duties (or abilities to alter the norms that impose duties). In fact, as has been indicated in my second chapter, legal powers are abilities to effect changes in legal positions (or legal norms) of any type. Some legal powers are indeed abilities to change or create or extinguish legal obligations, but sundry other legal powers are abilities to change or create or extinguish legal powers. Hart erred by suggesting otherwise.

As several commentators have observed (Green 2012a, 314; Hacker 1977, 19–21; MacCormick 2008, 130–4; Raz 1979, 178–9; Tapper 1973,

248–68), a more profound weakness in the passage quoted above is that Hart therein adduced multiple criteria for the demarcation between primary and secondary norms. Because those criteria are not extensionally equivalent – in other words, because they do not pick out the same sets of norms through the ways in which they specify the aforementioned demarcation – Hart did not present a univocal general standard for drawing the distinction on which his account of law as the union of primary and secondary norms is centered. First and most prominent among the ways in which he differentiated between primary norms and secondary norms was his equation of the former with duty-imposing norms and of the latter with power-conferring norms. Were the primary/secondary dichotomy to be understood solely and straightforwardly along these lines, it would be covered by Hart's quite rigorous meditations on duty-imposing norms and power-conferring norms in his critique of Austin. However, as we shall see, most of the secondary norms which Hart classified as such are not only power-conferring but also duty-imposing; that is, they comprise duty-imposing strands as well as power-conferring strands. Moreover, the simple dichotomy between duty-imposing norms and power-conferring norms does not neatly tally with some of the rest of the remarks in the passage above.

Most notably, that dichotomy does not perfectly tally with the suggestion by Hart that secondary norms are parasitic upon primary norms (whereas there is no similar relationship of dependence in the other direction). Hart was here using the term "parasitic" in a somewhat technical philosophical sense to mean that the contents of secondary norms presuppose the existence of other norms. He was seeking to make the same point which he articulated in his somewhat later assertion that secondary norms "may all be said to be on a different level from the primary rules, for they are all *about* such rules" (94, emphasis in original). Now, on the one hand, it is indeed true that the content of every power-conferring norm – as well as the content of every immunity-conferring norm – presupposes the existence of some additional norm(s). On the other hand, however, the contents of some duty-imposing norms and of some liberty-conferring norms also presuppose the existence of additional norms. For example, a judge can be under a legal duty to exercise a legal power of sentencing in specified circumstances; the content of the norm that imposes the duty presupposes the existence of a norm that confers the power of sentencing. Similarly, the judge is legally at liberty to exercise the power of sentencing in specified circumstances. That legal liberty has been conferred upon the judge by a norm whose content presupposes the existence of a norm that confers the power of sentencing. Hence, when the distinction between primary norms and secondary norms is drawn with reference to the property of being parasitic, it does not correspond to the distinction between duty-imposing norms and power-conferring norms. All power-conferring norms and immunity-conferring norms are parasitic, but not all parasitic norms are power-conferring or immunity-conferring. Some parasitic norms are duty-imposing, and some are liberty-conferring.

A third way of delimiting the categories of primary norms and secondary norms is distilled in the closing sentence of the passage quoted above. It too is focused on the contents of the norms. In that closing sentence Hart suggested that the contents of primary norms are specifiable purely in terms of physical conduct, whereas the content of every secondary norm pertains not only to physical conduct but also to some normative change(s). He subsequently echoed that suggestion, when he contended that "while primary rules are concerned with the actions that individuals must or must not do, ... secondary rules are all concerned with the primary rules themselves. They specify the ways in which the primary rules may be conclusively ascertained, introduced, eliminated, varied, and the fact of their violation conclusively determined" (94). This latest criterion for the demarcation between primary norms and secondary norms is extensionally equivalent to the preceding criterion and is therefore not extensionally equivalent to the first criterion.

Although the lengthy passage quoted above probably inclines most readers of *The Concept of Law* to conclude (at least initially) that the primary/secondary distinction is tantamount to the duty-imposing/power-conferring dichotomy, we should resist such a temptation and should recognize that the second of the three criteria inferable from the passage is determinative. That is, the decisive question for classifying norms as primary or secondary is whether the content of each norm presupposes the existence of other norms or not. Under such a criterion, all power-conferring norms and immunity-conferring norms are secondary – but so too are some duty-imposing norms and liberty-conferring norms. All primary norms are duty-imposing or liberty-conferring, but not all duty-imposing or liberty-conferring norms are primary in Hart's sense. Some are secondary, just as all power-conferring or immunity-conferring norms are. As has already been remarked, and as we are about to see, the paramount reason for embracing this understanding of the primary/secondary distinction is that it accords with what Hart said about the specific types of secondary norms which he identified as such.

5 Primary norms and secondary norms: Hart's thought-experiment

In the fifth chapter of *The Concept of Law*, Hart encouraged his readers to imagine a society in which there are no secondary norms. He pointed to three main sets of problems that would afflict any such society. First, there would be irresolvable uncertainty concerning the existence and contents of the prevailing primary norms. As Hart wrote: "[I]f doubts arise as to what the rules are or as to the precise scope of some given rule, there will be no procedure for settling this doubt, either by reference to an authoritative text or to an official whose declarations on this point are authoritative" (92). Second, a severe problem of stagnancy would obtain, as there would not exist any way in which the prevailing primary norms could be deliberately changed. Even more outlandish is that there would not exist any way in which the rights and duties and liberties bestowed by the prevailing primary norms could be deliberately changed (92–3). Third, there would be further irresolvable uncertainty concerning the occurrence or non-occurrence of contraventions of the prevailing primary norms. Even if the members of the fanciful society could all agree about the existence and content of some norm N, they might disagree intractably over the question whether N has been contravened in some particular setting. There would be no means of resolving such a question peacefully and authoritatively (93–4). Furthermore, even were there no doubt about the occurrence of some contravention, there would not be any authoritative way of administering a sanction or some other remedy in response to that contravention. Self-help, perhaps with assistance from the members of one's family or clan, would be the only recourse.

Even in a very small and simple assemblage of people, the three foregoing sets of problems would be grievous. Indeed, the second problem – the problem of stagnancy – would be fatally crippling even in such a small and simple assemblage. After all, its upshot would be that no one could ever acquire any rights of property. *A fortiori*, no one could ever transfer any such rights. Even the most mundane transaction, as a transfer of entitlements rather than merely as a transfer of possession, could not ever take place. No credibly possible society, even on a small scale, could emerge and endure in such conditions – which is one principal reason why Hart's thought-experiment is not to be understood as an anthropological hypothesis about some bygone state of affairs that underwent a transition to the institutions of legal governance. Instead, his thought-experiment is a means of prompting reflection on the extremely important functions that are performed by secondary norms. Those functions consist in averting or alleviating the three sets of problems which Hart recounted. (As has already been contended in my opening chapter, and as will be emphasized afresh in my penultimate chapter, the role of secondary norms in human society is not inherently moral. Although the operativeness of such norms is a necessary condition for the realization of various major ethical values in any community, it is scarcely a sufficient condition; and it is also a necessary condition for the realization of certain large-scale projects of evil such as the institution of chattel slavery. Thus, hugely important though the functions of secondary norms are, the moral character of those functions is proteanly dependent on the circumstances in which they are performed.)

Corresponding to the aforementioned three sets of problems are three types of secondary norms (94–8). First is the Rule of Recognition, which provides for the authoritative ascertainment of the norms that are laws in any given society. Despite the designation attached to it by Hart, which will be explained shortly, the Rule of Recognition is an array of norms. Some of those norms impose duties on legal officials to put into effect certain criteria for ascertaining the existence and contents of laws, and the remaining norms in the Rule of Recognition confer powers on the officials to bind other people with their law-ascertaining determinations. Through the imposition of those duties and the conferral of those powers, the problem of irresolvable uncertainty about the existence and contents of the regnant laws is addressed. To be sure, as we shall observe later, the alleviation of that problem is consistent with some disagreements among the legal officials themselves about the substance of the Rule of Recognition. Officials in a functional legal system converge with one another in their understandings of the key criteria laid down by their Rule of Recognition, but they can and frequently do diverge from one another over the details of the criteria – much as the speakers of English or some other natural language diverge from one another over details of usage and grammar. Still, the wide-rangingness of the convergence among the officials is what largely removes any irresolvable uncertainty about the laws that are applicable to people's conduct. (I will say a great deal more about the Rule of Recognition presently.)

Next among the secondary norms which Hart enumerated are the norms of change. These are many of the power-conferring laws to which he had adverted in his critique of Austin. For example, included in this category are the laws that enable individuals to form sundry legal arrangements such as contracts and marriages and wills and trusts and conveyances. Alongside the laws that confer those private powers are laws that confer public powers of legislation and administrative rule-making. Laws that confer these public powers enable the creation or modification or rescission of general legal norms, while laws that confer the private powers enable the creation or modification or rescission of the legal positions – such as claim-rights and duties and liberties and powers and immunities – that have been established under the general norms. Through these power-conferring laws, then, the problem of crippling stagnancy is averted.

Hart designated his final category of secondary norms as "rules of adjudication" (97), but he thereby exhibited his inordinate preoccupation with the activities of courts and his relative inattention to the activities of administrators. He displayed that inordinate preoccupation throughout his work in legal philosophy, but it is not integral to his analysis of the operations of legal systems or to his arguments in support of legal positivism. Hence, readers are well advised to eschew his excessive focus on adjudicators and to take equal account of the roles of administrators (who range from the directors of large agencies to low-level police officers). Of course, in most legal systems, the determinations of administrators are subject to being overturned by the rulings of adjudicators. However, much the same is true of the determinations reached by adjudicators in the lower tiers of the judicial hierarchy; those determinations are subject to being overturned by the rulings of upper-tier adjudicators. Moreover, unless the decisions of administrators are indeed overturned, they remain binding on everyone to whose conduct they are applicable. Consequently, the laws that bestow public powers on administrators as well as the laws that bestow public powers on adjudicators are the means by which a legal system of governance addresses the problem of irresolvable uncertainty concerning the occurrence and extent of any contraventions of the prevailing laws. Instead of labeling Hart's final category of secondary norms as "norms of adjudication," then, we should label it as "norms of adjudication and administration" or more pithily as "norms of law-application." In most legal systems, those norms establish arrangements for the centralized administration of sanctions and other remedies – though self-help measures are never completely superseded by such arrangements.

Before we move on to examine the Rule of Recognition in greater depth, four points should be broached here in closing. In the first place, we should note again that Hart (despite some of his careless wording) was not presenting an aetiological account of the emergence of secondary norms. Instead of seeking to shed light on the causes that have led to the devising of secondary norms, Hart was aiming to underscore the vital roles of such norms in the operations of government and in the everyday interaction of people. Precisely because the functions of such norms are so immensely important and pervasive, they can all too easily get overlooked in theorizing about law and government – just as the crucial role of oxygen in the atmosphere can get overlooked in one's thinking about human society. We can firmly grasp the import of the presence of oxygen in the atmosphere by imagining how human beings would fare without its presence, and we can likewise firmly grasp the import of secondary norms when we imagine how human beings would fare without their presence. Hart was prodding the imaginations of his readers in exactly that direction.

Another caveat to be entered here is that Hart's taxonomy of secondary norms can mislead readers into thinking that those norms are quite neatly compartmentalized. In fact, as Hart himself discerned, and as will be explored later in this chapter, the fundamental secondary norms in any legal system of governance are complicatedly interdependent. Some aspects of the interdependence are quite apparent; for example, without any law-ascertaining determinations reached implicitly or explicitly by reference to the Rule of Recognition in any particular jurisdiction, the norms of law-application in that jurisdiction could not ever be implemented. Other aspects of the interdependence of the fundamental secondary norms are more complex and subtle, as we shall see. For the moment, we should simply note that the demarcations among the basic secondary norms in any system of law are not nearly as tidy as Hart's tripartite classification might suggest.

A further point to be mentioned here is that my favored way of understanding the distinction between primary norms and secondary norms is vindicated by Hart's catalogue of secondary norms. Though some secondary norms confer powers that are not coupled with any duties, many of the secondary norms in Hart's catalogue confer powers that are indeed integrally bound up with duties. Most notably, as has been observed already and as will be discussed at greater length hereafter, the Rule of Recognition is both power-conferring and duty-imposing; it both authorizes and obligates legal-governmental officials to ascertain the laws of their jurisdiction in accordance with certain criteria. Similarly, the norms of law-application both authorize and obligate the adjudicative and administrative officials in a legal system of governance to give effect to the laws of the system broadly in accordance with their terms. Because so many of the Hartian secondary norms are duty-imposing as accompaniments to the Hartian secondary norms that are power-conferring, we can be confident that the primary/secondary distinction is not equivalent to the distinction between duty-imposing norms and power-conferring norms.

Finally, Hart's account of secondary legal norms might seem to be afflicted by tangles of circularity. After all, the norms of law-application are what confer upon certain people their statuses as adjudicators and administrators, yet those norms will not themselves be operative as laws unless they are ascertained as such under the prevailing Rule of Recognition by officials (adjudicators and administrators). Hence, the statuses of certain people as adjudicators and administrators might seem to be both preconditions and products of the processes whereby the norms of law-application are given effect. Now, although this chapter will address forthrightly these ostensible tangles of circularity, it will do so after expounding the nature of the Rule of Recognition. As will be seen, the key to dissolving this putative crux is to differentiate between two senses in which an ability to alter legal relations can be correctly classifiable as a legal power.

6 The Rule of Recognition: to whom is it addressed?

Let us begin our investigation of the Rule of Recognition by inquiring who its addressees are. A duty-imposing norm is addressed to anyone on whom it places a duty or on whom it confers a correlative claim-right, and a power-conferring norm is addressed to anyone on whom it bestows a power. On whom does the Rule of Recognition impose law-ascertaining duties, and on whom does it confer law-ascertaining powers?

Hart sometimes wrote as if the Rule of Recognition in any society were addressed to all members of the society – legal-governmental officials and private individuals alike. For example, he declared: "Wherever such a rule of recognition is accepted, both private persons and officials are provided with authoritative criteria for identifying primary rules of obligation" (100). When remarking on a fancifully simple Rule of Recognition that contains only one criterion, he similarly stated: "The existence of this simple form of rule of recognition will be manifest in the general practice, on the part of officials *or private persons*, of identifying the rules by this criterion" (101, emphasis added). Several pages later, he referred to "the practice of judges, officials, *and others*, in which the actual existence of a rule of recognition consists," and he affirmed that "the rule of recognition exists only as a complex, but normally concordant, practice of the courts, officials, *and private persons* in identifying the law by reference to certain criteria."[5] These statements make somewhat understandable the assertion by Dworkin (1986, 34) that Hart "said that the true grounds of law lie in the acceptance by the community as a whole of a fundamental master rule (he called this a 'rule of recognition')."

Nonetheless, any temptation to follow Dworkin's reading of Hart should be firmly resisted.[6] Both as a matter of what Hart contended and as a matter of what Hart should have contended, Dworkin erred in taking him to have held that the addressees of a Rule of Recognition are all the members of the society in which that Rule of Recognition obtains. In his more considered moments, Hart clearsightedly perceived that the addressees of a Rule of Recognition are legal-governmental officials – the people whose conduct and attitudes are also constitutive of the Rule of Recognition. Hart wrote, for example, that "[t]here is, of course, a difference in the use made by courts of the criteria provided by the [Rule of Recognition] and the use of them by others: for when courts reach a particular conclusion on the footing that a particular rule has been correctly identified as law, what they say has a special authoritative status conferred on it by other rules" (101–2). He similarly maintained that "in the case of conflict between unofficial statements of validity or invalidity and that of a court in deciding a case, there is often good sense in saying that the former must then be withdrawn" – though he rightly added that "it may be dogmatic to assume that [the private individual's statement] is withdrawn as a statement now shown to be *wrong*. ... For there are more reasons for withdrawing statements than the fact that they are wrong" (102, emphasis in original). Even more important is a later passage in which Hart explicitly denied that the operativeness of a legal system requires that citizens "generally share, accept, or regard as binding the ultimate rule of recognition specifying the criteria in terms of which the validity of laws [is] ultimately assessed" (114). As Hart comprehended, then, the people on whom a Rule of Recognition imposes law-ascertaining duties and confers law-ascertaining powers are legal-governmental officials rather than ordinary citizens. Only the officials are empowered to bind everyone else with the determinations which they reach as they ascertain what the law in their jurisdiction is.

Two caveats should be entered here, each of which is grounded in some remarks by Hart. First, there can exist very small and simple societies with legal systems in which the division between officials and citizens is highly tenuous. In such a society, as Hart observed (114), all adult citizens might well play roles in constituting the regnant Rule of Recognition and might therefore be empowered under that Rule of Recognition to play those roles. Still, although a state of affairs along such lines is quite possible in any of these marginal instances of legal systems, the central instances of legal systems in larger and more complex societies – the instances with which Hart was principally concerned – are marked by a clearer division between the roles of officials and the roles of citizens. In any central instance of a system of law, the Rule of Recognition is addressed distinctively to the officials by whose endeavors of law-ascertainment it is constituted.

Second, although the addressees of the Rule of Recognition in any central instance of a legal system are confined to legal-governmental officials, ordinary citizens (on their own or through their lawyers) can and often do become apprised of some of the criteria in the Rule of Recognition. Although their determinations and pronouncements about those criteria are not authoritative in the manner of the determinations and pronouncements undertaken by officials, and although they therefore do not directly contribute to constituting the substance of the Rule of Recognition, they can indirectly contribute to that substance by shaping the general network of expectations and attitudes within which the officials carry out the enterprise of ascertaining the law. Especially in liberal democracies, the expectations and attitudes that prevail among members of the general public are likely to influence the outlooks of officials over time. Notwithstanding that the members of the public lack legal powers to bind others with their conclusions about the Rule of

Recognition, their role – at least in liberal democracies – is not, or need not be, entirely passive. Indeed, a liberal-democratic system of governance can generally fare better when the ordinary citizens are engaged than when they are apathetically quiescent.

7 The Rule of Recognition: power-conferring and duty-imposing

My reflections on the Rule of Recognition have heretofore presented it as both power-conferring and duty-imposing. As I have argued elsewhere (2004, 104–5; 2013b, 28–30), the Rule of Recognition in any society is indeed a complicated array of norms – some of which are power-conferring and some of which are duty-imposing. Quite a few commentators have submitted that the Rule of Recognition is solely duty-imposing or solely power-conferring,[7] but neither of those positions is correct. Instead, the Rule of Recognition is a hybrid composed of both duty-imposing norms and power-conferring norms. Let us mull over this topic by first looking at a few of Hart's statements on the matter, and by then considering some arguments in favor of the proposition that the Rule of Recognition is a complex normative hybrid.

Hart sometimes wrote as if the Rule of Recognition were only power-conferring and not duty-imposing. For example, when discussing the so-called rules of adjudication, he commented: "Like the other secondary rules [including of course the Rule of Recognition] these are on a different level from the primary rules: though they may be reinforced by further rules imposing duties on judges to adjudicate, they do not impose duties but confer judicial powers" (97). When focusing on the Rule of Recognition itself, he declared: "Nor does the word 'obey' describe well what judges do when they apply the system's rule of recognition and recognize a statute as valid law and use it in the determination of disputes" (113). If we recall Hart's ruminations on the differences between power-conferring norms and duty-imposing norms – ruminations which I have recounted in my second chapter – we can notice that the language in this latest quotation echoes his earlier remarks about the distinctiveness of power-conferring norms. As Hart said in those earlier remarks, people who exercise powers by following some prescribed procedures are not thereby "obeying" the prescriptions which specify the procedures. With his extension of that observation to the implementation of the Rule of Recognition, he was strongly suggesting

82   Components of Hart's Jurisprudential Theory

that the Rule of Recognition is power-conferring and not duty-imposing. Indeed, his point in the quoted statement about the term "obey" was to assimilate the Rule of Recognition to the paradigmatically power-conferring norms that prescribe the conditions for the enactment of statutes. Just before that statement, he had written: "In no ordinary sense of 'obey' are legislators obeying rules when, in enacting laws, they conform to the rules conferring their legislative powers, except of course when the rules conferring such powers are reinforced by rules imposing a duty to follow them" (113). By denying that the language of "obedience" is applicable to the endeavors whereby the officials in a legal system give effect to the system's Rule of Recognition, Hart was apparently indicating that those endeavors consist in the exercising of powers rather than in the fulfilling of obligations.

A couple of pages later, Hart again proclaimed that the term "obedience" is "misleading as a description of what legislators do in conforming to the rules conferring their powers, and of what courts do in applying an accepted ultimate rule of recognition" (115). However, at that slightly later juncture in his text, what becomes clear is that – despite the initial appearances to the contrary – he was not really denying that the Rule of Recognition is duty-imposing. Instead, he was aptly denying that it is *solely* duty-imposing, and he was likewise denying that the duty-fulfilling aspect of the law-ascertaining activities of the officials in a legal system is exclusively a matter of obedience. Officials fulfill their duties under the Rule of Recognition not only by adhering to certain criteria for determining what counts as law, but also by displaying the full critical reflective attitude in relation to those criteria. As Hart stressed, their adoption of the full critical reflective attitude is vital for the functionality of their legal system (116):

> [T]he ultimate rule of recognition in terms of which the validity of other [legal] rules is assessed[,] ... if it is to exist at all, must be regarded from the internal point of view as a public, common standard of correct judicial decision, and not as something which each judge merely obeys for his part only. Individual courts of the system though they may, on occasion, deviate from [the criteria in the Rule of Recognition] must, in general, be critically concerned with such deviations as lapses from standards, which are essentially common or public. This is not merely a matter of the efficiency or health of the legal system, but is logically a necessary condition of ... the existence of a single legal system. If only some judges acted "for their part only" on the footing that what the Queen in Parliament enacts

is law, and made no criticisms of those who did not respect this [criterion] of recognition, the characteristic unity and continuity of a legal system would have disappeared.

In this passage as in quite a number of other passages, Hart over-emphasized the role of adjudicative officials and thus neglected the role of administrative officials. Nevertheless, he here perceptively captured why the Rule of Recognition has to be duty-imposing as well as power-conferring – and why the critical reflective attitude that prevails among the officials in a legal system is not only a product of the duties incumbent on them under their Rule of Recognition but is also the provenance of those duties.

Within the pages of *The Concept of Law*, then, there are ample grounds for concluding that the Rule of Recognition in any legal system is both power-conferring and duty-imposing. Furthermore, such a conclusion is justified philosophically as well as exegetically – for the duty-imposing character of a Rule of Recognition ties in directly with its power-conferring character. A legal system's Rule of Recognition lays obligations on the system's officials to treat certain sources of law as dispositive, and it bestows powers on the officials to engage in acts of law-identification which fulfill those obligations and which are binding on citizens. Whereas norms of law-application empower officials to ascertain authoritatively whether any violations of the prevailing laws have occurred, the Rule of Recognition empowers the officials to ascertain authoritatively the existence and contents of those very laws. (Of course, as has been glancingly mentioned in §5 of this chapter, law-ascertaining determinations are essential for any violation-detecting determinations. Consequently, when something of the former kind takes place, it often is an element of something of the latter kind. Nonetheless, the two types of determinations can be distinguished analytically, even though differentiating between them in practice will sometimes be fiendishly difficult.) Precisely because the law-ascertaining endeavors of the officials are legally decisive – that is, precisely because the officials legally bind citizens and other officials with their findings, and because they thereby alter people's legal positions – their engaging in those endeavors of law-ascertainment consists in their exercising of legal powers vested in them by their Rule of Recognition.

Were the Rule of Recognition not duty-imposing, the officials in a system of governance would be legally at liberty to identify any norms at all as the laws of their system. Were the Rule of Recognition not power-conferring, the officials would be unable to identify the law in a legally binding fashion and would thus be unable to carry out their adjudicative and administrative responsibilities as officials. They would not be able to undertake authoritatively the processes of law-ascertainment which they are duty-bound to undertake in accordance with the requirements which their Rule of Recognition imposes upon them. In short, only the hybrid composition of a Rule of Recognition provides both the structured constrainingness and the dynamic operability of a legal system.

8 The unity of the Rule of Recognition: disagreements over details

As I have argued at far greater length elsewhere (1999, 142–6; 2004, 105–6; 2013b, 44–9), there need not be and typically will not be a wholly univocal Rule of Recognition in any particular system of law. Typically, the officials in such a system do not all adhere to exactly the same set of criteria for ascertaining the law. Commonly, there are some variations among the officials' understandings of the regnant criteria – which is why the officials in certain knotty cases disagree with one another at the level of their Rule of Recognition rather than exclusively at the level where the uniformly embraced standards in their Rule of Recognition are brought to bear on problematic matters of classification. Those divergences among the officials are fully compatible with the functionality of a legal system of governance, so long as the points of contention among them concern only the ancillary layers of their Rule of Recognition. If officials converge with one another on the chief criteria for identifying the norms that count as laws which belong to their system, they can diverge from one another over the remaining criteria without jeopardizing the system's regularity and stability.

On the one hand, intractable disagreements about all the paramount criteria in a Rule of Recognition would lead to civil war or revolution or governmental chaos that would undermine the rule of law in the country where those disagreements persist. On the other hand, a lack of unanimity on some of the lesser criteria in a Rule of Recognition is quite consistent with the regularity and functionality of a legal system as such. Given as much, we have no reason to believe that there will always or typically be unanimity on those lesser criteria. Much more likely is that the officials in any

Components of Hart's Jurisprudential Theory   85

particular system of law will indeed diverge from one another in their understandings of the details of their Rule of Recognition. They can do so while arriving at convergent determinations in the large majority of circumstances to which the laws of their system apply.

Especially in a large system of law, any thorough consentaneity among the system's officials on all the minutiae of their law-ascertaining criteria is formidably unlikely. Hence, if the notion of a single overarching Rule of Recognition somehow implied full agreement among all the officials on those minutiae, we would have to conclude that there never has existed any legal system (no central instance of a legal system, at any rate). After all, there never has existed a Rule of Recognition with a content that is undisputed in every detail among the officials who uphold it. In fact, of course, we should instead realize that no such thorough consentaneity among the officials is necessary for the existence of a single overarching Rule of Recognition and thus for the existence of a legal system. We can correctly maintain that a single Rule of Recognition exists in this or that legal system even though the officials therein do not all subscribe to exactly the same set of criteria for legal validity – just as we can correctly maintain that the people in some community speak a single language even though they do not all adhere to precisely the same set of semantic and syntactic rules. Exhaustive uniformity is not prerequisite to the unity that is a hallmark of a legal system. (Hart emphasized as much throughout the final section of the seventh chapter in *The Concept of Law*, where he dwelt on the inevitability of disagreements among legal-governmental officials about the peripheral aspects of their Rule of Recognition. In my next chapter, we shall scrutinize his exploration of this matter.)

9 The unity of the Rule of Recognition: multiple criteria

Joseph Raz (1979, 95–6) has submitted that a legal system can comprise multiple Rules of Recognition, each of which specifies an ultimate source of law. Either those multiple specifications of sources will be unranked, or else each of them will independently indicate how it is to be ranked in relation to the other Rules of Recognition. So Raz argues.

Yet, with reference to any legal system that has been operating as such for more than an extremely short period, nobody can plausibly suggest that its criteria for legal validity remain largely or entirely unranked. In any credible setting, the potential for conflicts among the criteria will have occasioned the prioritization of some of them over others. Whether explicitly through what the officials of a legal system say or implicitly through what they do, their prioritization of the sources of law within the system will be discernible by any careful observer. To be sure, the rankings will very likely remain unsettled in some of their details – either because the officials take disparate views of those details or because many questions to be answered by the intricacies of their scheme of prioritization have not yet been addressed. Nevertheless, the unsettledness of the Rule of Recognition in such matters of detail is something that Hart rightly and readily acknowledged. As has been mentioned above, he famously contended that any Rule of Recognition will partake of an open texture on its periphery (147–54). He was correct in thinking that the functionality of a legal system as a unified array of institutions does not necessitate the unequivocality of its Rule of Recognition in every jot and tittle. Some involuted questions pertaining to the rankings of the criteria in the Rule of Recognition, as well as some involuted questions pertaining to the contents of those criteria, might lack determinate answers at any given juncture. To allow as much is scarcely to deny or doubt that a single Rule of Recognition exists in the society where the determinate answers to those questions about minutiae are missing.

Let us turn, then, to the other possibility delineated by Raz: his suggestion that each of the multiple Rules of Recognition in some legal system might independently indicate its own superiority or subordination in relation to each of the other Rules of Recognition in the system. One difficulty afflicting such a suggestion is that we would be hard pressed indeed to tell whether any particular scheme of prioritization exemplifies what Raz has posited or not. That is, we would be hard pressed to tell whether any such scheme derives from specifications of rankings that are internal to the power-conferring and duty-imposing norms in which the various law-validating criteria of a Rule of Recognition are embedded, or whether it instead derives from a set of priority rules that complement those norms. If the officials in a system of law are sufficiently self-aware to indicate explicitly whether the rankings in their Rule of Recognition are internal to the aforementioned norms or are complementary to those norms, then we will be able to tell. Otherwise, however, an

Components of Hart's Jurisprudential Theory 87

observer will be reduced to conjectures about something in regard to which there might not be any determinate fact of the matter. If a Rule of Recognition can be equally well formulated through either of the two main ways of encapsulating the rankings among its criteria – namely, through an encapsulation that locates the rankings in the power-conferring and duty-imposing components of the Rule of Recognition, or through an encapsulation that locates the rankings in a concomitant set of priority rules – there will not be any need to choose speculatively between those two ways. If a difference does not make a difference, we need not attend very closely to it.

Moreover, even when we can be confident that the scheme of prioritization in a Rule of Recognition is internal to its power-conferring and duty-imposing constituents, we should not follow Raz in labeling each of those constituents as a separate Rule of Recognition. On the one hand, when the phrase "Rule of Recognition" is employed to designate the whole assortment of power-conferring and duty-imposing standards in which are embedded the ultimate criteria for legal validity in some jurisdiction, it is admittedly quite misleading – since it tends to convey the erroneous impression that the foundation of the processes of law-ascertainment in the specified jurisdiction is a single norm. On the other hand, despite the misleadingness of that phrase, Hart adduced a solid reason for using it. Writing about a Rule of Recognition with multiple criteria, he explained that "[t]he reason for still speaking of 'a rule' at this point is that, notwithstanding their multiplicity, these distinct criteria are unified by their hierarchical arrangement" (1983, 360). Whether a scheme of prioritization is internal to the power-conferring and duty-imposing norms that contain the law-validating criteria, or whether it instead ensues from supplementary rules of ranking that are also comprised by the Rule of Recognition, it ties the power-conferring and duty-imposing norms together as a coherently interrelated set of standards. The integratedness which it bestows upon them is what justifies us in affirming that those norms and their rankings are an overarching Rule of Recognition. Although the label "Rule of Recognition" is misleading in the respect that has already been touched upon, it well captures the unity of a throng of law-ascertaining touchstones that stand in quite clear relationships of superiority and subordination to one another. (Of course, the order of priority among the law-validating standards need not be perfectly comprehensive. As has already been argued, the unity of the Rule of Recognition in any particular legal system is consistent with a modicum of indeterminacy in the rankings among those standards.)

10 The unity of the Rule of Recognition: institutional hierarchies

Raz has posed another objection to the idea of a single Rule of Recognition in each legal system. He raises *en passant* the possibility that "there are various rules of recognition, each addressed to a different kind of officials" (1980, 200). Raz's fleeting suggestion has been illuminatingly scrutinized by Kent Greenawalt, who probes it against the background of the institutional stratification that obtains in virtually every legal system (1987, 635–6). Any typical system of law involves multiple tiers of officials. At each level in the hierarchy, the officials have to defer to the determinations reached by the officials in any of the levels above them. Now, some readers might be inclined to join Raz in thinking that officials located at different tiers of a legal system are adhering to different Rules of Recognition. After all, the officials in the topmost level of the hierarchy will not have to defer to anyone else in the system. They will therefore always be directly guided by the law-ascertaining standards that directly guide the other officials only when any relevant issues have not yet been resolved by rulings in the uppermost tier of the hierarchy. On many occasions, the lower-tier officials will be guided not by the aforementioned standards but instead by a standard that instructs them to uphold whatever the topmost officials have decided. For the topmost officials, by contrast, that additional standard is beside the point. They do not have to heed a directive that is addressed only to lower-rank officials. Accordingly, some readers might be tempted to endorse the view that is expressed in the quotation from Raz above.

That view might seem to find further support in a fact pointed out by Greenawalt (1987, 634–6). On a key question relating to the Rule of Recognition in the United States – the question whether a constitutional amendment has been properly adopted – the American courts defer unreservedly to determinations by the Congress. Those Congressional determinations are themselves guided by the prescriptions set forth in the amending clause of the US Constitution. Hence, the Congress adverts directly to the prescriptions in the amending clause, whereas the courts advert directly to the conclusions of the Congress concerning whether those prescriptions have been fulfilled. Once again, then, some readers might be tempted toward Raz's view. It may seem that the members of the Congress are following one Rule of Recognition while the members of the American judiciary are following another.

Greenawalt wisely rejects the Razian view, but his alternative position is not entirely satisfactory. He contends that the best approach to ferreting out a single Rule of Recognition is to "understand the rule of recognition as the ultimate standards of law used by officials who are not simply accepting the judgments of other officials" (1987, 636). In other words, the officials at the top of the hierarchy of a legal system are always guided by the system's Rule of Recognition when they ascertain the law, whereas the officials in the lower strata of the hierarchy are frequently guided instead by the law-ascertaining judgments of their superiors. Much the same can be said – under Greenawalt's approach – about the members of the Congress and the members of the judiciary in the United States. Members of the Congress orient themselves toward the American Rule of Recognition when handling matters of constitutional amendments, whereas the members of the judiciary orient themselves instead toward the decisions of the Congress on such matters.

Although Greenawalt's stance is preferable to Raz's position, it still portrays the processes of law-ascertainment in the United States as more fractionated than they are. Even more important, it obfuscates the respects in which the lower-tier officials (or the members of the American judiciary) take their guidance from the prevailing Rule of Recognition when they acquiesce unreservedly in the conclusions reached by the upper-tier officials (or by the members of the US Congress). Rather than opting for Greenawalt's approach to this matter, we should grasp that – subject to the qualifications already presented, concerning divergences among officials on points of detail – the sundry officials in each legal system adhere to a single Rule of Recognition. Their Rule of Recognition includes standards that direct the lower-rank officials to treat the law-ascertaining determinations of the upper-level officials as binding. The lower-tier officials manifest their adherence to those standards by indeed treating such determinations as dispositive. Naturally, the officials in the uppermost tier do not manifest their acceptance of those standards through compliance therewith, since such officials are not subordinate to anyone else. Norms in their Rule of Recognition that call for deference are not addressed to them and do not directly guide their own ascertainment of laws. Nevertheless, those topmost officials do accept the deference-prescribing norms and are disposed to manifest their acceptance in other ways. They are disposed to criticize any deviations from those norms by lower-tier officials, and they are disposed to go further – with penalties for contumacious subordinates – if the deviations are not rapidly corrected. Through their preparedness to engage in criticism and (when necessary) in punitive measures, the officials at the top of a legal system's hierarchy join the lower-echelon officials in upholding a single Rule of Recognition. They do not themselves seek to comply with the deference-prescribing directives in that Rule of Recognition, since those directives are not addressed to them; but they are firmly disposed to ensure that those directives are heeded by their subordinates, to whom the directives are addressed. In that crucial respect, the upper-echelon officials are adhering to the same Rule of Recognition to which the subordinate officials adhere. The overarching unity of their Rule of Recognition is comparable to that of a religious code of appropriate observances which includes some provisions that are addressed only to men and some provisions that are addressed only to women. Everyone in a society can be upholding the one code even though its precise bearing on each person's behavior will differ between the sexes.

In sum, so long as we keep in mind that the deference-requiring prescriptions in a Rule of Recognition carry different implications for the officials in different strata of a legal system's hierarchy, we should encounter no difficulty in apprehending the integratedness of that Rule of Recognition and the integratedness of the system that is undergirded by it. Those deference-requiring prescriptions directly guide some of the law-ascertaining determinations of the officials in the lower strata of the system. *Pari passu*, they directly guide the officials in the paramount stratum (and in the subordinate strata) as those officials gauge the correctness of the law-ascertaining decisions that have been reached by the lower-echelon functionaries. Thus, although the deference-prescribing norms in a legal system's Rule of Recognition impinge on the behavior of the system's officials in varying ways and to varying degrees, they impinge on every official's behavior to some extent. They constitute a common point of reference for the officials' law-ascertaining endeavors – that is, they set standards toward which the officials orient themselves for varying purposes in the course of those endeavors – just as do the other norms in the regnant Rule of Recognition. Hence, while containing those deference-requiring provisions, a Rule of Recognition can perfectly well function as an overarching assortment of touchstones that are presupposed and upheld by the

11 The ultimacy of the Rule of Recognition

As Hart explained at some length (107–10), the Rule of Recognition that underpins a legal system is ultimate in that its authoritativeness throughout the system does not derive from any other laws that belong thereto. Whereas every one of the other laws of the system owes its status as a law to its being picked out directly or indirectly by some standard(s) contained in the Rule of Recognition, the Rule of Recognition does not similarly owe its status to any other norms of the system. As has already been remarked, the Rule of Recognition comprises an array of power-conferring and duty-imposing standards in which are embedded the various criteria that specify the fundamental sources of any laws that belong to the system. In Hart's parlance, a norm is *valid* within a legal system if and only if it belongs to the system as a law that is to be given effect by virtue of its having emanated from one or more of the aforementioned sources.[9] Hence, while all the other laws of the system are valid, the Rule of Recognition itself as the basis of all validity is neither valid nor invalid. As Hart declared, we have to draw on the notion of legal validity "to answer questions which arise *within* a system of [legal] rules where the status of a rule as a member of the system depends on its satisfying certain criteria provided by the rule of recognition. No such question can arise as to the validity of the very rule of recognition which provides the criteria; it can neither be valid nor invalid but is simply accepted [by the officials of the system] as appropriate for use in this way" (109, emphasis in original).

Precisely because the Rule of Recognition is ultimate in this fashion, not every standard for legal validity in a given jurisdiction is comprised by the Rule of Recognition therein. Some such standards are derivative of the fundamental norms which make up the Rule of Recognition. For example, if there arises a question whether a regulation issued by some administrative agency is a valid law, the answer to the question most likely resides in the legislative enactment under which the agency has been authorized to promulgate regulations. Any standards laid down by that enactment are derivative, rather than directly constitutive, of the prevailing Rule of Recognition. They obtain as determinative standards because some of the norms in the Rule of Recognition provide that officials are to treat certain materials (statutory enactments or constitutional provisions) as binding laws.

12 The Rule of Recognition: the foundational level and the codified level

Clearly related to the distinction between ultimate and derivative standards for legal validity is the distinction between the foundational incarnation and the codified incarnation of the Rule of Recognition (Kramer 2004, 110–14). As has been stated, the Rule of Recognition in any legal system exists as an array of power-conferring and duty-imposing norms in which are embedded the criteria that specify the fundamental sources of the system's laws. Those norms underlie and structure the law-ascertaining activities of the system's officials, who rely upon the norms implicitly or explicitly while determining what counts as legally binding and what does not. The standards in the Rule of Recognition are operatively presupposed even if they remain unarticulated by the officials whose determinations are grounded on them. Perhaps the officials would not be able to articulate some of the criteria in their Rule of Recognition even if they attempted to do so, or perhaps they simply do not attempt to do so. Whatever may be the reason for the fact that those criteria remain unexpressed (if they do indeed remain unexpressed), they can guide and undergird the officials' law-ascertaining endeavors all the same. In this respect, the standards that constitute a Rule of Recognition are similar to the rules of a natural language. Competent speakers of a language adhere to any number of semantic and syntactic and stylistic rules even if those rules are never articulated overtly – and indeed even if the speakers are incapable of articulating any of them. Whether or not such rules ever get stated explicitly by anyone, they inform the speakers' discourses. They exist as norms that are presupposed by the multitudinous utterances and interpretations which the users of the language undertake in their daily activities of communication and understanding. The operativeness of those norms as basic presuppositions and guides is in no way dependent on their being explicitly enunciated by the users.

Now, what has been described in the preceding paragraph is the Rule of Recognition at the foundational level of its existence. That level, where the standards in the Rule of Recognition obtain as a matrix of normative presuppositions that antecede any formulations of their contents, is the only level of the Rule of Recognition in some legal systems. In many other such systems, however, a second level also emerges. Quite frequently, the contents of some of the criteria in a Rule of Recognition come to be codified in statutory enactments or constitutional provisions. Any such codifications constitute the Rule of Recognition in its formulated incarnation. In that incarnation, the Rule of Recognition exists not as a network of presupposed norms that are prior to any articulations of their contents, but instead as some articulated norms. Its statutory or constitutional encapsulation is the guise in which it obtains at the formulated level. Of course, that formulated level never supplants the foundational level. A Rule of Recognition can exist in its foundational incarnation without existing in any codified incarnation, but not vice versa. After all, any constitutional provisions or statutory enactments are endowed with legally binding force only because standards in the foundational Rule of Recognition direct the relevant officials to treat those provisions or enactments as authoritative. Hart perceptively grasped as much: "Even if [the content of a Rule of Recognition] were enacted by statute, this would not reduce it to the level of a statute; for the legal status of such an enactment necessarily would depend on the fact that the [Rule of Recognition] existed antecedently to and independently of the enactment" (111). Nonetheless, although a Rule of Recognition in its formulated incarnation is always dependent on its foundational incarnation, the codification of it is frequently a focus of attention for officials and citizens.

Just as a Rule of Recognition at the foundational level is analogous in some important respects to the network of syntactic and semantic rules that give shape to a natural language such as English, so too a Rule of Recognition at the formulated level is roughly analogous to various works – such as dictionaries – that are produced as distillations of linguistic rules. On the one hand, a natural language can perfectly well function as a complex medium of communication even if no one has sought to formulate its underlying rules. On the other hand, lexicographers and linguists and grammarians often do compile works that quite rigorously recount the structural or semantic or stylistic apparatus of a language. Dictionaries and grammatical manuals and other such publications bring some underlying norms to the surface, and they thereby render explicit the standards on which the competent users of the language rely when communicating with one another. In that regard, those publications are broadly comparable to statutory or constitutional provisions that formulate the criteria in a legal system's Rule of Recognition.

Dictionaries and other guides to some natural language are derivative of the patterns of usage that actually prevail in a linguistic community. Unlike works of fiction (such as J.R.R. Tolkien's invention of an elaborate vocabulary for the world of the hobbits and elves in his novels), the guidebooks to a natural language present themselves as reflective of the rules or patterns of discourse that are actually operative in the employment of the language by competent speakers and writers. To be sure, lexicographers and grammarians do not eschew prescriptive ambitions entirely. Within the bounds of their roles, they typically favor some of the observed patterns of usage, and they discountenance the remaining patterns. All the same, unless their accounts of linguistic features do accurately represent the fabric of the language to which those features are ascribed, the accounts will not be successful in fulfilling their assigned functions. If dictionaries and other such publications are not to be fictional or antiquated, they will have to reflect the norms that are actually presupposed in the communications of the users of the relevant language. Once again, then, we can perceive an analogy between the domain of language and the domain of officials' law-ascertaining activities. In a legal system where the officials aim to codify their Rule of Recognition in a constitutional or statutory form, their efforts will be unavailing if they fail to capture the ultimate norms that are actually presupposed by their law-ascertaining endeavors. Of course, the officials might instead be aiming to set new criteria for legal validity that will modify the underlying criteria which have theretofore been presupposed by their endeavors. (Any such transfigurative ventures will themselves depend on other presupposed standards, which direct the officials to attribute binding force to the statutory or constitutional provisions that contain the new criteria for legal validity.) Still, if the officials are trying to formulate rather than alter their Rule of Recognition, they will have to strive for accuracy in their recapitulation of it. The Rule of Recognition at the codified level is derivative of the Rule of Recognition at the foundational level, not only in that the former is dependent on the latter for its binding force, but also in that the content of the former has to match the content of the latter.

Yet, notwithstanding the twofold derivativeness of any Rule of Recognition in its codified incarnation, the codification can influence the foundational Rule of Recognition. Before considering this point in connection with law, we should glance again at the workings of language. As has been noted, dictionaries and other such guides to a language are designed to encapsulate the semantic or structural characteristics which are actually present in that language. Their role is predominantly that of recapitulation or distillation, rather than invention. Nonetheless, such works can affect the substance and the structuring of the very language which they aspire to chart. This influence can operate in either of two main ways. (I shall concentrate here on dictionaries, since they are especially likely to engender the sorts of effects which I am envisaging.)

First, if the compilers of a dictionary inadvertently or deliberately depart from some prevailing patterns of usage, they might bring about certain changes in some of those patterns. It may be that the communicative practices of the users of the relevant language will adapt to what is specified in the dictionary. In that event, the dictionary will have transmuted some of the elements of the practices which it purports to recount. Admittedly, such adaptations will normally be quite circumscribed in scope. Normally, a dictionary will be effective in prompting such adaptations only if it enjoys high esteem by capturing accurately most of the regnant patterns of usage. If a compilation of definitions were instead to include sweeping departures from the existent norms of the language, its ability to induce people to shift their linguistic propensities would be greatly impaired if not altogether eliminated. Striking though a dictionary's innovative power can sometimes be, its endowment with such power is generally dependent on its overall reliability as a summation of the meanings that are actually attached to words by users in the relevant linguistic community. Nevertheless, within limits, the potential for innovation abides.

A second respect in which a dictionary can influence a language is conservative rather than innovative. On the one hand, the prestige of a dictionary typically derives from the proficiency with which its compilers have executed their task of assembling the senses that are respectively associated with words. On the other hand, once that prestige has been gained, the dictionary will often take on a life of its own. In addition to gauging the estimableness of a dictionary on the basis of its accuracy in tracking how words are employed, people start to gauge the semantic propriety of their utterances on the basis of their conformity to the definitions enumerated in the dictionary. Instead of serving only as a looking glass or a reflection, the dictionary becomes also a lodestar. Having distilled the ways in which myriad words are used, it tends to entrench those ways by investing them with the aura of a certified status. To some extent, then, it retards change in the medium of communication from which it has emerged as a mirroring encapsulation.

Although the analogy between the communicative activities of the speakers of a natural language and the law-ascertaining activities of the officials in a legal system is far from perfect, the codification of a Rule of Recognition by officials can affect their law-ascertaining criteria in broadly the same fashion in which a dictionary can influence the meanings of words. One of the two principal aspects of the codification's potential influence has already been briefly broached. If officials introduce some statutory or constitutional standards for legal validity that do not accurately correspond to the criteria which have been presupposed theretofore by their law-ascertaining endeavors, they might effect some modifications in those criteria thenceforward. Such an upshot is not inevitable – since the statutes or constitutional provisions might remain wholly unimplemented – but it is quite plausible. Indeed, the innovative force of constitutional or statutory formulations may well prove more far-reaching than the innovative force of a dictionary. Whereas extensive changes in the patterns of usage of a natural language over a short period are extremely unlikely, some quite sweeping changes in the law-ascertaining practices of a country could realistically be sought through the codification of new criteria. In such circumstances, major adjustments in a legal system's foundational Rule of Recognition could come about through the elaboration of its codified Rule of Recognition. (Of course, as has already been noted, any such process of transformation depends on standards in the foundational Rule of Recognition which enjoin officials to treat the codified Rule of Recognition as legally authoritative. In other words, the innovative impact of any codification of a legal system's Rule of Recognition is always ultimately attributable to the presupposed norms that constitute the system's Rule of Recognition in its foundational incarnation.)

Like a dictionary, the codification of a Rule of Recognition can play a conservative role at least as robustly as a transformative role. Let us suppose that the officials in some legal system accurately formulate many of the criteria in their Rule of Recognition and that they enshrine those criteria in constitutional provisions. Such provisions are derivative of the system's foundational Rule of Recognition in the two respects already mentioned. That is, the provisions are binding because the foundational Rule of Recognition deems them to be binding, and their contents reflect the contents of the criteria embedded in the power-conferring and duty-imposing standards that make up the foundational Rule of Recognition. In turn, the constitutional provisions can serve to reinforce various elements in the foundational Rule of Recognition. Like a dictionary, a Rule of Recognition in its codified incarnation can take on a life of its own. Within the system to which the constitutional formulations belong, those formulations can become the foci of the enterprise of law-ascertainment undertaken by the system's officials – who may come to justify their determinations (to themselves and to their fellow officials) chiefly by drawing upon the constitutional language. Since the standards in the foundational Rule of Recognition that impute binding force to the constitutional provisions might be much more resistant to change than any of the criteria that are given expression in those provisions, the codification of the criteria can greatly strengthen their durability. In such a context, the disinclination of each official to deviate from the formulated criteria will be primarily ascribable not to the contents of the criteria but instead to the sheer fact of their having been enshrined in the articles of a constitution. In short, although the standards for legal validity in a codified version of a Rule of Recognition are always dependent on standards for legal validity in the foundational incarnation of that Rule of Recognition, the flow of influence between the foundational level and the codified level will often be bidirectional rather than unidirectional.

13   The intertwining of the Rule of Recognition and other secondary norms

As has been briefly remarked in §5 of this chapter, the Rule of Recognition in any jurisdiction is intertwined with the other fundamental secondary norms therein. In §5, I have mentioned one quite apparent aspect of the intertwining: namely, the fact that officials cannot exercise the powers conferred by norms of law-application unless they have exercised the powers conferred by the Rule of Recognition. If an adjudicator or administrator has not ascertained the existence and contents of the laws that are applicable to some set of circumstances, she will not be able to ascertain whether any laws have been contravened in those circumstances. Hart grasped as much when he wrote that "if courts are empowered to make authoritative determinations of the fact that a rule has been broken, these cannot avoid being taken as authoritative determinations of what the rules are" (97). However, he slightly muddied the water when he added that the operative norms of law-application will therefore "also be a rule of recognition, identifying the primary rules through the judgments of the courts and these judgments will become a 'source' of law" (97). Although Hart was correct in pointing out that any authoritative judgment about the fulfillment or contravention of some law will depend on an authoritative judgment about the existence and content of that law, he erred in suggesting that a judgment of the latter kind will perforce be endowed with precedential bindingness. Adjudicative determinations concerning the existence and contents of laws are endowed with precedential bindingness in many legal systems but not in all legal systems; and, even where they are so endowed, their precedential force does not derive from the sheer fact that such determinations are prerequisite to any decisions by adjudicators about the occurrence or non-occurrence of contraventions of laws.

At any rate, the interdependence of the Rule of Recognition and other fundamental secondary norms is more extensive and somewhat more subtle than might be gathered from the one point of interdependence that has been touched upon so far. For example, when the standards in a legal system's Rule of Recognition provide that the norms ordained by some person or body of people are legislative enactments that are to be given effect as laws of the system, those law-ascertaining standards presuppose the operativeness of secondary norms which confer legislative powers on that person or body of people (Hart 1982, 258–9). Those standards also presuppose the operativeness of secondary norms that confer powers of law-application on certain people as officials who are to effectuate laws. Conversely, of course, the secondary norms that confer the powers of legislation presuppose the operativeness of the standards in the Rule of Recognition which ultimately authorize and obligate officials to hold that the norms introduced through exertions of those powers of legislation are laws that belong to the prevailing system. Similarly, the secondary norms that confer the powers of law-application presuppose the operativeness of the standards in the Rule of Recognition which ultimately authorize and obligate officials to hold that those secondary norms themselves are among the laws of the system.

Because of these and sundry other modes of interdependence among the fundamental secondary norms, quite a few readers of Hart have worried that his account of such norms is untenable or even incoherent. Two principal types of queries have emerged. First, some critics have contended that the Rule of Recognition is

Components of Hart's Jurisprudential Theory 99

reducible to other secondary norms: to the norms of change or to the norms of law-application. Second, as has been mentioned in §5 of this chapter, some critics have submitted that Hart's exposition of the structure and functioning of a legal system is plagued by vicious circularity – since the norms that establish the positions of certain people as legal-governmental officials are operative only because those norms are treated as laws by officials. Let us ponder some objections of these two main sorts.

14   Interdependent but distinct: a riposte to Shapiro

While arguing that any Rule of Recognition is only duty-imposing and not power-conferring, Scott Shapiro declares that the attribution of a power-conferring dimension to the Rule of Recognition would conflate its standards with the secondary norms of change (2009a, 239–40):

> Is it possible, then, to understand the rule of recognition as either a power-conferring or a duty-imposing rule? I think that the first option cannot be Hart's position. For if we suppose that the rule of recognition in Britain is "The Queen in Parliament has the power to create British law," we inadvertently convert Britain's rule of recognition into its rule of change. Moreover, the rule of recognition can validate certain types of customs [as laws], and since customs need not be (and usually are not) created through the exercise of legal authority, the rule that validates them cannot be power-conferring. The only alternative, then, is to treat the rule of recognition as a duty-imposing rule.

Shapiro's reasoning goes awry because of his misrepresentation of the ways in which a Rule of Recognition is power-conferring. Shapiro has failed to note that the criteria in a Rule of Recognition which specify the authoritative sources of law for some society are embedded in the power-conferring norms and duty-imposing norms that constitute the Rule of Recognition. Thus, the portion of the British Rule of Recognition that pertains to enactments by Parliament is not correctly formulated as "The Queen in Parliament has the power to create British law." Instead, the correct formulation is "Every legal-governmental official in the United Kingdom is empowered as well as obligated to hold authoritatively that any norms enacted by Parliament as statutes are laws which belong to the UK's system of governance and which are therefore to be given effect by legal-governmental officials in the UK."[10] Likewise, in a somewhat simplified version, the portion of the English Rule of Recognition that pertains to customary laws is correctly formulated as follows: "Every legal-governmental official in England is empowered as well as obligated to hold authoritatively that customary norms endowed with certain properties – such as longstandingness, reasonableness, and prevalent operativeness within this jurisdiction – are laws which belong to the English system of governance and which are therefore to be given effect by legal-governmental officials in England."

As these formulations make clear, the powers directly conferred by the Rule of Recognition are powers of law-ascertainment rather than powers of law-alteration. In other words, once the norms that bestow those powers are correctly encapsulated, we can see that Shapiro errs when he contends that any ascription of a power-conferring role to the British Rule of Recognition would efface the distinction between two types of secondary norms. To be sure, the components of the British Rule of Recognition which have been distilled here also nicely reveal how intertwined that Rule of Recognition is with other secondary norms. Each of those components presupposes the operativeness of some secondary norms of law-application which confer powers on certain people as officials who give effect to norms that belong to the relevant system of governance as laws thereof. Furthermore, the first component also presupposes the operativeness of some secondary norms which confer legislative powers on Parliament and which specify the qualifications for membership in Parliament. Still, although the interdependence of the Rule of Recognition and other secondary norms is manifest in the strands of the UK's Rule of Recognition that have been formulated here, the distinctiveness of the Rule of Recognition is also evident in those strands. The power-conferring and duty-imposing constituents of the Rule of Recognition establish powers and duties that are specifically concerned with the ascertainment of legal norms.

In short, my rejoinder to Shapiro's mischaracterizations of some power-conferring elements in the British Rule of Recognition has underscored the correctness of John Gardner's observation that "a legal system's ultimate rules of recognition, change, and adjudication … cannot but cross-refer, and hence depend on each other for their intelligibility, yet each has its own normative force." As Gardner adds: "Each regulates different actions, or different agents, or the same actions of the same agent in a different way. Each is therefore a distinct rule" (2012, 106).

15 Interdependent but distinct: a riposte to Waldron

Shapiro is not the only prominent legal philosopher who has misguidedly declared that the Rule of Recognition somehow collapses into norms that confer legislative powers. In quite a different manner, Jeremy Waldron (2009) has reached just such a conclusion. The gist of his reasoning is as follows. According to Hart, the fundamental norms of a legal system are social rules that exist if and only if they are accepted and implemented among the group of people to whom they are addressed. Suppose that the fundamental norm of change in a legal system invests a monarch or a legislature with the power to alter citizens' legal positions through the issuance of statutes. That norm of change prescribes the procedures that are to be followed for the enactment of such statutes. Now, if that norm of change is existent as a fundamental norm of the system, it is accepted and implemented among the legal-governmental officials to whom it is addressed. Yet, if the officials accept and effectuate that norm, there is no real work to be done by a Rule of Recognition. When the officials ascertain that a statute has been passed through the prescribed procedures, and when they accordingly administer that statute in conformity to its terms, they are giving effect to the fundamental norm of change which they accept. Their acceptance of that fundamental norm consists in just such law-ascertaining and law-administering behavior. Consequently, Waldron maintains, the role of the Rule of Recognition in providing for the ascertainment of laws is redundant. Because such a role is integral to the fundamental norm of change as an accepted and practiced norm, there is no need for a Rule of Recognition to perform it – or so Waldron argues.

The fatal weakness in such a line of reasoning is that it leaves Waldron unable to explain how a fundamental norm of change – a norm that confers law-making powers on a monarch or legislature – would exist. Let us recall from §2.4 of my second chapter that Hart's model of social norms, with its focus on the critical reflective attitude as the hallmark of people's acceptance of such norms, is apposite solely for norms that impose duties. Without supplementation, the model does not extend to power-conferring social norms (or immunity-conferring social norms). Hence, without supplementation, it does not extend to the fundamental norm of change envisaged by Waldron.

Suppose that that fundamental norm of change does exist in some society because it is accepted and regularly implemented by most of the officials there, and suppose that a few maverick officials quite frequently decline to recognize the normative alterations that are produced when the legislative powers conferred by that norm of change are exercised. Suppose further that many officials who do accept the fundamental norm of change nonetheless occasionally fail to identify correctly those normative alterations. Both the maverick officials and the occasionally wayward officials will be subject to censure from their fellow functionaries. Objections addressed to them will be framed at least partly in deontic terms. That is, the maverick or occasionally wayward officials will be reproached for contravening some of the duties which they bear. What is the source of those duties? Given that the fundamental norm of change is a power-conferring norm only, it cannot be the source of the duties incumbent on officials to recognize that norm itself and to recognize the normative adjustments produced when the legislative powers which it establishes are exercised. Instead, those duties are imposed by the officials' Rule of Recognition, which – as this chapter has emphasized – is made up of duty-imposing norms as well as of power-conferring norms. Whether the obligations imposed by the Rule of Recognition are explicitly invoked or are tacitly taken for granted as presuppositions, they are the guiding points of reference for the dispositions of officials to condemn any fellow officials who decline to acknowledge the existence and effects of the fundamental norm of change in the jurisdiction.

What is crucial here is that the dispositions just mentioned are indispensable as elements of the collective attitudes (among officials) that constitute the existence of the fundamental norm of change. Both in Hart's model of the acceptance of social norms and in my second chapter's outline of the internal point of view for power-conferring norms, dispositions to take exception to deviant behavior are vital. In the absence of such dispositions harbored by all or most officials, the fundamental norms of a legal system would not be accepted by the officials and would therefore not exist. Hence, in the absence of such dispositions harbored by all or most officials, Waldron's fundamental norm of change would not be accepted by the officials and would therefore not exist. Yet those dispositions, oriented as they are toward the duties of officials to recognize the existence and effects of that fundamental norm of change, are underlain by the Rule of Recognition – since the Rule of Recognition, rather than the fundamental norm of change itself, is the fount of such duties. Ergo, contrary to what Waldron repeatedly suggests, the role of the Rule of Recognition in providing for the ascertainment of legal norms is not redundant. Only because the Rule of Recognition is operative in legally obligating as well as legally empowering officials to ascertain such norms, are all the dispositions operative that constitute the fundamental norm of change. The fundamental norm of change on its own does not account for some of the dispositions that amount to its being accepted. Without the Rule of Recognition, the fundamental norm of change does not suffice to account for its own existence.

16 Interdependent but distinct: a riposte to MacCormick

We have just seen that, although the Rule of Recognition and any fundamental norm of change are intertwined, they are distinct. Neither of them is redundant, and neither of them is collapsible into the other. Much the same is true of the relationship between the Rule of Recognition and the norms of law-application. Interdependent though the Rule of Recognition and any fundamental norm of law-application are, neither is subsumable into the other. Instead of *establishing* any powers and duties of law-application, the Rule of Recognition *presupposes* the operativeness of those powers and duties. The powers and duties which it itself establishes are powers and duties of law-ascertainment (the operativeness of which is presupposed by any norms of law-application).

Quite a few philosophers have gone astray in their reflections on this matter,[11] but I will concentrate here on a couple of sentences by Neil MacCormick: "Whereas the secondary rules of adjudication and change are power-conferring, the rule of recognition lays down duties binding on those who exercise public and official power, especially the power to adjudicate ... [T]hose who have power to act as judges are also duty bound as judges to *apply* all and only those rules that satisfy more or less clearly specified criteria of validity" (2008, 32–3, emphasis added). MacCormick's conflation of the Rule of Recognition with norms of law-application – his contention that the Rule of Recognition imposes duties of law-application rather than, or in addition to, duties of law-ascertainment – was here bound up with his mistaken view that the Rule of Recognition is solely duty-imposing and with his equally mistaken view that the norms of law-application are solely power-conferring. As this chapter has already maintained, the Rule of Recognition comprises both power-conferring standards and duty-imposing standards; similarly, the norms of law-application include both power-conferring standards and duty-imposing standards. Whereas the powers conferred and duties imposed by the Rule of Recognition are powers and duties of law-ascertainment, the powers conferred and duties imposed by norms of law-application are powers and duties of adjudication or administration. MacCormick erred in submitting that the Rule of Recognition imposes duties of adjudication. Those latter duties are presupposed, rather than established, by the standards that make up the Rule of Recognition. (The fact that duties of law-application are presupposed by the standards in any Rule of Recognition is evident from the formulations of two such standards in my rejoinder to Shapiro in §14 of this chapter.)

Of course, because the duties and powers of law-application are presupposed by the standards in the Rule of Recognition, and because the duties and powers of law-ascertainment are presupposed by the norms of law-application, the Rule of Recognition and the norms of law-application are deeply and complicatedly interdependent – as this chapter has sustainedly emphasized. Moreover, although the activities of law-ascertainment and law-application can be distinguished clearly enough *in abstracto*, one's endeavors to differentiate between them in practice will frequently be much more problematic. Powers and duties of law-ascertainment and powers and duties of law-application are often established simultaneously, and any exercises of the latter powers have to involve exercises of the former powers. At a practical level, as opposed to a philosophical level of analysis, the functions of norms are not readily susceptible to compartmentalization.

Still, despite the messiness of the relevant contrasts in practice, and despite the intricate interdependence of the Rule of Recognition and the norms of law-application even in theory, a legal philosopher can and should descry their distinctness as well as their complex interwovenness. At the level of high abstraction on which such a philosopher contemplates the nature of law, the difference between duties of law-ascertainment and duties of law-application is clear-cut. By eliding that difference, MacCormick led his readers away

17 The problem of circularity

As has been signaled at the end of §5 of this chapter, the interdependence of the fundamental norms in a legal system might seem to generate a problem of vicious circularity. That problem is normally posed as a conundrum about the origins of any legal system. If the prerogatives of people as officials are always due to norms that confer powers of law-ascertainment or law-application or legislation upon them, and if those norms are operative in a jurisdiction only because they are treated as operative by the officials therein, the fundamental norms that confer such powers might seem to lack any point of entry. How can those fundaments ever come into existence, given that their existence presupposes the very statuses – the statuses of certain people as officials – which the fundaments themselves establish?

Shapiro (2011, 42) designates this problem as the "Possibility Puzzle," which he traces to two putatively compelling theses. He labels the first of those two theses as the "Egg Principle," which he formulates as follows:

> "Some body has power to create legal norms only if an existing norm confers that power."

Shapiro labels the other thesis as the "Chicken Principle," and he formulates it as follows:

> "A norm conferring power to create legal norms exists only if some body with power to do so created it."

Those two theses in combination generate the crux which I have recounted in the preceding paragraph. As Shapiro states, somebody could invoke those two theses in an effort "to show that no assertion of legal authority is compatible with the Chicken and Egg principles without resorting to vicious circles or infinite regresses" (2011, 40).

As has been suggested at the close of §5 of this chapter, the most straightforward route for resolving the chicken-and-egg crux lies in differentiating between two senses of the phrase "legal power."

Every legal power is an ability of some person to alter people's legal positions through the adoption of some course of conduct. Hence, the phrase "legal power" can properly be used in a relatively expansive sense to denote any such ability regardless of the origins of that ability. (As has been remarked in my second chapter, Hart presumed that an ability to alter legal positions is not a legal power unless the possession of it is generally beneficial for people who are endowed with it. That restriction imposed by Hart does not affect my current discussion, and can therefore be taken for granted here without being expressly indicated.) Though most legal powers in the capacious sense just specified are products of a legal system – in that they owe their existence to legislative processes or other law-making events within such a system – not all legal powers in that capacious sense are such products. Some of them exist without having been created by legislative processes or other law-making events. In recognition of that fact, the phrase "legal power" can alternatively be employed more narrowly. So employed, the phrase denotes an ability-to-alter-legal-positions only if that ability owes its existence to the law-making operations of a legal system.

Now, what is clear is that the foundational powers of a legal system – the powers that enable the system to be brought into existence, and the powers that are the bedrock of the workings of the system thereafter – are legal powers only in the relatively capacious sense and not in the narrower sense. As the underpinnings of the system's operations, they do not owe their existence to those operations. Thus, if we glance again at Shapiro's Egg Principle, we can see that it mistakenly assumes that all abilities of people to create or alter legal norms and positions are legal powers in the narrower sense. Having grasped that some such abilities are legal powers only in the more expansive sense and not in the narrower sense, we should reject the Egg Principle. That is, we should reject the notion that every ability of anyone to create legal norms has itself come into existence by way of some antecedent legal norm(s). Foundational powers do not come into existence in that fashion.

Through the repudiation of the Egg Principle, we escape the vicious circularity that would engulf us if we were to embrace both of Shapiro's chicken-and-egg theses. However, the dismissal of his Egg Principle should not be accompanied by any uncritical endorsement of his Chicken Principle. More specifically, the Chicken Principle should also be rejected unless the second instance of the term "power" in its formulation is construed as referring to legal powers in the relatively expansive sense rather than only in the more restrictive sense. A power-conferring norm in a legal system can be created by somebody whose own ability to establish that norm authoritatively – an ability that is of course a legal power in the expansive sense – has not been bestowed by any of the system's law-making processes.

My point here about the two senses of the phrase "legal power" is quite closely related to Hart's musings on the question whether the standards in the Rule of Recognition should be classified as legal or as pre-legal (111–12). On the one hand, the standards in the Rule of Recognition are properly classifiable as legal because the powers conferred by them and the duties imposed by them are legal. When officials exercise the powers of law-ascertainment bestowed upon them by their Rule of Recognition, they alter the legal positions of other people by legally obligating those others to heed the law-ascertaining determinations that have been reached. Similarly, noncompliance by officials with the duties of law-ascertainment imposed on them by their Rule of Recognition will render them liable to undergo legal penalties at the hands of their fellow functionaries. At the same time, the standards in the Rule of Recognition are properly classifiable as pre-legal because they do not owe their existence to any of the law-creating operations of the legal system in which they obtain; they are instead presupposed by all such operations, as the foundational norms that are immanent in the law-ascertaining practices of the system's officials. Their effects or implications are all internal to the system, but their provenance is anterior to it. Much the same is true of the other foundational norms of a legal system, which are intertwined with those comprised by the Rule of Recognition.

18   Necessary and sufficient conditions

This chapter will close by briefly mulling over Hart's presentation of the two individually necessary and jointly sufficient conditions for the existence of any central instance of a legal system. Hart stated the two conditions as follows: "On the one hand, those rules of behaviour which are valid according to the system's ultimate criteria of validity must be generally obeyed, and, on the other hand, its rules of recognition specifying the criteria of legal validity and its rules of change and adjudication must be effectively accepted as common public standards of official behaviour by its officials" (116).

Hart submitted that the first of these two conditions is a specification of the minimum pattern of conduct that must be exhibited by citizens (including officials qua private individuals) if a central instance of a legal system is to exist. Such a system cannot function unless most citizens, in relation to most of the system's duty-imposing laws, generally evince at least the first of the three behavioral dispositions that constitute the critical reflective attitude. That is, unless most citizens usually comply with most of the duty-imposing laws that are addressed to them by the institutions of legal governance that preside over their society, those institutions cannot endure. Hart readily granted and indeed emphasized that a system of governance will normally be much more robust if most citizens not merely *obey* most of its duty-imposing laws but also fully *accept* those laws by exhibiting toward them all three of the dispositions in the critical reflective attitude. He nevertheless believed that, if the mere obedience of most citizens to most of their society's duty-imposing laws is combined with the second of the two conditions which he specified, it can be sufficient to secure the functionality of a central instance of a legal system.

By proclaiming that the role of citizens in sustaining the operations of a central instance of a legal system can consist in mere compliance with duty-imposing laws, Hart once again strangely neglected the import of power-conferring laws. Having striven in his critique of Austin to highlight the distinctiveness and significance of laws that confer private powers on citizens, Hart appeared to forget about those laws when specifying his necessary and sufficient conditions for a central instance of a legal system. Given the indispensability and far-reachingness of exertions of private powers in the arranging and transforming of the legal relationships of citizens, the wholesale failure by Hart to mention such powers at this juncture in his text is bewildering. Had he taken account of such powers in his specification of the conditions necessary and sufficient for the existence of a central instance of a legal system, he would have had to fill the lacuna that yawns most widely in his theory. In other words, he would have had to supply an exposition of the internal point of view in relation to power-conferring norms. With such an exposition, he could have filled the additional lacuna that has been exposed here; that is, he could have carved out an adequate place for exertions of private powers by citizens in his cogitations on what is essential for the functionality of a central instance of a legal system.

By failing to provide any analysis of the internal point of view in relation to power-conferring norms, Hart also detracted from the cogency of his effort to specify the crucial role of officials in the workings of a legal system. In the statement quoted above, he averred that a central instance of a legal system cannot function and endure as such unless its officials accept its Rule of Recognition and its norms of change and norms of law-application as "common public standards of official behaviour." We know that, in Hart's parlance, the acceptance of a duty-imposing norm by anyone consists in her adoption of the critical reflective attitude toward that norm. Now, given that the Rule of Recognition and the norms of law-application are duty-imposing as well as power-conferring, Hart's reference to the acceptance of them by officials is readily intelligible. Because the duties imposed by the Rule of Recognition and the norms of law-application are indeed incumbent on adjudicative and administrative officials, we can understand quite clearly what Hart meant when he asserted that those officials "must regard these [norms] as common standards of official behaviour and appraise critically their own and each other's deviations as lapses" (117). However, both in this latest quotation and in the statement quoted at the outset of this section, Hart was adverting not only to the Rule of Recognition and to the norms of law-application but also to the norms of change. Though some norms of change (such as norms pertaining to the promulgation of administrative regulations) do impose duties on adjudicative or administrative officials, most do not. Most norms of change are only power-conferring. Moreover, even among the relatively few norms of change that impose duties, the duties are more often incumbent on legislators or on private citizens than on adjudicative and administrative officials. Hence, given that Hart omitted to elucidate the internal point of view in relation to power-conferring norms, he left thoroughly unclear what he meant when he referred to the acceptance of the norms of change by adjudicators and administrators. He needed something like the first of the two explications of the internal viewpoint for power-conferring norms which I have propounded in §2.4 of my second chapter, but he did not provide any such explication. Having rightly deplored Austin's inattentiveness to power-conferring laws, Hart damagingly left some significant gaps in his own theory by not fully absorbing the lesson to be drawn from his excoriation of his great predecessor.

4

Hart on Legal Interpretation and Legal Reasoning

As has been emphasized throughout this book, Hart distanced himself from the command theory of law by insisting that the structure and operations of any legal system are fundamentally normative. A system of legal governance is a system of norms, which are introduced and administered within it. Having proclaimed as much, Hart knew that the success of his jurisprudential endeavors would hinge on his ability to provide a satisfactory account of the nature and functioning of norms. He began to build that account during his critique of the command theory – for example, through his distinction between norm-guided behavior and merely habitual behavior, and through his contrast between the internal point of view and the external points of view – and he continued to develop his analysis of norms generally and of legal norms specifically as he maintained that any system of law is a union of primary and secondary norms. Not until the seventh chapter of *The Concept of Law*, however, did Hart devote any sustained attention in that text to the matter of legal reasoning and legal interpretation. He could scarcely go without addressing that matter, for his affirmation of the normativity of law was premised on the assumption that norms are meaningfully operative in legal institutions. Legal reasoning and legal interpretation are key ingredients in the processes through which the norms of a legal system are brought to bear on particular situations. They are key ingredients, that is, in the processes through which the norms of a legal system become meaningfully operative. Hence, Hart could not vindicate his general model of law without adequately explaining how legal reasoning and legal interpretation

Legal Interpretation and Legal Reasoning 111

work. With the seventh chapter of *The Concept of Law*, he sought to meet that challenge.

In his effort to rise to the challenge just mentioned, Hart succeeded only partly. His seventh chapter contains quite a few valuable insights and several memorable lines of discussion, but it also contains some confusion and missteps and oversimplifications that left Hart needlessly vulnerable to certain criticisms subsequently leveled against him by Ronald Dworkin. Though many of Dworkin's objections to legal positivism arose from his own misrepresentations and strange misunderstandings, a few of his strictures exposed genuine failings in Hart's ruminations on legal reasoning and interpretation.[1] Moreover, Hart's ruminations were marred by some significant shortcomings beyond those to which Dworkin took exception.

To some extent, the weaknesses of Hart's meditations on legal reasoning and legal interpretation were due to the brevity of those meditations and to the variability of such reasoning and interpretation across jurisdictions. As has been remarked in §5 of my opening chapter, the techniques of legal reasoning and interpretation employed by officials in their activities of adjudication and administration are jurisdiction-specific to quite a high degree. Although some illuminating observations about those techniques can be made across jurisdictions, and although Hart indeed advanced some such observations, most aspects of legal reasoning and interpretation do not lend themselves to the strongly jurisdiction-transcendent plane of analysis on which the philosophy of law proceeds. Most such aspects vary among legal systems or among types of legal systems (for example, systems in the common-law tradition versus those in the civil-law tradition). Accordingly, Hart – who was writing at a philosophical level of abstraction – encountered some fairly sharp limits on the extent to which he could elucidate the nature of legal reasoning and interpretation. For instance, he could make some laconic and perceptive comments on the role of precedents in English adjudication (134–5), but he wisely refrained from trying to extend those comments to the modes of adjudication in other common-law jurisdictions; and, of course, he refrained from trying to extend those comments to the modes of adjudication in jurisdictions outside the common-law tradition. Hence, because he generally aspired to furnish analyses that would be applicable to all central instances of legal systems, he was understandably quite sparing in his analyses of the patterns of legal reasoning and interpretation.

Still, the inadequacies in Hart's exploration of legal reasoning and interpretation did not stem principally from the constraints faced by any such exploration that aspires to a philosophical level of generality. (Indeed, Hart's reticence in response to those constraints was more a manifestation of commendable circumspection than an inadequacy.) Far more important in rendering Hart vulnerable to complaints by critics was his unattunedness to some pregnant distinctions that should have informed his reflections. Thus, before we turn to the specifics of those reflections, we should mull over the distinctions to which Hart did not sufficiently attend.

One point in defense of Hart should be noted straightaway as a preliminary matter, however. In his seventh chapter, as elsewhere in *The Concept of Law*, he concentrated inordinately on adjudication and largely neglected the role of administration. Nevertheless, as we shall see hereafter, he did ponder the latter role quite prominently at one juncture. Moreover, his excessive focus on the judiciary was somewhat more pardonable in his seventh chapter than elsewhere in his text – since the reasoning of courts, especially the reasoning of appellate courts, is such a cynosure in the eyes of lawyers and other legal experts. Hence, although my misgivings about the unduly judge-centered orientation of Hart's philosophy of law are applicable to his cogitations on the nature of legal reasoning and interpretation, I will henceforth put those misgivings aside.

1 Crucial distinctions

Notwithstanding the laudableness of many of Hart's pronouncements about legal reasoning and interpretation, his approach to the matter suffered from his tendency to disregard some crucial distinctions. Those distinctions mainly pertain to the differences between ontological phenomena and epistemic phenomena; more specifically, they mainly pertain to the differences between (1) the actual substance or implications of legal norms and (2) the beliefs held by people about the substance or implications of legal norms. Such differences will turn out to be subtly multifaceted, as we shall behold.

1.1 Indeterminacy versus indemonstrability

An answer to a legal question in some jurisdiction can be *determinately* correct – that is, either uniquely correct or within a small range of answers that differ from all other answers in being correct – even though its correctness is persistently denied by some reasonable people who have reflected carefully on the matter. If a way of resolving a legal dispute is determinately correct, it is so regardless of whether anyone discerns as much. By contrast, a resolution of a dispute is *demonstrably* correct only if its singular appropriateness will be perceived and endorsed by virtually every sensible person who competently ponders the arguments in favor of it. As should be apparent, determinate correctness does not entail demonstrable correctness. The latter involves more than the former. As should likewise be apparent, the right answers to the questions at issue in the knotty cases addressed by the appellate courts in any system of governance are very seldom demonstrably correct. Yet, because determinate correctness does not entail demonstrable correctness, the absence of the latter property does not entail the absence of the former; there may be some determinately correct answer to any major question at issue in an appellate case, even though the answer will very likely not be demonstrably correct.

Adverting to the intractability of the disagreements among jurists over the answers to the questions at issue in difficult appellate cases, legal philosophers and other legal theorists have too often taken for granted that none of those answers is determinately correct. Yet, although there might indeed not be any determinately correct answers in some difficult cases, the sheer fact that jurists (or other people) differ fiercely with one another about the suitable outcome in any particular case is far from sufficient to establish that no outcome is determinately correct. The tenacity of the disagreement does not in itself have any bearing on the possibility of a uniquely correct resolution of the crux to which the disagreement pertains. Only by effacing the distinction between determinacy and demonstrability could anyone think otherwise. Instead of simply referring to the persistence of divergences among jurists in hard cases, a theorist who wishes to justify claims about indeterminacy in those cases will have to back up her position with pertinent arguments. She will have to explain why the lastingness of the divergences is attributable to the absence of determinately correct answers rather than to the temperamental or intellectual or ideological limitations of some of the jurists involved. (Let us glimpse here at a situation in a different domain. Tens of millions of well-informed Americans disagree vigorously with one another over the question whether Lee Harvey Oswald was participating in a large-scale conspiracy – organized by some Communist regime or by some organized-crime syndicate, for example – when he assassinated President John Kennedy in November 1963. There is a determinately correct answer to that question, notwithstanding the abidingness of the tussles over it among experts.)

Hart was not wholly blind to the distinction between indeterminacy and indemonstrability, but he failed to grasp its full import. On the one hand, he sought to stress that his account of the "open texture" of legal norms – an account which we shall examine later – was concerned with indeterminacy, rather than merely with indemonstrability, in the law. In the Postscript to the second edition of *The Concept of Law*, he wrote as follows (252, emphases in original):

> My view advanced in this book is that legal rules and principles identified in general terms by the criteria provided by the rule of recognition often have what I call frequently "open texture," so that when the question is whether a given rule applies to a particular case the law fails to determine an answer either way and so proves partially indeterminate. Such cases are not merely "hard cases," controversial in the sense that reasonable and informed lawyers may disagree about which answer is legally correct, but the law in such cases is fundamentally *incomplete*: it provides *no* answer to the questions at issue in such cases. They are legally unregulated and in order to reach a decision in such cases the courts must exercise the restricted law-making function which I call "discretion."

Having reaffirmed that the questions at issue in various difficult cases are without any determinately correct answers, Hart acknowledged that his position was at odds with Dworkin's insistence that there are uniquely correct answers to the questions at issue in all instances or virtually all instances of legal proceedings. Hart aptly observed that, in Dworkin's view, an answer to such a question can be uniquely correct while also being intractably controversial – since "its controversial character is perfectly compatible with there being facts (in many cases moral facts) in virtue of which it is true" (253). Now, as will be discussed in my next chapter, Hart was an Inclusive Legal Positivist rather than an Exclusive Legal Positivist. That is, he believed that the compatibility of a norm N with some requirement(s) of moral legitimacy can be a necessary condition for the status of N as a law in this or that jurisdiction. He also believed that the correctness of N as a moral principle can be a sufficient condition for the status of N as a law in this or that jurisdiction. Given as much, and given that moral principles are the grounding for the existence of uniquely correct answers to the questions at issue in some difficult cases of law, Hart's Inclusive Legal Positivism would be inconsistent with his claims about the indeterminacy of the law in those particular difficult cases. Hart appeared to think that Dworkin was accusing him of such inconsistency. Let us label that Dworkinian accusation as the "Moral Principles Objection."

Hart touched upon the Moral Principles Objection while also responding to another allegation by Dworkin of inconsistency. Dworkin (1978, 349; 1984, 250) maintained that Hart's Inclusive Legal Positivism was at odds with the putative aspiration of positivists to keep their accounts of law noncommittal on the matter of the objectivity of morality. Let us label this latter allegation of inconsistency as the "Aloofness Objection." Before we probe Hart's reaction to the Aloofness Objection, we should very briefly note two points about that objection itself. First, although Dworkin was correct in contending that Hart wished to retain a noncommittal stance on the matter of the objectivity of morality, such a stance is not integral to legal positivism generally or to Inclusive Legal Positivism specifically. Second, as Dworkin himself subsequently strove to emphasize, and as will become apparent in my penultimate chapter – and as should already be apparent from my comment on minimalism at the end of my opening chapter – the objectivity of morality is itself fundamentally a moral matter rather than an austerely metaphysical matter.[2] Hence, one principal reason why Inclusive Legal Positivists should eschew Hart's aspiration to remain noncommittal on the objectivity of morality is that they will not be saddling themselves with any abstruse metaphysical theses when they uphold that objectivity. Instead, they will simply and rightly be rejecting any thoroughgoing version of moral skepticism.[3]

At any rate, Hart unwisely confirmed that in his view a theory of law "should avoid commitment to controversial philosophical theories of the general status of moral judgments and should leave open ... the general question of whether they have what Dworkin calls 'objective standing'" (253–4, quoting Dworkin 1984, 250). Hart then appeared to concede that his inclination to remain aloof from debates over the objectivity of morality would also require him to distance himself from Inclusive Legal Positivism: "Of course, if the question of the objective standing of moral judgments is left open by legal theory, as I claim that it should be, then [Inclusive Legal Positivism] cannot be simply characterized as the theory that moral principles or values may be among the criteria of legal validity, since if it is an open question whether moral principles and values have objective standing, it must also be an open question whether [Inclusivist] provisions purporting to include conformity with them among the tests for existing law can have that effect or instead, can only constitute directions to courts to *make* law" (254, emphasis in original). Hart here in effect capitulated to Dworkin's Aloofness Objection.

Dismaying and gratuitous though Hart's capitulation to the Aloofness Objection was, the upshot of his surrender might seem to have supplied a route of escape from Dworkin's Moral Principles Objection. After all, if Hart was now suspending his advocacy of Inclusive Legal Positivism, he might seem to have evaded the inconsistency between his espousal of that doctrine and his claims about indeterminacy in difficult cases. Given that Hart never returned in his Postscript to the Moral Principles Objection, he may indeed have presumed that he had resolved it. If he did think as much, however, he was making yet another error.

A noncommittal stance on the objectivity of morality and on Inclusive Legal Positivism would entail a noncommittal stance on the question whether there are any cases in which moral principles incorporated into the law under the prevailing Rule of Recognition have filled up some gaps left by statutes and other legal materials. If the Rule of Recognition in some jurisdiction provides that the correct principles of morality are incorporated into the law as substantive legal norms, and if the officials in the jurisdiction frequently and intractably diverge from one another when they seek to identify discrete principles, then the actually correct principles of morality belong to the law despite the persistence of the disagreements over their contents. In every case where one of those principles does fill a gap left by the black-letter law – in that the correct principle of morality determinately yields an outcome whereas the black-letter law on its own does not – there is a determinately correct outcome even though there is not a demonstrably correct outcome. Now, if someone who would otherwise subscribe to Inclusive Legal Positivism is suspending judgment on the objectivity of morality, then she is suspending judgment on whether there are ever any cases of the sort just recounted. She is suspending judgment on whether the indeterminacy at the level of the black-letter law is ever offset by determinacy at the level of the moral principles that have been incorporated into the law under the regnant Rule of Recognition. Yet Hart did not indicate that he was retreating at all from his claims about indeterminacy in difficult cases where jurists disagree intractably. In his Postscript he simply reiterated those claims and adverted to Dworkin's trenchant contestation of them (endeavors of contestation in which Dworkin pertinently accentuated the distinction between indeterminacy and indemonstrability). Hart did not state that he would have to curtail his claims about indeterminacy by suspending judgment on the question whether gaps in the black-letter law are sometimes filled by moral principles that have been incorporated into the law. Instead, he implicitly let his original pronouncements about indeterminacy stand. Thus, in spite of his awareness of the distinction between indeterminacy and indemonstrability, Hart appeared to be inferring the former from the latter. He appeared to assume that, because jurists will diverge from one another when identifying the correct principles of morality that might seem to fill some of the gaps left by the black-letter law of a jurisdiction, those principles will not actually fill such gaps by enhancing the determinacy of the law into which they have been incorporated. *Pro tanto*, he was not remaining noncommittal on the matter of the objectivity of morality; rather, he was adopting a skeptical position on that matter.

1.2 Indeterminacy versus uncertainty

Closely related to the distinction between indeterminacy and indemonstrability, but not identical to it, is the distinction between indeterminacy and uncertainty. Like the former distinction, the latter is a contrast between an ontological phenomenon and an epistemic phenomenon.[4] Uncertainty is a state of inadequate beliefs (an epistemic state), whereas indeterminacy is a state of equipollent or incommensurable justifications (an ontological state). When somebody is uncertain about the correct answer to some legal question and is furthermore uncertain whether there is any determinately correct answer to that question, she is hardly in a position to deny the existence of such an answer. She should be withholding judgment on its existence, just as much as on its specific content. Her beliefs are insufficient for any verdict on either of those points. Conversely, if anyone announces that there is no determinately correct answer to some legal question, she is not giving voice to uncertainty. She is instead maintaining that neither an affirmative reply nor a negative reply to the question is superior to the other. (If the question is not appositely answerable with a "yes" or "no" response – for example, a question about the appropriate level of the minimum wage – then the denial of determinate correctness amounts to the claim that none of the principal competing answers to the question is superior to any others.) To substantiate one's insistence that each answer is no better than the rival answer(s), one has to show that the counterpoised considerations are evenly balanced or that they are insusceptible to being ranked. Far from being a product of uncertainty, any such substantiation will have to be grounded on solid argumentation at least as much as will any satisfactory effort to show that some particular answer is better than every other. Uncertainty is no basis at all for the arguments that would vindicate one's position.

In any context where the main matters in contention are of gnarled complexity and where there are significant justificatory grounds on each side of a dispute, many knowledgeable observers may be inclined to feel uncertainty not only about the correct disposition of the dispute but also about the very idea that a determinately correct disposition is attainable even in principle. Yet, as has just been indicated, any observers who do feel considerable uncertainty about those points are not in a position to deny that a determinately correct resolution of the dispute is possible. Until their uncertainty has been overcome, they should be refraining from either affirming or gainsaying the existence of a determinately correct answer to the question of how the dispute should be handled. Their verdict should instead be a verdict of indecision. All too often, however, when legal theorists examine difficult cases and report their own uncertainty or the uncertainty of other knowledgeable observers about the possibility of determinately correct outcomes in those cases, they then deem the law in those cases to be indeterminate. Such slippage from uncertainty to declarations of indeterminacy is to be resisted. It is manifestly a non sequitur, and it leads jurisprudential theorists to overestimate the scale of the indeterminacy to which the legal regulation of people's conduct is prone.

Hart was guilty of such slippage at numerous junctures in his discussion of legal reasoning and interpretation. Again and again, he switched abruptly from talking about uncertainty to talking about indeterminacy – or vice versa. Let us look at only a couple of passages, which are representative of many other portions of the seventh chapter in *The Concept of Law*. Quite early in that chapter, Hart wrote that legal "standards of behaviour, ... however smoothly they work over the great mass of ordinary cases, will, at some point where their application is in question, prove indeterminate; they will have what has been termed an *open texture*. ... [U]ncertainty at the borderline is the price to be paid for the use of general classifying terms in any form of communication" (128, emphasis in original).

Hart's lurching between assertions of indeterminacy and assertions of uncertainty often occurred through his references to the presence of doubts or to the absence of clarity. Whereas the presence of doubts and the absence of clarity are tantamount to uncertainty, Hart tended to treat them as also tantamount to indeterminacy. Consider, for example, the following passage in which he was mulling over the rule of parliamentary sovereignty in England (150, emphases added):

> [A]s with every other rule, the fact that the rule of parliamentary sovereignty is *determinate* at this point [namely, on the question whether a parliamentary enactment can be entrenched against future efforts to repeal it] does not mean that it is so at all points. Questions can be raised about it to which at present there is no answer which is *clearly* right or wrong. These can be settled only by a choice, made by someone to whose choices in this matter authority is eventually accorded. Such *indeterminacies* in the rule of parliamentary sovereignty present themselves.

Like the term "unsettled," the term "settled" – which appears in the latter of these two quoted passages – is such that it straddles the epistemic/ontological divide between uncertainty and indeterminacy. A question about the applicability of some law to certain types of circumstances can come to be settled in that the answer to the question is now clear and is no longer shrouded in uncertainty, or it can come to be settled in that there now has emerged a determinately correct answer to it. Though terms such as "settled" and "unsettled" or "resolved" and "unresolved" are valuable and are hardly to be abjured, their straddling of the epistemic/ontological division can abet the drawing of unwarranted inferences from uncertainty to indeterminacy. When someone is not careful to avoid those invalid inferences, the use of that terminology can facilitate confusion by concealing the fact that just such an inference has been drawn.

This subsection should close with a caveat. Although I have here underscored the distinctness of uncertainty and indeterminacy, I have decidedly not implied that those two properties are somehow mutually exclusive. Frequently, people are unsure about the answerability of questions to which there are indeed no determinately correct answers. This subsection has not aimed to deny or obscure that obvious way in which the extension of the concept of uncertainty intersects the extension of the concept of indeterminacy. Instead, the aim has been solely to warn against invalid inferences of the sort mentioned in the preceding paragraph. From the sheer fact that jurists and other people are uncertain about the implications of some law, we cannot validly infer that those implications are indeterminate.

1.3 Types of mind-independence

Some readers might worry that the foregoing two subsections have overlooked the key role of officials' conduct and attitudes in constituting the norms of a legal system as laws. Such readers might think that, if officials persistently disagree with one another about the implications of some law L or if most officials are uncertain about those implications, there cannot be any determinately correct answers to the questions on which the disagreement or uncertainty is centered. After all, such readers might reason, a norm exists as a law of a legal system only when the officials of the system converge in treating that norm as a law. If the officials do not converge with one another in identifying some of the implications of L, then those implications do not exist as elements of the system to which L belongs. Accordingly, these readers might contend, I have erred in maintaining that widespread disagreement or uncertainty among jurists does not entail indeterminacy in the law.

To grasp why any such line of thought is facile, we need to attend to some distinctions among the ways in which the norms of a legal system are mind-dependent or mind-independent.[5] One such distinction lies between (i) beliefs held by any particular individual and (ii) beliefs held in common by individuals who collaborate in the running of a legal system or in some other collective enterprise.[6] Sometimes when theorists affirm the mind-independence of certain matters, they are simply indicating that the facts of those matters transcend the beliefs or attitudes of any given individual. They mean to allow that those facts are derivative of the beliefs and attitudes shared by individuals who interact as a group (such as the judges and other legal officials who together conduct the operations of a legal system). These theorists contend that, although the views of any single individual are not decisive in ordaining what is actually the case about the matters in question, the understandings which individuals share in their interactions as a group are indeed so decisive. Let us designate as "weak mind-independence" the type of objectivity on which these theorists insist when they ascribe a dispositive fact-constituting role to some group of individuals while denying any such role to each separate individual.

That modest species of objectivity is obviously to be contrasted with *strong* mind-independence, which obtains whenever the nature or existence of some phenomenon is determined neither by the views of any separate individual nor by the common views and convictions that unite individuals as a collectivity. Insofar as strong mind-independence prevails within a domain of enquiry, a consensus on the bearings of any particular state of affairs in that domain is neither necessary nor sufficient for the actual bearings of the specified state of affairs. How things are is independent of how they are thought to be.

Before we turn to a second major division between types of mind-independence, a brief clarificatory comment is advisable. When some phenomenon is weakly mind-independent, its existence or nature is ordained by the beliefs and attitudes (and resultant patterns of conduct) that are shared among the members of a group. However, the beliefs and attitudes need not be shared among *all* the members of a group. In any large-scale association or community, very few beliefs and convictions will be shared by absolutely everyone. What typically underlies the existence of a weakly mind-independent entity – an entity that can equally well be characterized as "weakly mind-dependent" – is not some chimerical situation of unanimity, but instead a situation of convergence among *most* of a group's members. Consider, for example, the diffuse group of people throughout Canada who competently use the English language. If most of those users of the language regard the employment of "ain't" as improper in any formal speaking or writing (except when the term is deliberately wielded for comical effect), and if most of them accordingly forgo the use of that slang term in formal contexts, then Canadian English includes a weakly mind-independent rule proscribing the employment of "ain't" in formal discourse. Probably, some competent users of the English language in Canada do not eschew "ain't" in formal contexts. Such a fact, if it is a fact, is perfectly compatible with the existence of the aforementioned rule. Indeed, the exact difference between the status of some entity X as a weakly mind-independent phenomenon and the status of some entity Y as a strongly mind-*dependent* phenomenon is that the existence or nature of X (unlike the existence or nature of Y) is not ordained by the outlook of any particular individual. Instead, it is ordained by the outlooks and conduct that prevail among most of the members of some group. Typically, convergence among a preponderance of a group's members – which falls short of convergence among all of those members – will be sufficient to ground the existence or to establish the nature of some weakly mind-independent phenomenon. Note furthermore that, when there is very little convergence among a group's members on some proposition, and when the lack of convergence negates the existence of some weakly mind-independent entity X (such as a linguistic norm that allows the use of "ain't" in formal contexts), the weakly mind-independent character of X is evidenced by the very inexistence of such an entity. Precisely because X is weakly mind-independent rather than strongly mind-independent, the meagerness of the convergence among the outlooks of the group's members is something that matters to X's existence.

Now, before we can come to grips with the question whether legal requirements are strongly mind-independent or weakly mind-independent (or neither), we need to attend to another major dichotomy: the dichotomy between existential mind-independence and observational mind-independence. Something is *existentially* mind-independent if and only if its occurrence or continued existence does not hinge on the existence of some mind(s) and the occurrence of mental activity. Not only are all natural objects mind-independent in this sense, but so too are countless artefacts such as pens and houses. Although those artefacts would never have materialized as such in the absence of minds and mental activity – that is, although in their origins they were existentially mind-dependent – their continued existence does not similarly hinge on the presence of minds and the occurrence of mental activity. A house would persist for a certain time as the material object that it is, even if every being with a mind were magically and permanently whisked out of existence.

Something is *observationally* mind-independent if and only if its nature (comprising its form and substance and its very existence) does not hinge on how any observer construes that nature. Whereas everything that is existentially mind-independent is also observationally mind-independent, not everything that is observationally mind-independent is existentially mind-independent. Consider, for example, an intentional action. The occurrence of any such action depends on the existence of a mind in which there arises the intention that animates the occurrence, yet the nature of the action does not hinge on what any observer(s) – including the person who has performed the action – might believe it to be. Even if every observer thinks that the action is of some type B, it may in fact be of some contrary type C.

Varieties of mind-independence

	Existential	Observational
Weak	The occurrence or continued existence of something is not dependent on the mental activity of any particular individual.	The nature of something is not dependent on what it is thought to be by any particular individual.
Strong	The occurrence or continued existence of something is not dependent on the mental functioning of any members of any group individually or collectively.	The nature of something is not dependent on what it is thought to be by any members of any group individually or collectively.

When pondering the mind-independence of laws, then, we should be attuned to both the strong/weak distinction and the existential/observational distinction. A bit of reflection on the matter should reveal that, if the *existential* status of laws is our focus, most general legal norms are weakly mind-independent while most individualized legal directives are not even weakly mind-independent. Quite evident is the fact that most general legal norms are at least weakly mind-independent. The existence of those norms does not stand or fall on the basis of any individual's mental activity; it is not the case that the cessation of the mental processes of any particular individual brings about the disappearance of general legal norms. Whereas someone's beliefs and fantasies and attitudes and convictions are existentially dependent on the mind of the particular individual who harbors them, the existence of any general legal norm differs in not being radically subjective. (There can be exceptions in rather unusual circumstances. In a monarchy, the officials might adhere to a practice whereby some general laws go out of existence whenever the mental activity of the reigning king or queen has permanently ceased. Such an arrangement would be peculiar, but it would plainly be possible. Still, in a legal system that is to endure beyond a single person's lifetime, the incidence of any such strongly mind-dependent general laws would have to be highly circumscribed.)

When we move away from general laws and concentrate on individualized legal directives, we seldom find any existential mind-independence. Typically, if not always, an order addressed to a particular person – by a judge or some other legal official – will not remain in effect as such if its addressee's mental activity permanently ceases. If the result sought through the issuance of the individualized order is to be achieved, it will usually have to be pursued through some other means (perhaps through the issuance of a directive to some alternative individual or set of individuals who will act in lieu of the original addressee). Typically, then, an individually addressed legal requirement is strongly mind-dependent existentially; its continued existence as a legal requirement hinges on the occurrence of mental activity in a particular person's mind.

By contrast, the continuation of the sway of general legal norms will almost always transcend the mental functioning of any given individual. Even so, the existential mind-independence of such norms is weak rather than strong. They cannot persist in the absence of all minds and mental activity. They abide as legal norms only while certain people (most notably, judges and other legal officials) collectively maintain certain attitudes and beliefs concerning them. Unless legal officials converge in being disposed to treat the prevailing laws as authoritative standards by reference to which the juridical consequences of people's conduct can be gauged, those laws will cease to exist. To be sure, some of the general mandates within a functional legal system – such as ordinances that prohibit jaywalking – can continue to exist as laws even though they are invariably unenforced. The requirements imposed by such mandates are inoperative practically, but they remain legal obligations. However, the very reason why inoperative legal duties continue to exist as legal duties is that myriad other legal obligations are quite regularly given effect through the activities of legal officials, who converge in being disposed to treat those other obligations as binding requirements. Only because those manifold other legal requirements are regularly given effect, does a system of law exist as a set of functional institutions. In the absence of the regularized effectuation of most mandates and other norms within a legal system of governance, the system and its sundry components will have gone by the wayside. In sum, the continued existence of laws (including inoperative laws) as laws will depend on the decisions and endeavors of legal officials. Yet, because those decisions and endeavors inevitably involve the beliefs and attitudes and dispositions of conscious agents, the continued existence of laws as laws is not strongly mind-independent. The existential mind-independence of general legal norms is only weak.

Let us now investigate the observational mind-independence of legal norms. Is their observational mind-independence strong or only weak? We can know straightaway that general legal norms are at least weakly mind-independent observationally. After all, as has already been remarked, everything that is existentially mind-independent is also observationally mind-independent. The outlooks and mental processes and behavioral patterns that constitute the existence of a legal system are those shared by many officials in their interactions with one another. The nature of any of those outlooks and mental processes and behavioral patterns is manifestly independent of what any particular individual presumes.

Matters become more intricate, however, when we turn from inquiring whether legal norms are observationally mind-independent to inquiring whether their observational mind-independence is strong or weak. Here we come back to the conundrum that has occasioned this whole discussion of mind-independence – a conundrum that can now be addressed rigorously. Quite a few legal philosophers, such as Andrei Marmor, have had no doubt that the observational mind-independence of laws is merely weak. Marmor first notes that, when a concept pertains to something that is strongly mind-independent, "it should be possible to envisage a *whole community of speakers* misidentifying [the concept's] real reference, or extension." He then declares: "With respect to concepts constituted by conventional practices [such as the operations of a legal system], however, such comprehensive mistakes about their reference [are] implausible. If a given concept is constituted by social conventions, it is impossible for the pertinent community to misidentify its reference." He emphatically proclaims: "There is nothing more we can discover about the content of the [norms of our social practices] than what we already know" (2001, 138, emphasis in original). Actually, however, things are more complicated than Marmor suggests. His comments are not completely wrong, but they are simplistic. (In the following ruminations on the strong observational mind-independence of laws, there is no need for me to distinguish between general norms and individualized directives. In each case, the observational mind-independence is always strong.)

On any matter of law, the whole community of legal officials in some jurisdiction can indeed be mistaken. Legal officials can collectively as well as individually be in error about the attitudes and beliefs – concerning some matter of law – which they themselves share. They can collectively be in error about the substance and implications of those shared beliefs and attitudes, and can therefore collectively be in error about the nature of some legal norm(s) which those beliefs and attitudes sustain. To assume otherwise is to fail to differentiate between (i) their harboring of the first-order attitudes and beliefs and (ii) their second-order understandings of the contents and products of those first-order mental states. The fact that the officials share certain attitudes and beliefs and behavioral patterns in regard to the existence and content of some legal norm is what establishes the existence and fixes the content of that norm; but the officials can collectively misunderstand what has been established and fixed by the attitudes and beliefs and behavioral patterns which they share. A gap of misapprehension is always possible between people's first-order beliefs and their second-order beliefs about the contents and implications of those first-order beliefs.

Indeed, Marmor's elision of the first-order/second-order distinction will land his analysis in incoherence when it is applied to many credible situations. Suppose that the courts in some jurisdiction declare that their previous interpretation of a particular law was incorrect. They now maintain that that law should have been understood and applied (and will henceforth be understood and applied) in some alternative way. They affirm that, had the earlier interpretation been correct at the time of its adoption, it would still have been correct now; however, it was mistaken at the time of its adoption and is mistaken now. If the members of the judiciary are collectively infallible at the current juncture when they pronounce on this matter of legal interpretation, then they were fallible at the earlier juncture when they espoused the now-disowned reading of the specified law. Conversely, if they were collectively infallible at that earlier juncture, then they are currently mistaken when they deem themselves to be rectifying an error. However Marmor might try to analyze such a situation, he will be led to the conclusion that legal officials have collectively erred about a matter of legal interpretation. His insistence on the officials' collective infallibility will have undermined itself.

The observational mind-independence of legal norms is therefore strong rather than weak. Nevertheless, Marmor is not flatly incorrect. If the legal officials in a jurisdiction do collectively err in their understanding of the substance and implications of some legal norm(s) which their own shared beliefs and attitudes and behavioral patterns have brought into being, and if they do not correct their misunderstanding, that misunderstanding will thenceforth be determinative of the particular point(s) of law to which it pertains. It will in effect have replaced the erstwhile legal norm(s) with some new legal norm(s). Such an upshot will be especially plain in any areas of a country's law that are covered by doctrines of precedent akin to those in Anglo-American jurisdictions, but it will ensue in other areas of the law as well. The new legal norm(s) might be only slightly different from the previous one(s) – the differences might lie solely in a few narrow implications of the norm(s) – but there will indeed be some differences, brought about by the legal officials' mistaken construal of the substance and implications of the superseded norm(s). Subsequent judgments by the officials in accordance with the new legal standard(s) will not themselves be erroneous, since those judgments will tally with the law as it exists in the aftermath of the officials' collective misstep. The officials go astray in perceiving the new legal standard(s) as identical to the former legal standard(s), but, once their error has brought the new standard(s) into being, they do not thereafter go astray by treating the new standard(s) as binding. (There can be limited exceptions to this general point. If the officials in a legal system adhere to a norm requiring them to undo any mistaken judgment whenever they come to discern their mistake within a certain period of time, and if they comply with that norm in most circumstances to which it is applicable, then their nonconformity with it in some such set of circumstances would temporarily vitiate the new legal standard that has been engendered by a misstep which they have acknowledged but not corrected. However, the additional error of nonconformity will itself quickly be absorbed into the workings of the legal system, along with the now-acknowledged but uncorrected misstep, as something that is binding on the officials.)

Of course, a new legal norm engendered by the officials' collective misunderstanding of a pre-existent legal norm may itself become subject to misapplication in the future. If it does indeed undergo distortion in that manner, it will have been displaced by some further legal norm that is the product of the distortion. Such a process in its general contours, through which a collective error on the part of the officials has led to the supersession of some legal standard(s) by some other legal standard(s), is open to recurring indefinitely. Legal change can occur by many routes, but a succession of errors is one of them.

Thus, although Marmor is incorrect in contending that the observational mind-independence of legal norms is weak rather than strong, his remarks can serve to alert us to the fact that the *existential* mind-independence of those norms is never strong. Legal officials can collectively be wrong about the implications of the laws which their own shared beliefs and attitudes and behavioral patterns sustain, but their errors (unless subsequently corrected) quickly enter into the contents of those laws and thereby become some of the prevailing standards. Moreover, we should note that – in the remarks quoted above – Marmor does not initially assert that community-wide mistakes about the extensions of conventional concepts are impossible. He initially asserts merely that they are implausible. Such an assertion is overstated, but it is not entirely misguided. There is some truth in the thesis that our epistemic access to the products of our own practices is more intimate than our epistemic access to the phenomena of the natural world. Though that thesis should never obscure the possibility of disaccord between people's first-order beliefs and their second-order beliefs about the contents and implications of those first-order beliefs, it aptly suggests that we should sometimes feel greater confidence in our grasp of our own ideas than in our grasp of entities which we have not fashioned. Within limits that prevent it from hardening into a dogma about the infallibility of our apprehension of our own practices, a tenet about relative levels of confidence is pertinent. That tenet is particularly germane in connection with very narrowly and precisely delimited conventions such as the rules of chess, but it also has some force in connection with conventions that are more diffuse – such as those that make up a large legal system.

In short, when we ponder whether the general norms of a legal system are objective in the sense of being mind-independent, we should arrive at a complex conclusion. Such norms are both existentially and observationally mind-independent, but their existential mind-independence is weak, whereas their observational mind-independence is strong. Though discrepancies between officials' perceptions and the actualities of the norms can arise because of the norms' strong observational mind-independence, the weakness of the norms' existential mind-independence minimizes those discrepancies. It does so not by ensuring that the officials who run a legal system are collectively infallible in their interpretations of legal materials, but instead by ensuring that any of their uncorrected errors will quickly be incorporated into the law of the relevant jurisdiction. In other words, any incongruities between the officials' collective perceptions and the substance of the law are quite rapidly removed through the recurrent reshaping of the substance in accordance with the perceptions. Furthermore, because legal officials are so familiar with their own practices and the products of those practices, any incongruities between what is collectively perceived and what is actual should be relatively uncommon.

Now, when the types of mind-independence are properly demarcated, we can see how evident is the potential for divergences between indemonstrability and indeterminacy – and between uncertainty

Legal Interpretation and Legal Reasoning 129

and indeterminacy – in the workings of legal systems. Many philosophers appear to assume that, if there is widespread disagreement or uncertainty among the legal officials in a given jurisdiction about the content and very existence of a determinately correct answer to some legal question, there cannot be any such answer to that question. An assumption along those lines would be well founded if the observational mind-independence of legal norms were like the existential mind-independence thereof in being only weak. In fact, however, although legal norms as legal norms are constitutively underlain by the shared first-order beliefs and attitudes of legal officials, they are endowed with contents and implications that can exceed the officials' own second-order grasp. Think, for example, of a constitutional provision or some other legal norm that prohibits the infliction of severely cruel punishments. Legal officials will need to reflect on the tenor of that norm in order to ascertain how it bears on various punitive measures. In so doing, the officials might disagree with one another intractably about the legitimacy of some specific type of punishment, or most of the officials might feel deeply uncertain about the matter. Nonetheless, there may well be a uniquely correct answer to each question about which the officials disagree or about which they feel uncertain. Their wrangling or perplexity over some of the implications of a legal norm – a norm that exists because of their law-creating activities – is not a bar to the determinacy of those implications.

As we shall see later in this chapter, Hart himself descried the distinction between the weak existential mind-independence and the strong observational mind-independence of laws. Though he did not analyze that distinction with the precise and somewhat technical philosophical categories of this subsection, he perceptively understood that the *finality* of the decisions rendered by the topmost court in a legal system does not amount to the *infallibility* of those decisions (141–7). Like the other officials who run a system of legal governance, the officials who occupy positions on the topmost court can collectively be mistaken about the contents and implications of the laws which they apply. By powerfully insisting as much, Hart evinced his awareness of the difference between the weak existential mind-independence and the strong observational mind-independence of those laws. On the one hand, every law in a jurisdiction possesses its status as such through the practices whereby the legal-governmental officials there collectively identify the norms that belong to their system of governance as laws. Those norms belong to that system because they are treated as belonging thereto by the officials, whose practices of law-ascertainment uphold the standards of legal validity – including most notably the ultimate standards in the Rule of Recognition – under which the norms are endowed with the status of laws. On the other hand, although the very existence of laws as laws is due to the collective endeavors of the officials in sustaining and applying the aforementioned standards of legal validity, the officials collectively as well as individually can go astray when construing the standards of legal validity or when construing any of the laws that are recognized as such by reference to those standards. Hart was correct in his stance on this point; he was correct to deny that legal-governmental officials are ever collectively infallible in their interpretations of legal norms. By proleptically rebutting Marmor's contrary stance on the matter, Hart implicitly apprehended the divide between the weak existential mind-independence and the strong observational mind-independence of legal norms. *Malgré lui*, however, he thereby underscored the unwisdom of his own tendency to overlook the distinction between indeterminacy and indemonstrability and also the cognate distinction between indeterminacy and uncertainty.

1.4 *Semantics versus pragmatics*

A final distinction to be noted in this preliminary section of the chapter is the contrast between the semantics and the pragmatics of legal utterances. That is, we need to differentiate between the meanings of legal statements and the characteristic purposes for which those statements are articulated. If any instance of communication is to be construed properly, then both the semantics and the pragmatics of that instance have to be taken into account. Frequently, of course, the purpose for which a statement has been articulated is to impart the information that is conveyed by the semantics of the statement. In many other cases, however, instances of communication will be misunderstood if their addressees are not alert to the potential for dissimilarities between underlying aims and semantic surfaces.

Let us glance at an elementary example. Suppose that, while conversing with Miranda, Ferdinand opens a window on his side of the room. After a short time, Miranda utters the following statement: "A cold draft is blowing through that open window into the room." In most circumstances, Ferdinand will have misunderstood Miranda's act of communication if he takes her purpose to consist simply in imparting to him the information conveyed by the semantics of her statement. Her purpose is predominantly instead to direct him to close or lower the window. Ferdinand will have failed to engage with Miranda's utterance adequately if he does not fathom that the speech-act constituted by the utterance is principally that of a request or directive and only secondarily that of an assertion.

As this homely example illustrates, the semantics and the pragmatics of a statement can diverge in interesting ways. Often, of course, the divergences will be more substantial or much more complicated than in the scenario of Miranda and Ferdinand. Because of the potential discontinuity between the semantic dimension and the pragmatic dimension of any act of communication, someone who interprets such an act will generally have to take account of both dimensions in order to come up with an accurate understanding of what has been communicated.[7] This point is especially important in the context of legal interpretation, where complex and specialized conventions bear on many aspects of the semantics and pragmatics of legal texts.

Hart in his later work clear-sightedly comprehended the distinction between the semantics and the pragmatics of utterances (1982, 135–6; 1983, 4–5, 7–8, 93–4, 106), but, as he self-chidingly acknowledged, he had not adequately attended to it at the time when he wrote the seventh chapter of *The Concept of Law*. Consequently, in much of that book's discussion of legal reasoning and legal interpretation, he was inordinately preoccupied with semantic matters. To be sure, those matters – such as the question whether roller skates and bicycles are covered by the meaning of the term "vehicle" in a prohibition on the use of vehicles in a public park[8] – can be of great significance in legal contexts and indeed are frequently the foci of legal disputation. Nevertheless, an account of legal interpretation that highlights such matters while devoting far less attention to the complexities of the pragmatics of legal discourse is simplistic and distortive. Hart in his later writings was right to upbraid himself for his overemphasis on the semantics of legal formulations in the seventh chapter of *The Concept of Law*.

Three caveats should be entered here. First is a point that has been made in §5 of my opening chapter. Although philosophers of language in recent decades have sophisticatedly shed light on the intricately ramified distinction between the semantics and the pragmatics of acts of communication, we should not presume that the philosophy of language supplies a general template for the interpretation of legal texts. It alerts us to the subtlety and multiplicity of the factors that affect the contents of acts of communication, but those factors vary markedly across jurisdictions. Indeed, they can vary across different domains of the law even within a single jurisdiction. Pragmatic aspects and semantic aspects, as well as the relationships among those aspects, are operative in diverse forms. Thus, as my first chapter has observed, there are quite sharp limits on the extent to which the philosophy of language or any other area of philosophy can guide the efforts of jurists and lawyers and laypeople to come to grips with the contents of legal norms. Given that the appropriateness of the techniques for interpreting those contents is so heavily a jurisdiction-specific matter, a general philosophical distinction such as that between semantics and pragmatics is valuable for legal interpreters not because it offers them any very concrete guidance but instead because it can expand their horizons by alerting them to complexities which they might otherwise have neglected.

Second, although Hart was correct to reproach himself later for his overemphasis on matters of semantics in his musings on legal reasoning and interpretation, we should not infer that he ignored matters of pragmatics throughout *The Concept of Law*. On the contrary, his distinctions among viewpoints (internal, external, simulative) were fundamentally focused on the pragmatics of legal utterances. That focus is especially evident in relation to the contrast between the internal point of view and the simulative point of view. Any statement articulated from the former point of view can be articulated, with the same semantics, from the latter point of view. Hence, if we are to differentiate between the internal perspective and the simulative perspective, we have to do so by reference to their pragmatics – as Hart indeed did in his discussion of the teacher of Roman Law and the White Russian, to which I have referred in my third chapter. Whereas a statement uttered from the internal perspective expresses a genuine commitment to some norm or practice or institution, a semantically identical statement uttered from the simulative perspective expresses only a feigned commitment. Whereas someone who articulates an internal legal statement always pragmatically presupposes that the system containing the relevant law(s) is generally efficacious, someone who articulates a simulative legal statement might or might not be making a similar presupposition. Contemporary philosophers of law are indebted to Hart for the penetratingness of his endeavors to chart these nuances of the pragmatics of legal utterances.

A third caveat is related to the second one. As we shall see in my next chapter, some philosophers of law in recent years have attributed to Hart the view that internal legal statements are not expressive of any cognitive contents and are instead expressive only of desires or emotions or volitions. When I contest the attribution of such a view to Hart, I will maintain that those philosophers mistake his account of legal pragmatics for an account of legal semantics. As has just been noted, he was concerned principally with matters of pragmatics rather than principally with matters of semantics in his expositions of the different viewpoints that might be adopted by legal theorists and by jurists. Thus, when we mull over his analysis of the internal perspective and of the statements articulated from that perspective, we are encountering his reflections on legal pragmatics. Keeping this point in mind will be invaluable when we assess the recent efforts by some philosophers to portray Hart as a non-cognitivist. We shall return to this topic in my next chapter, where I will expound the gist of the doctrine of non-cognitivism and then argue against any classification of Hart as a proponent of that doctrine.[9]

2 Hart on formalism and rule-skepticism

Chapter 7 of *The Concept of Law* is entitled "Formalism and Rule-Scepticism" – a title that bespeaks the concerns to which Hart addressed himself throughout his reflections on legal reasoning and interpretation. He took formalism to consist in the proposition that the laws of any well-functioning system of governance prescribe a determinately correct answer to every legal question that might arise therein. According to formalists, there is consequently no occasion for any discretionary decision-making by the officials of such a system. Hart took rule-skepticism to consist in the proposition that the laws of every system of governance never prescribe a determinately correct answer to any legal question that might arise therein. According to rule-skeptics, every occasion for decision-making by the officials of such a system is consequently an occasion for a discretionary choice. As is evident, each of these theories goes well beyond simply denying the truth of the other. Each of them goes to the opposite extreme by claiming that what the rival theory deems to be always true is in fact never true. Thus, the debate encapsulated in the title of Hart's seventh chapter is a starkly polarized dispute between outlandishly extreme positions.

Hart ventured to steer a path between those extremes, albeit closer to the formalist position than to rule-skepticism. While staying clear of those extremes, however, he took from them his focus on the extent of the determinacy of legal norms. His contemplation of the nature of legal reasoning and interpretation was centered largely on questions about that very extent (though, as has been observed, he did not adequately distinguish such questions from questions about indemonstrability or uncertainty). Indeed, his approach to the topic can quite accurately be understood as an exploration of the considerations that have been adduced by various legal theorists in support of rule-skepticism. Hart showed that some of those considerations do not carry any rule-skeptical implications at all, and he defused the remaining considerations by showing that their rule-skeptical implications are modest. Though he overstated the degree of the indeterminacy in central instances of legal systems – chiefly because of his failure to differentiate sharply enough between indeterminacy and indemonstrability and between indeterminacy and uncertainty – he was correct both in claiming that there is some indeterminacy and in claiming that the indeterminacy is far from rampant.

2.1 The difficulties of identifying rules

Early in his discussion of legal reasoning and interpretation (125, 126), Hart broached some of the renowned meditations by Ludwig Wittgenstein on the difficulties of identifying the rules that are followed in various social practices. Though Hart was well aware of the importance of those meditations, he put them aside after touching upon them at the outset of his enquiry into the determinacy of legal norms. He was wise to do so, for – as I have argued at considerable length elsewhere (Kramer 2007, 21–5) – Wittgenstein's profound and fascinating investigations do not bear on the determinacy or indeterminacy of legal norms or any other norms.[10]

Summarized with the utmost terseness, the fundamental problem highlighted by Wittgenstein is that any norm-governed patterns of conduct are consistent with a limitless abundance of norms rather than only with some norm N that is immanent in those patterns as their point of reference. We are hard pressed to specify the basis for the proposition that the envisaged patterns of conduct are oriented toward N rather than toward any of the countless other norms with which they are consistent. Still, in spite of the depth of this conundrum, it does not really have anything to do with the determinate correctness of answers to legal questions (or of answers to questions in other domains). The cruxes which it exposes are not any snags in the actual following of norms within multitudinous activities, but are instead snags in philosophical efforts to provide a criterion for the identification of those norms. Wittgenstein's work in this area is best read as a challenge to the idea that the task of philosophy is to come up with the foundations for norm-governed activities, which rest instead on themselves as their own foundations.

When Wittgenstein is understood in the way favored here, we can perceive that his central objective was to show that no comprehensively applicable criterion for singling out the norms immanent in practices is available. Efforts to come up with a noncircular philosophical criterion of that kind are as futile and misdirected as are any efforts to come up with a noncircular philosophical foundation for the Law of Noncontradiction or for the inferability of future regularities from past regularities. If we attempt to show that some norm-governed patterns of conduct are oriented toward a norm N rather than toward the miscellaneous other norms with which those patterns are consistent, we shall have to take for granted what we are purporting to demonstrate.

Construed in this fashion, the Wittgensteinian critique of the notion of following a rule does reveal that the matter of identifying the norms which are immanent in human practices is opaque to noncircular philosophical analyses. Wittgenstein's critique hardly implies, however, that the following of rules is itself futile or problematic. No inferences about indeterminacy can validly be derived from his critique. Questions about the implications of rules in various domains will continue to be answerable in determinately correct ways, just as will questions about the conformity or nonconformity of sundry propositions with the Law of Noncontradiction. Norms that guide patterns of conduct will continue to require certain decisions, and to disallow contrary decisions, by the people whose behavior is subject to them. Although philosophical analysis cannot explain why we are correct in singling out those norms rather than the myriad of other norms with which the patterns of conduct are consistent, that fact does not detract one whit from the decision-prescribing force of the norms that have been correctly singled out. Far from disclosing that everything is unsettled in activities such as the operations of a legal system, Wittgenstein's critique leaves those activities entirely as they are. To believe otherwise is to fail to grasp that the unanalyzable fundamentals of some practice are indeed fundamentals of that practice. Though their unanalyzable character thwarts philosophical elucidation, it does not even slightly impair their operativeness within the practice. That operativeness scarcely depends on our being able to provide a noncircular philosophical account of it.

2.2 *Determinacy and unforeseeability*

Hart began by pondering whether legislation with its explicitly formulated norms is less susceptible to problems of indeterminacy than are judicial or administrative rulings that are endowed with precedential force (124–7). He did not completely dismiss the common view that legislation is indeed less prone to those problems, but he contended persuasively that such a view is highly simplistic at best. Despite some genuine advantages of statutes over precedents as vehicles for the issuance of legal norms, all laws are brought into existence by human beings whose ability to anticipate the future is quite limited. As Hart wrote: "It is a feature of the human predicament (and so of the legislative one) that we labour under two connected handicaps whenever we seek to regulate, unambiguously and in advance, some sphere of conduct by means of general standards to be used without further official direction on particular occasions. The first handicap is our relative ignorance of fact: the second is our relative indeterminacy of aim" (128). In other words, because human beings even with the assistance of computers cannot perfectly foresee the endlessly diverse contingencies that might arise henceforth, the objectives which human beings pursue through the issuance of legal norms are to some degree open-ended. Only if people were gods who could peer omnisciently into the future, would they be able to fix upon objectives that are fully determinate. Because people in fact fall markedly short of divinity and omniscience, the aims which they seek to further through the promulgation of statutes and other laws are not fully definite. Consequently, even when those aims are duly taken into account by the adjudicative and administrative officials who are responsible for interpreting and applying the laws, some of the questions that might arise in legal proceedings will not be determinately answerable by reference to any relevant laws.

Having thus argued that some indeterminacy in the law of any jurisdiction is inevitable, Hart mulled over two main techniques through which the systems of legal governance in modern Western societies have handled the medleys of situations to which the broadly formulated laws of those systems are applicable: the promulgation of regulations by administrative agencies (131–2), and the rendering of judgments by courts that establish precedents (132–3, 134–5). Often, a statute framed in highly abstract terms will delegate to some administrative agency the task of bringing the statute's requirements to bear on the concreteness of people's circumstances. Such an agency will typically conduct enquiries with opportunities for input from people and organizations who are likely to be affected by its determinations. Recurrently over time, the agency will issue regulations that flesh out the abstractions of the statute under which the regulations are authorized. The regulations are intermediate between those abstractions and the minutiae of people's activities to which the regulations will be applied by the agency itself or by the courts.

Alternatively or additionally, a system of legal governance can deal with certain aspects of people's lives predominantly through rulings by judges in response to mishaps or disputes that have to be resolved through the intervention of public authorities. Apart from providing some fine-grained directives and guidance to the parties involved in those mishaps or disputes, the adjudicative rulings – especially at appellate tiers of the judicial hierarchy – are typically accompanied by reasoned justifications that sometimes include intermediate-level principles. Insofar as those justifications are vested with precedential force, the principles included in them are functionally similar in some respects to the regulations promulgated by administrative agencies (132). As Hart observed, this mode of legal governance has been exemplified in England and the United States by the doctrine of negligence in tort law.

2.3 *A source of indeterminacy: vagueness*

In his discussion of administrative regulations and adjudicative principles, Hart assumed that the abstractions of highly general statutes or highly general principles give rise to indeterminacy in the law of any jurisdiction. To some extent, his assumption on that point derived from his conflation of indeterminacy with indemonstrability and uncertainty. However, to some extent, Hart had glimpsed a genuine source of indeterminacy: the vagueness of general terms. Here I am using the word "vagueness" in a technical philosophical sense that only partly corresponds to its everyday sense. Vagueness in that technical sense has been explored rigorously and extensively by philosophers during the past few decades. Though

Hart wrote his books before the efflorescence of philosophical work on the topic in recent years, the problem of vagueness – in the technical sense – has been recognized by philosophers since ancient times. Indeed, it is often known as the "sorites paradox," because the most prominent version of the problem among the ancient Greeks was focused on the existence of a heap (*sōros*). Hence, notwithstanding that Hart abstained from any explicit references to the sorites paradox as he explored the "open texture" of the formulations of legal norms, we can safely presume that he was familiar with the matter. Since the problem of vagueness is genuinely a source of some indeterminacy in the workings of legal systems, a brief account here of that problem is very much in accordance with Hart's cogitations on the open texture of law.[11]

Of course, a full-scale treatment of the matter of vagueness is far beyond the scope of this book; a laconic sketch of one mundane instance of the problem will suffice for my present purposes. Suppose that a period of six months is unreasonably long as an interval during which students are kept waiting to be informed of their examination results, and suppose that a period of three days is reasonably short as such an interval. Yet, if a period of six months is unreasonably long, then so is a period of six months minus one tenth of a second. Any basis for deeming the former to be unreasonable in length would apply as well to the latter. Conversely, if a span of three days is reasonably short, then a span of three days plus one tenth of a second is likewise reasonable. Any distinction that might classify the former span as reasonable and the latter span as unreasonable would be preposterously without any basis. In this context, much the same can be said about a reasonableness/unreasonableness distinction between any span of length L and a span of L-plus-one-tenth-of-a-second or a span of L-minus-one-tenth-of-a-second. Whatever may be the numerical value of the "L" variable, a reasonableness/unreasonableness distinction between L and L-plus-one-tenth-of-a-second or between L and L-minus-one-tenth-of-a-second would be ludicrously arbitrary. Given as much, however, someone who tries to pin down the distinction between the reasonably short and the unreasonably long will proceed indefinitely in contemplating the addition of tenths of seconds to the length of three days – and will likewise proceed indefinitely, until reaching zero, in contemplating the subtraction of tenths of seconds from the length of six months. No increment of one tenth of a second, whether added to the length of three days or subtracted from the length of six months, will constitute a point of transition from the reasonableness of the former length to the unreasonableness of the latter. We therefore seem impelled toward the verdict that an open-endedly long period of time is reasonably brief and that an extremely short period is unreasonably protracted.

Naturally, the sorites paradox bears *mutatis mutandis* on a host of dichotomies rather than only on the reasonableness/unreasonableness dichotomy. What it reveals is that each of those dualities is associated with a gray area of borderline cases. Within that gray area – the boundaries of which are themselves vague – there is no determinate answer to the question whether any particular borderline phenomenon falls on one side or the other of the relevant duality. Now, among the vague concepts and properties that give rise to such gray areas are many of the major concepts and properties that figure in legal systems. Those juridical concepts and properties differ among one another in the extent of their vagueness (and in the degree of its practical importance), but each of them can generate questions to which there are no determinately correct answers. The potential for some such questions is ineliminable, since any means of closing off vagueness in one or more of its manifestations will rely on concepts that are themselves not impervious to lines of reasoning which broadly resemble the argument sketched in the foregoing paragraph. Although vagueness within a legal system can usually be reduced, and although it can always be shifted from one focal point to another, it cannot ever be overcome completely.

2.4 *A specious focus of rule-skepticism: exceptions*

Whereas the presence of vagueness in the law of any jurisdiction is genuinely a source of indeterminacy, some of the other considerations adduced by rule-skeptics in support of their doctrine are much more dubious. For example, as Hart eloquently contended, some of the rule-skeptics base their cynical doctrine on the sheer fact that many of the norms which belong to systems of governance as laws are subject to exceptions that cannot be exhaustively specified in advance. Having grasped that an extreme formalist position is untenable, these rule-skeptics infer that any invocation of norms in the decision-making operations of legal systems is deluded or mystifying. As Hart wrote (138–9):

> The rule-sceptic is sometimes a disappointed absolutist; he has found that rules are not all they would be in a formalist's heaven, or in a

140   Legal Interpretation and Legal Reasoning

world where men were like gods and could anticipate all possible combinations of fact, so that open texture was not a necessary feature of rules. The sceptic's conception of what it is for a rule to exist, may thus be an unattainable ideal, and when he discovers that it is not attained by what are called rules, he expresses his disappointment by the denial that there are, or can be, any rules.

Quite rightly, Hart was disdainful of these rule-skeptics who have reached their conclusions by adhering to an extravagantly demanding position on whether anything counts as a norm-governed mode of conduct: "To argue in this [rule-skeptical] way is to ignore what rules actually are in any sphere of real life. It suggests that we are faced with the dilemma: 'Either rules are what they would be in the formalist's heaven and they bind as fetters bind; or there are no rules, only predictable decisions or patterns of behaviour.' Yet surely this is a false dilemma" (139). Hart delivered a famous riposte to this version of rule-skepticism: "It does not follow from the fact that ... rules have exceptions incapable of exhaustive statement, that in every situation we are left to our discretion and are never bound to [comply with rules]. A rule that ends with the word 'unless ...' is still a rule."[12]

2.5 *Another specious focus of rule-skepticism: instincts*

An even shakier consideration highlighted by some rule-skeptics is that judges and other legal decision-makers frequently arrive at conclusions about the legal consequences of situations without consciously adverting to the laws under which those consequences are ordained (139–41). When a rule-skeptic does marshal such a consideration in support of her doctrine, she is submitting that legal decision-makers rely on hunches or instincts which they then seek to vindicate by dressing up their conclusions as deductions from legal norms. According to this rule-skeptical line of thought, the norms are not genuinely guiding or governing the processes of decision-making in a legal system. Instead, they are ornaments that are drawn upon to rationalize conclusions which have been reached intuitively. Hunches, rather than norms, are the provenance of the determinations rendered by adjudicators and administrators in the operations of a system of governance.

Hart countered this line of thought principally by emphasizing that the officials who apply the laws of a system of governance can be acting under the guidance of those laws even when the officials are not consciously reflecting on the terms thereof. If the laws in question have long been familiar to the officials, the endeavor of applying those laws can often be performed in a routinely unreflective manner without any conscious deducing of conclusions from premises. Consider here an analogy that was broached *en passant* by Hart. A player of chess will typically make many moves in a game without consciously attending to the rules under which those moves are open to her. Her attention will instead typically be trained on the strategic ebb and flow of the competition, as she and her opponent vie to outwit each other. Nonetheless, she is complying with the rules and is being guided by them, in that she harbors all the dispositions of the internal point of view in relation to them. (My invocation here of the internal point of view includes my second chapter's extension of that point of view to power-conferring norms.) Much the same is true of legal-governmental officials on occasions when they straightaway reach conclusions, in an unreflective manner, about the legal consequences of people's actions. Because officials will typically be closely familiar with the contents of many of the laws which they are called upon as adjudicators or administrators to apply in sundry settings, they will often concentrate their attention on ascertaining what has happened in those settings, and they will draw upon the contents of the laws as taken-for-granted elements of their everyday outlooks through which they view what has happened. Precisely because those contents have entered into the everyday outlooks of the officials – who harbor all the dispositions of the internal point of view in relation to them – the laws are effectively guiding the officials' determinations without being consciously pondered in most cases.

Indeed, as is apparent from the success of people in communicating sophisticatedly to one another in natural languages such as English, the guiding role of norms can be operative even if the people who are swayed by them are not able to articulate them fully. When people are proficient in speaking such a language, they partake of all the dispositions of the internal point of view in relation to syntactic and semantic norms which they might well not be able to formulate. Both in their own compliance with those norms and in their monitoring of other people's compliance therewith, the users of a language are guided by the norms to form inclinations which they act upon intuitively rather than through studied deductions. Of course, because the officials who run the operations of a legal system are far more often required to justify their judgments than are the speakers of a natural language, the likelihood that the officials will be unable to articulate many of the legal norms to which they give effect is considerably lower than the likelihood that the speakers of a language will be unable to articulate many of the syntactic and semantic norms to which *they* give effect. Still, as has been observed in my third chapter, the officials who run a legal system might be unable to formulate some of the standards in the foundational Rule of Recognition by which they are decisively guided in their law-ascertaining endeavors. And, in any event, the broader point here is that norms can orient the judgments of their addressees even in numerous circumstances where the addressees are not consciously adverting to the norms – including, obviously, any circumstances in which an addressee of the norms is not capable of articulating their contents with any precision.

This discussion should close with a caveat. Hart wisely allowed that there can of course be occasions in the workings of a legal system when judges or other officials invoke norms to rationalize some decisions which they have reached through wholly unguided hunches (140–1). Though such occasions can undoubtedly arise, the clear possibility of them does not warrant any rule-skeptical conclusions – because, as Hart contended, there is no basis for thinking that such occasions are pervasive in the operations of legal systems of governance. As he declared, "for the most part decisions, like the chess-player's moves, are reached either by genuine effort to conform to rules consciously taken as guiding standards of decision or, if intuitively reached, are justified by rules which the judge was antecedently disposed to observe and whose relevance to the case in hand would generally be acknowledged" (141).

2.6 *A further specious focus of rule-skepticism: finality*

In §1.3 of this chapter, we have glanced at Hart's astute distinction between finality and infallibility (141–7). A decision is final in a legal system of governance if and only if the decision is not appealable within that system. Thus, for example, most decisions by the US Supreme Court are final within the American legal system of governance – because most of the Court's decisions cannot be appealed any further in that system. To be sure, the broader upshot of a decision by the US Supreme Court can eventually be countered through the workings of American governmental institutions. For example, a later judgment by the Court itself can overturn some earlier ruling(s); a constitutional amendment can undo the effects of some constitutional decision(s) by the Court; and a statute enacted by the US Congress can undo the effects of some non-constitutional decision(s) by the Court. Still, the very reason why such measures are necessary for displacing the consequences of any determinations handed down by the US Supreme Court is that those determinations stand as unappealably final in the meantime. Finality does not consist in a thoroughgoing insusceptibility to modifications in the future, but it always amounts to the absence of any further opportunities for appeals in the current system of governance.

Infallibility is quite a different property. A decision is infallible in a system of governance if and only if the very fact that the decision has been reached is sufficient to make it correct by providing the full justificatory basis for it. Any decision that endeavors to apply a norm N to some set of circumstances is not infallible (though of course it may well be correct), since the endeavor to apply N might misconstrue the content of that norm or might misconstrue the circumstances on which N is brought to bear. In other words, the sheer occurrence of the endeavor to apply N to those circumstances is not sufficient to guarantee the correctness of the application by supplying the full justificatory basis for it. Hence, whereas the decisions of the US Supreme Court are unappealably final in the American system of governance, they are not infallible. Decisions by that court involve applications of constitutional provisions or other laws to various situations, and can thus err either by misconstruing the laws or by misconstruing the situations.

Hart broached a fanciful game known as "scorer's discretion," to illustrate how the decisions reached by someone in a given context could be infallible (142, 143–4). Whereas nearly every genuine game is structured by some rules with contents that are independent of the discretion of anyone who applies those rules, the sole rule about the attaining of touchdowns in the game of scorer's discretion is that a touchdown has been attained when and only when the scorer declares that a touchdown has been attained. Simply by declaring that a touchdown has been attained, the scorer has made his decision correct by supplying it with its full justificatory basis; conversely, simply by refraining from any declaration that a touchdown has been attained, the scorer has made his decision correct by supplying it with its full justificatory basis. Every declaration by the scorer about the attaining of touchdowns is self-justifyingly correct, since the only rule about the attainment of touchdowns has set forth a standard with a content that is wholly dependent on the scorer's discretion. There is no possibility of his erring in his pronouncements about the attainment or non-attainment of touchdowns.

As is evident, the game of scorer's discretion is strikingly different from virtually any real-world game. Yet, by the reckoning of a rule-skeptic, the game of scorer's discretion closely resembles the operations of a legal system. According to a rule-skeptic, the substantive norms of such a system are vacuous as bases for legal decision-making and are thus not constitutive of any independent constraints on the discretion of the officials who engage in that decision-making. Because those norms are vacuous, any applications of them by the officials are self-justifyingly correct. Hence, by the reckoning of a rule-skeptic, the officials of a legal system are infallible in performing their roles as legal decision-makers. There is no possibility that the officials will reach any legally incorrect outcomes when they perform those roles, because the discretion of the officials is the only touchstone by reference to which the legal correctness of any outcomes can be gauged.

As Hart perciptiently observed (141–2), rule-skeptics over the decades have quite often sought to vindicate their outlandish depiction of the operations of legal systems by resorting to slogans such as "The American Constitution means what the US Supreme Court says that it means." For the purposes of a rule-skeptic, the serviceability of such a maxim derives from its ambiguity – ambiguity that straddles the divide between finality and infallibility. On the one hand, the rule-skeptics intone the aphorism about the American Constitution in order to ascribe infallibility to the constitutional decisions reached by the US Supreme Court. Such an ascription of infallibility is at the heart of rule-skepticism. On the other hand, among people not already convinced of the soundness of rule-skepticism, the adage about the American Constitution is likely to gain acceptance only when it is construed as an attribution of finality to the constitutional judgments rendered by the US Supreme Court. So construed, the adage is true. So construed, however, it is not supportive of rule-skepticism at all. As we have already seen, decisions that are final within a system of governance can nonetheless be mistaken. Although the judgments of the US Supreme Court on constitutional matters are indeed final within the American system of governance, those judgments can be erroneous in their interpretations of constitutional provisions (as well as in other respects).

Rule-skeptics can strive to win adherents to their doctrine by trading on the ambiguity just outlined. Having themselves conflated finality and infallibility, they can lead other people into similar

Legal Interpretation and Legal Reasoning 145

confusion through seductive sloganeering. Thus, by exposing the ambiguity of the slogans and the confusion that might result from it, Hart resisted a particularly insidious version of rule-skepticism. As he cogently maintained, the need for finality in any legal system is scarcely a ground for concluding that such a system does not actually contain any laws which prescribe determinately correct answers to the questions at issue in the legal disputes that are addressed by adjudicators and administrators.

2.7 One more specious focus of rule-skepticism: ultimacy

In the final main section of his chapter on legal reasoning and interpretation, Hart returned to a matter which he had broached in his discussion of the Rule of Recognition. That is, he contemplated some of the circumstances under which the Rule of Recognition in this or that particular jurisdiction is itself not fully settled (147–54). Though Hart in his reflections on this matter often conflated indeterminacy with indemonstrability or uncertainty, those reflections make clear that there is some degree of indeterminacy in the implications of any Rule of Recognition – just as there is some degree of indeterminacy in the implications of any law validated under a Rule of Recognition.

Yet the presence of indeterminacy in the ultimate criteria of the Rule of Recognition might seem to provide a route for the rule-skeptics to clinch their position. After all, the Rule of Recognition in any jurisdiction lays down the standards under which all the other laws of that jurisdiction possess their status as laws. Among those laws are the norms of law-application that invest certain people with the status of officials who are authorized to resolve legal points of contention. Given as much, the adjudicators and administrators in the relevant jurisdiction may seem to lack any footing from which they can confer determinacy on an indeterminate Rule of Recognition. As Hart formulated the putative problem (152, emphasis in original):

> The courts will have made determinate at this point the ultimate rule by which valid law is identified. Here "the constitution is what the judges say it is" does *not* mean merely that particular decisions of supreme tribunals cannot be challenged. At first sight the spectacle seems paradoxical: here are courts exercising creative powers which settle the ultimate criteria by which the validity of the very laws, which

confer upon them jurisdiction as judges, must itself be tested. How can a constitution confer authority to say what the constitution is?

Hart dispelled this ostensible crux by reiterating the paramount message to be gleaned from his jousting with rule-skepticism. Though he badly conflated indeterminacy with uncertainty in his dissolution of that seeming crux – as he repeatedly adverted to doubts and doubtfulness – he did not thereby greatly lessen the cogency of his response. In that response, he made clear once again that his rejection of formalism aligned him with rule-skepticism only to a modest degree (152):

> But the paradox vanishes if we remember that though every rule may be doubtful at some points, it is indeed a necessary condition of a legal system existing, that not every rule is open to doubt on all points. The possibility of courts having authority at any given time to decide these limiting questions concerning the ultimate criteria of validity, depends merely on the fact that, at that time, the application of those criteria to a vast area of law, including the rules which confer that authority, raises no doubts, though their precise scope and ambit do.

In the closing sentence of Chapter 7 in *The Concept of Law*, at the end of his discussion of the indeterminacy engendered by the ultimate standards that make up a Rule of Recognition, Hart underscored afresh the point made in this latest passage. In other words, he again emphasized that any indeterminacy in a functional legal system is situated within the wide-ranging expanses of determinacy throughout the system's workings: "Here, at the fringe of these very fundamental things, we should welcome the rule-sceptic, as long as he does not forget that it is at the fringe that he is welcome; and does not blind us to the fact that what makes possible these striking developments by courts of the most fundamental rules is, in great measure, the prestige gathered by courts from their unquestionably rule-governed operations over the vast, central areas of the law" (154).

Having positioned himself between rule-skepticism and formalism at every juncture in his meditations on legal reasoning and interpretation, Hart rightly located his stance much closer to the latter doctrine than to the former. Though his development of that stance was tarnished by the lapses which I have recounted and criticized in the first half of this chapter, his central thesis – his contention that the very functionality of a legal system depends on the determinacy of the implications of the system's norms in most settings – was solid. Both at the level of a foundational Rule of Recognition and at the level of the norms that are validated as laws by that Rule of Recognition, rule-skepticism is pertinent only at the periphery. Cases that arise on the periphery can be of great importance, of course, and they generally receive far more attention from law students and legal academics than do cases in which the implications of the applicable laws are not only determinate but also clear-cut. Nonetheless, the cases on the periphery are not representative of the vast array of situations that are covered by the laws in a functional system of governance. Representative, instead, are the circumstances in which the legal bearings of people's conduct are both determinate and unexcitingly clear-cut.

5

Law and Morality

Hart was the foremost Anglophone philosopher of law in the twentieth century, and he was rivaled only by Hans Kelsen as the foremost philosopher of law in any language during that century.[1] Among his many sterling accomplishments in the philosophy of law was his reinvigoration of the tradition of legal positivism. His revival of that tradition greatly strengthened it by transforming it in some major respects – not least by severing it from the command theory of law. Yet, in spite of the distance that Hart put between himself and his illustrious predecessors such as Jeremy Bentham and John Austin, he was firmly aligned with them in his emphasis on the distinction between what legal institutions are and what legal institutions morally ought to be. With his general insistence on the separability of law and morality, he established himself as an opponent of natural-law theorists and their efforts to show that law is an inherently moral phenomenon. Indeed, the arguments through which he impugned a multiplicity of such efforts are one feature of *The Concept of Law* that has cemented its place as a classic text with which generations of legal philosophers will perennially grapple.

Although Hart scarcely attempted to conceal his allegiance to legal positivism during the first several chapters of *The Concept of Law*, he did not overtly take up the cudgels on behalf of that doctrine until the penultimate chapter – the ninth chapter – of his book. He did not entirely avoid confusion and misjudgments in his discussions of legal positivism, but those discussions overall have been invaluable in enhancing the rigor and clarity of subsequent treatments of the topic. Both by elaborating some of the principal theses of legal positivism and by assailing many of the misconceptions about it that have been propagated by its opponents, Hart sharpened the thinking of legal philosophers about the sundry relationships between law and morality. Writing at a time when the horrors of fascism and Communism had led numerous jurisprudential theorists to denounce legal positivism for what they perceived as its excessively deferential attitude toward the directives of legal-governmental officials, he cogently maintained that such strictures against positivism were based on badly distortive misapprehensions about its orientation. Albeit positivism does not in itself commit its proponents to any particular positions on matters of politics or legal interpretation, its tenets are highly serviceable for theorists who are vigilantly distrustful of the demands issued by governments. Hart himself was such a theorist, whose espousal of legal positivism stemmed partly from his resistance to the idea that legal requirements are always morally binding. By making clear that positivism can fruitfully be drawn upon in furtherance of social justice against the legal mandates that emanate from the institutions of government, he helped to dispel one of the most pernicious jurisprudential misconceptions. In so doing, he performed a service not only for the advocates of legal positivism but also for its detractors.

1 Separability theses

One commendable aspect of the ruminations by Hart on legal positivism, which quite a few contemporary philosophers of law have not fully absorbed, is that he recognized the diversity of the points of contention that have pitted the devotees of positivism against the devotees of natural-law theories. Whereas some present-day philosophers of law are inclined to refer to "the separability thesis" of legal positivism – with the definite article "the" as a signal that there is one defining point of dispute between legal positivists and their opponents – Hart knew that there is no single such thesis.[2] He countered the notion of a single defining thesis, indeed, in the opening sentence of his chapter on positivism: "There are many different types of relation between law and morals and there is nothing which can be profitably singled out for study as *the* relation between them" (185, emphasis in original). Hart was keenly aware that natural-law theorists have postulated numerous connections between law and morality which putatively clinch the character of law as an inherently moral phenomenon, and he rightly held that legal positivism poses a challenge to nearly every one of those connections and also to the claim that any unchallenged connection serves to establish the inherently moral character of law. Far from being confined to a solitary separability thesis, legal positivism consists in a wide-ranging affirmation of the separability of law and morality – an affirmation that contests the multifarious endeavors of natural-law theorists to present law as intrinsically moral.

To be sure, Hart himself inadvertently abetted the tendency of later philosophers of law to equate legal positivism with one pithy thesis. In the second paragraph of his chapter on positivism, he announced that he would "take Legal Positivism to mean the simple contention that it is in no sense a necessary truth that laws reproduce or satisfy certain demands of morality, though in fact they have often done so" (185–6). Although Hart here broached the proposition that was most saliently at issue in the debates between legal positivists and their opponents during past centuries – and although that proposition continues to be quite a prominent focus of controversy in the present day, both among legal positivists and between legal positivists and their adversaries – he went astray in suggesting, even *en passant*, that legal positivism is concerned with only one main way in which law and morality have sometimes been viewed as indisseverable. Later in his ninth chapter, and in some of his subsequent writings, Hart revealed that any such suggestion is unfounded. There he charted and entered some of the other principal tussles between legal positivists and natural-law theorists that have occurred both in recent decades and in bygone eras. Moreover, immediately before the somewhat ill-advised suggestion that has just been quoted, Hart readily accepted that the phrases "Legal Positivism" and "Natural Law" have each "come to be used for a range of different theses about law and morals" (185).

Thus, we can best begin an exploration of legal positivism by pondering the complex diversity of the debates between positivists and their opponents. Those debates concern the relationships between law and morality, but there is no single understanding of morality that runs through all of them. Of course, one reason for the profuseness of the conceptions of morality which are operative in those debates is that the participants therein subscribe to varying substantive moral standards. At least as important, however, is that different aspects or dimensions of morality are at issue across the sundry disputes between positivists and natural-law theorists. Each of those aspects or dimensions can illuminatingly be approached through a distinction between morality and something else that serves as a point of contrast.[3]

1.1 Four aspects or dimensions of morality

Let us here contemplate four distinctions. Three of them pertain to aspects or dimensions of morality that have figured conspicuously in controversies over the separability of law and morality, whereas the fourth distinction pertains to an aspect or dimension of morality that is not genuinely at issue in any of those controversies. The reason for including that fourth dichotomy will become clear in my next subsection, after which we shall glance at some of the disputes that have been associated with the other three facets of morality that are delineated here.

First, then, is a contrast between morality and immorality. It is a distinction that gets invoked pervasively in everyday life, and is construable in either of two chief ways. On the one hand, it is construable as a division between the permissible and the impermissible or between the legitimate and the illegitimate or between right and wrong (where those three pairings are taken to be interchangeable). On the other hand, it can additionally be construed as a division between the morally commendable and the morally deplorable or between the morally salutary and the morally noxious or between virtue and vice (where, again, those three pairings are taken to be interchangeable). Obviously, these two ways of interpreting the morality/immorality diremption are closely related. However, whereas every morally commendable mode of human conduct in ordinary circumstances is morally permissible, not every morally permissible mode of human conduct in ordinary circumstances is morally commendable. Some morally permissible modes of conduct, such as one's scratching of one's nose in any ordinary circumstances, are not properly classified as either commendable or deplorable. Likewise, whereas every morally noxious mode of conduct is morally impermissible, not every morally impermissible mode of conduct is morally noxious. Some morally impermissible modes of conduct, such as one's breaking of a minor promise in any ordinary circumstances, are not properly classified as either salutary or noxious.

Second is a distinction between morality and prudence. Here the term "prudence" is used in a technical philosophical sense that only tenuously corresponds to its quotidian sense. The morality/prudence dichotomy relates to the reasons that might underlie the actions of any person P. A prudential reason for some action by P is focused exclusively or primarily on the interests of P and only derivatively if at all on the interests of anyone else. A moral reason for some action by P is focused exclusively or primarily on the interests of other people and only derivatively if at all on the interests of P. Suppose for example that P is deliberating whether she will desist from her habit of smoking cigarettes. Among the prudential reasons for an affirmative decision are that the discontinuation of her habit will save her a lot of money, and that it will improve her health, and that it will keep the stench of tobacco from permeating her clothes and breath and furniture, and that it will halt the discoloration of her teeth. Among the moral reasons for her to terminate her habit of smoking are that such a decision will enhance her ability to support her children and other dependents, and that it will lessen the burdens which she imposes per annum on the public healthcare service in her country, and that it will cut off her financial contributions to an industry that imperils the health of countless other people. Now, as should be evident from this example of P and her habit of smoking, prudential reasons and moral reasons are readily combinable and are often overlapping even though they are distinguishable. Moreover, although the distinctness of prudential reasons and moral reasons can be encapsulated straightforwardly at an abstract level, the task of differentiating between them at concrete levels will sometimes be much more difficult.

Before we move on to a third distinction, we should note that the moral/prudential contrast is quite different from the moral/immoral contrast. Though of course many factors that can underlie people's actions are both nonprudential and morally benign, many other such factors are nonprudential but morally odious. For example, if an official in a Communist system of governance imposes harsh penalties on political dissidents in order to protect the system against ideological impurity, or if an official in a fascist system of governance authorizes the slaughter of the members of a downtrodden racial or religious group in order to enhance the purity of a master race, the official is acting on the basis of a nonprudential but morally evil consideration. Furthermore, though of course many factors that can underlie people's actions are both prudential and morally impermissible, many other such factors are both prudential and permissible. For example, each prudential consideration listed above as a reason for P to desist from her practice of smoking is a morally permissible reason for action. Hence, notwithstanding a sizeable overlap between the morality/immorality duality and the morality/prudence duality, there are also numerous divergences between them.

A third dichotomy to be noted here is the division between moral matters and empirical matters. Roughly stated, that division lies between what morally *should* be done and what *is* being done or what *has* been done or what *will* be done. This distinction between moral facts and empirical facts is a feature of everyday life but is also of far-reaching importance in philosophy. It has for example been enshrined by philosophers in what is often known as "Hume's Law," which holds that there is at least one moral premise in every argument that validly draws a moral conclusion from logically consistent premises (Kramer 2009a, 6–9). In other words, a moral conclusion is never validly inferable from any logically consistent premises that are wholly descriptive. Whether in a somewhat technical philosophical form or in an everyday form, the moral/empirical dichotomy captures an aspect or dimension of morality – its focus on what morally ought to be rather than solely on what was or what is or what will be – that is different from the aspect or dimension captured by each of the other two dichotomies that have been outlined above. When this moral/descriptive distinction is elaborated along epistemic lines, it amounts to a contrast between moral reasoning and purely empirical or logical or mathematical reasoning.

Finally, a fourth distinction is the divide between moral phenomena and non-moral phenomena. In the sense that is relevant here, non-moral phenomena are those things to which moral concepts or categories are not appositely applicable (Kramer 2017c, 189–90). Virtually all natural processes and states of affairs are non-moral in this sense. For example, suppose that we inquire whether the strong-force interconnectedness of the protons and neutron(s) in some atom of helium is morally permissible or morally impermissible. The appropriate answer to such a question is that neither moral permissibility nor moral impermissibility can ever appositely be predicated of such a state of affairs. If someone ascribes either of those properties to such a state of affairs, she commits a daft conceptual error as well as a moral error. Even more plainly misdirected would be anyone's application of ethical notions such as worthiness and virtue or unworthiness and villainy to the interconnectedness of the subatomic particles in an atom of helium. So applied, such notions would be ludicrously out of place.

By contrast, the doings and decisions and practices undertaken by human beings are always appropriately susceptible to some moral assessments. In precisely that respect, all such doings and decisions and practices are moral rather than non-moral. To be sure, some courses of conduct by human beings are such that the only moral concept pertinently applicable to them is that of permissibility. Such courses of conduct impinge only trivially if at all on the interests of other people. For example, if we ask whether Joe's scratching of his nose in any ordinary circumstances is morally virtuous or morally vicious, the answer to our question is that neither of those ethical properties is germanely predicable of such a mode of conduct in such circumstances. Similarly, if we ask whether Alice's choice between playing solitaire and putting together a jigsaw puzzle as a pastime in any ordinary circumstances is morally commendable or morally deplorable, the answer to our question is that neither of those ethical categories is applicable to such a choice. Still, although neither Joe's action nor Alice's decision is properly assessable with these somewhat thicker ethical concepts, both his action and her decision are properly assessable as morally permissible. In that regard, though only in that regard, both his action and her decision are moral rather than non-moral.

1.2 The fourth distinction: no debates

Each of the first three aspects or dimensions of morality delineated above is associated with a number of debates between legal positivists and natural-law theorists. We shall glance at some of those debates shortly. However, what should be noted straightaway is that the fourth aspect or dimension of morality – the moral versus the non-moral – is not associated with any genuine disputation between positivists and their opponents. As is glaringly evident, the operations of legal systems of governance are run by human beings whose attitudes and beliefs and conduct are integrally constitutive of those operations. Hence, given that all the doings and decisions and practices undertaken by human beings are appositely susceptible to moral appraisal, the operations of legal systems are appositely susceptible to moral appraisal. Moreover, as is also glaringly apparent, those operations in any jurisdiction impinge far more than trivially on the interests of people who reside or work or visit there. Legal requirements and judgments and institutions affect people's lives wide-rangingly and far-reachingly. Indeed, the effects of those requirements and judgments and institutions on people's lives are often momentous. Accordingly, the full repertory of moral concepts can pertinently be applied to the workings of legal systems of governance. Any such system as a whole, along with most of its elements, can germanely be assessed not only as morally legitimate or illegitimate but also as morally salutary or noxious. Although particular moral judgments about a legal system or about some laws and decisions within a legal system can of course be mistaken, the sheer fact that moral concepts have been applied to such a system or to such laws and decisions is never itself inapposite.

Thus, if we are asking whether law is inherently moral, and if the contrast implicit in the question is between the moral and the non-moral, the answer is that law is indeed inherently moral. No legal positivist in his or her right mind has ever suggested otherwise, because no legal positivist in his or her right mind has ever doubted the points made in the preceding paragraph. As has been emphasized in that paragraph, it is obvious that legal systems and their components can always properly be subjected to moral assessment. Far from denying or doubting that those systems are always open to moral appraisal, positivists such as Hart have emphatically proclaimed the vital need for such appraisal. Precisely because Hart's predecessors Bentham and Austin were so keenly determined to gauge the moral quality of every legal system by reference to the precepts of utilitarianism, they staunchly insisted on the distinction between what the law is and what the law ought to be. Not all positivists are utilitarians, fortunately, but every positivist would join Bentham and Austin in recognizing that the subjection of legal systems to rigorous moral scrutiny is an entirely germane endeavor (Kramer 1999, 123–5, 189–91, 200–4).

In short, because every legal positivist is perfectly well aware that legal systems and norms can suitably undergo moral assessments, no positivist has sought to maintain that law is non-moral rather than moral. Every legal positivist would agree that, insofar as "moral" is contrasted with "non-moral," law is an inherently moral phenomenon. This point is worth stressing because some opponents of legal positivism have egregiously overlooked it. Lon Fuller, for example, submitted that positivists look upon law as "simply a datum of nature" and that their approach to legal institutions is "like [that of] the scientist who discovers a uniformity of inanimate nature" (1969, 148, 151). Confronted with such calumnies, Hart quite understandably reacted with exasperation. Specifically with reference to Fuller's phrase "simply a datum of nature," Hart stingingly retorted: "Surely this last phrase merely darkens counsel.

... The author's use of this opaque philosophical phrase suggests that those who, like myself, attempt to analyse the notion of legislative powers in terms of rules are committed to eliminating from their analysis any reference to anything but the inanimate" (1983, 359).

Contrary to what is suggested by Fuller's superfluous remonstrations – and by some equally misguided remonstrations from other anti-positivist writers such as Michael Detmold and Ronald Dworkin (Kramer 1999, 123–5, 189–91) – there are no genuine debates between legal positivists and their foes over the question whether law is moral or non-moral. Every philosopher of law who is at least minimally sensible, whether a positivist or an anti-positivist, concurs on the answer to that question. No such philosopher has failed to grasp that moral concepts are applicable to laws and to legal systems, and therefore no such philosopher has failed to grasp that laws and legal systems in that respect are always moral. Consequently, when legal positivists affirm the separability of law and morality, they are not addressing the moral/non-moral question. They are instead focusing on the other aspects or dimensions of morality that have been summarized in §1.1 above.

1.3 *Morality contrasted with immorality: some debates*

Whereas no legal positivist has ever contended that law is non-moral, virtually every legal positivist contends that the efforts by natural-law theorists to portray law as inherently benign or legitimate – that is, as inherently moral rather than immoral – are unfounded. In other words, when morality is contrasted with immorality rather than with non-moral phenomena, there have indeed occurred sundry genuine debates between positivists and their opponents over the proposition that law is inherently moral. Before we glimpse at some of those debates, we should note a couple of caveats that also apply to the next two subsections of this chapter. First, here and in those succeeding two subsections, this chapter will be tersely outlining some debates rather than entering into them. Though I have elsewhere actively participated in the controversies that will be synopsized here, the confines of this chapter do not leave room for such participation (even in §2 of the chapter, where I will expand upon Hart's approach to one of those controversies). Second, although each of the altercations sketched here does pit a positivist insistence on the separability of law and morality against a natural-law insistence on the inseparability thereof, not all philosophers who are aptly classifiable as legal positivists would endorse the positivist stance unswervingly in every one of those altercations. Even while subscribing to the positivist stance on most of the relevant points of contention, some philosophers deviate from that stance occasionally. Though I myself have defended the positivist affirmation of the separability of law and morality in every one of the disputes that will be broached here, most other legal positivists are somewhat less robust. Even Hart, who steadfastly upheld the positivist banner in most of those disputes, abandoned that banner in a few contexts that will be remarked upon below. (We have already encountered one of those contexts in §6.5 of my opening chapter, where we looked at Hart's limited embrace of a moralized methodology in his theorizing about the nature of law.)

Morality as contrasted with immorality is the focus of the debates to which Hart alluded when he offered his one-sentence encapsulation of legal positivism which I have quoted near the outset of §1 above. Those debates are what Bentham and Austin were addressing when they strenuously proclaimed the distinction between what the law is and what the law ought to be. That is, some natural-law theorists over the centuries have declared that the status of any norm N as a law in any legal system is always dependent on the norm's satisfaction of some test of moral legitimacy. Unless the substance of N is at or above a threshold of moral soundness, N is not genuinely a law in any system of governance – even if the officials in some such system treat N as though it were a law. So have proclaimed a bevy of natural-law theorists from ancient times through the present day. Notwithstanding that a number of contemporary natural-law philosophers distance themselves from such a position in order to concentrate on other connections between law and morality, the notion of a test of moral legitimacy for the status of norms as laws has continued to play quite a prominent role in anti-positivist theorizing (Kramer 2004, 228 n7). Legal positivists are unanimous in rejecting the idea that any such test is an essential feature of law. To be sure, as we shall see in §3 of this chapter, some positivists – Inclusive Legal Positivists – allow that the consistency of N with correct principles of morality can be a necessary condition for the status of N as a law within this or that jurisdiction. However, those positivists maintain that the operativeness of such a moral test for legal validity in any particular jurisdiction is a contingent aspect of the system of law in that jurisdiction rather than an essential aspect of every system of law. Such a test will be operative in a given system of governance only if the officials there uphold a Rule of Recognition under which the test is among the criteria that have to be satisfied by every norm that belongs to the system as a law. Hence, Inclusive Legal Positivists are like other legal positivists in contending that the status of every law as such within any jurisdiction is fundamentally grounded in the practices of officials. Inclusivists hold that any moral test for legal validity in a particular jurisdiction is attributable to those practices rather than to the nature of law.

With the focus still on morality in opposition to immorality, another area of disputation between positivists and their foes is concerned with the general function of legal systems of governance. Most natural-law theorists have submitted that the central function of law is inherently commendable and that every ongoing system of law is itself therefore inherently commendable. Whether the function is deemed to be the securing of basic orderliness and coordination or the governance of human beings as rational agents or the expression of reciprocity between the rulers and the ruled – or any other desideratum or combination of desiderata – the claim by antipositivist theorists is that the operativeness of a legal system is sufficient as well as necessary for the realization of morally commendable states of affairs. Those theorists accordingly conclude that law is an inherently moral phenomenon. In rebuttal, legal positivists have in some cases challenged the premises of the natural-law arguments and have in other cases accepted the premises while rejecting the conclusions that have been drawn from them. We shall encounter a version of the latter strategy in §2 of this chapter, when we examine Hart's argument about the minimum content of natural law. As will become apparent there, legal positivists can and do accept that in any sizeable society the existence of a functioning legal system of governance is necessary for the realization of various morally commendable states of affairs. However, positivists deny that the existence of such a system is *sufficient* for the emergence of any morally commendable states of affairs, and they further deny that the role of such a system as a necessary condition for the realization of certain moral values is something that endows law with the status of an inherently moral phenomenon.

Yet another flashpoint of contention between positivists and their opponents is the way in which any legal system presents itself through the pronouncements of its officials. As I have discussed elsewhere (1999, 101–8; 2004, 216–22), some natural-law philosophers contend that every legal system presents itself and its mandates as morally legitimate. Although these theorists are postulating a necessary connection between law and morality at the level of discourse rather than at the level of underlying substance, they do indeed maintain that officials' legal pronouncements are inextricably bound up with assurances of moral legitimacy (which are usually implicit rather than explicit). Moreover, some of these philosophers have argued that the authoritative utterances of the officials cannot retain any credibility if the assurances of moral legitimacy implicit within them are preposterous. Consequently, in the eyes of these philosophers, nothing counts as a genuine system of law without surpassing some threshold of moral legitimacy. In other words, by reflecting on the presuppositions of the utterances of officials, these philosophers proceed to elaborate a traditional natural-law position – albeit with a test of moral legitimacy applied to the workings of any legal system as a whole rather than to individual laws. Legal positivists, then, have ample grounds for contesting the claims of these philosophers about the assurances that are ostensibly presupposed by the authoritative pronouncements of officials.

One more area of dispute that should be outlined here is the proposition that every system of law attains at least a minimal level of moral worthiness by dint of the procedural or administrative justice that is involved in giving effect to laws in accordance with their terms. Somewhat curiously, Hart went quite a long way toward endorsing that proposition in *The Concept of Law* (160–1, 206–7). However, he later came to have grave doubts about his conciliatory stance (1983, 18), and his conciliatoriness has been criticized in varying ways by some other legal positivists (Kramer 1999, 21–36; Lyons 1973). As Hart came to realize, a few of his later arguments against the efforts by Fuller to ascribe an inner morality to law could be turned upon his own apparent preparedness to acquiesce – however hesitantly – in the proposition about procedural or formal justice.

1.4 *Morality contrasted with prudence: some debates*

When morality contrasted with prudence is the orienting concern, the thesis most commonly propounded by natural-law philosophers is that there are no credible prudential reasons for the officials in any system of governance to abide by the rule of law. These philosophers submit that, in any system of governance, the sole credible reasons for officials to uphold the restrictions integral to the rule of law are moral rather than self-interested. Now, as has been observed in some earlier chapters of this book, Hart expressly left open the nature of the considerations that would motivate the officials in a system of governance to run it as a legal system. He thereby positioned himself against the conclusions of the natural-law philosophers who rule out prudential factors as credible bases for the self-restraint involved in the operation of a legal system. Their conclusions have been impugned at much greater length by me in my previous books and articles on legal positivism.[4] Among the points to be made in the challenges to their anti-positivist conclusions is a distinction between the rule of law and the Rule of Law (Kramer 2007, ch. 2). Whereas the rule of law consists in the individually necessary and jointly sufficient conditions for the existence of a legal system, the Rule of Law consists in the existence of a legal system that exemplifies the values of liberal democracy both procedurally and substantively. Though the claims of the natural-law philosophers about the reasons-for-action that can credibly account for officials' patterns of conduct are largely sustainable in connection with the Rule of Law, those claims are unsustainable in connection with the rule of law. There are credibly possible systems of governance in which the officials who run the systems have strong prudential reasons for complying with rule-of-law requirements to quite high levels in furtherance of exploitative repression.

Another area of controversy involving the morality/prudence distinction is concerned with the reasons-for-action which the officials of any legal system implicitly or explicitly invoke when they advert to legal mandates in justification of their decisions. Although Joseph Raz is predominantly a legal positivist, he and his followers have persistently argued that officials' invocations of legal directives assert or imply that there are moral reasons (nonprudential reasons) for citizens to comply with those directives. Whether or not the officials believe all the implications of what they are asserting, their references to legal mandates as the bases for their adjudicative or administrative rulings imply that the addressees of the rulings have been morally bound to obey those mandates. By adverting to legal requirements as grounds for demanding that people behave in specified ways, the officials are adverting to interest-independent reasons for action – that is, reasons for action that are moral rather than prudential. So runs Raz's line of thought, in a number of interesting variations. Hart endeavored to cast doubt on that line of thought (1982, 153–61, 262–8; 1983, 9–10), and I have elsewhere sought at length to strengthen and amplify Hart's objections (Kramer 1999, ch. 4). While my rejoinders to Raz are multiple, they concentrate on the credible possibility of systems of legal governance in which no punishment-independent reasons for action are asserted or implied by officials' invocations of legal mandates as bases for their decisions. Challenges to Raz's position on this matter are crucial for legal positivism, since his line of thought easily lends itself to being appropriated by natural-law theorists who would deny that legal officials in any credible system of governance are systematically mendacious or deluded in the claims which they make concerning the justifiability of their own decisions.

Also eliciting resistance from legal positivists are some arguments by natural-law philosophers who seize upon the fact that law and morality share a wide-ranging deontic vocabulary. Both in morality and in law, key terms such as "rights" and "duties" and "obligations" and "liberties" and "permissions" and "authority" and "justice" and "powers" and "immunities" are prominently wielded. In the eyes of some natural-law theorists, the terminological affinities between morality and law are indicative of deeper connections between those two domains. In the course of arguing that the reasons-for-action communicated by officials in their authoritative pronouncements are moral rather than prudential, these philosophers have taken for granted that the terminology of "duties" or "obligations" carries the same meaning in legal contexts as in moral contexts. On exactly that point, I have joined Hart in contesting the natural-law position – not by suggesting preposterously that the terminological correspondences between law and morality are unaccompanied by any conceptual overlap, but instead by maintaining that the conceptual overlap is formal rather than substantive. On the one hand, a legal obligation is like a moral obligation in that each of them is a requirement established by some norms that are applicable to human conduct. To fulfill a legal obligation is *pro tanto* to act in accordance with the terms of any legal mandate by which it has been imposed, and to fulfill a moral obligation is *pro tanto* to act in accordance with the content of any moral principle by which it has been imposed. To contravene a legal obligation is to act at odds with the terms of the legal mandate by which it has been imposed, and to contravene a moral obligation is to act at odds with the content of the moral principle by which it has been imposed. To contravene a legal obligation is to commit a legal wrong, and to contravene a moral obligation is to commit a moral wrong. In these respects as well as in some other respects, the deontic structure of the legal domain is homologous to that of the moral domain. On the other hand, however, those several formal parallels between the two domains are accompanied by a major substantive divergence between them. Whereas the correct principles of morality that impose moral duties are always constitutive of objectively binding reasons for compliance with what they require, the legal directives that impose legal duties in any particular jurisdiction do not necessarily constitute such reasons. Some legal directives in some jurisdictions, indeed, do not generate any punishment-independent reasons for their addressees to comply with what those directives require. Not all legal obligations are moral obligations, and not all legal wrongs are moral wrongs; consequently, the language of "obligations" or "duties" is fully available to systems of governance whose officials do not assert or imply the existence of any punishment-independent reasons for citizens to obey the legal requirements that are incumbent on them. The sharing of that deontic vocabulary between law and morality is consistent with the credible possibility of legal systems in which punishment-centered prudential reasons are the sole reasons for obedience that are implicitly or explicitly invoked by many of the pronouncements issued from officials to citizens.

1.5 Morality contrasted with empirical facts: some debates

Let us finally turn to the distinction between morality and empirical facts. Here one principal source of disagreements between legal positivists and their foes is the issue or set of issues highlighted by many of the philosophers who refer to "the separability thesis." Jules Coleman, for example, has largely echoed Hart as follows: "Interpreted as a claim about the relationship between substantive morality and the content of the criteria of legality, the separability thesis asserts that it is not necessary that the legality of a standard of conduct depend on its moral value or merit."[5] With such an orientation, legal positivists submit that the endeavors of officials in ascertaining the existence and contents of laws are not necessarily guided by any moral assumptions. Those endeavors can instead concentrate strictly on matters of empirical fact. In this or that jurisdiction, it can be the case that moral soundness is neither a necessary condition nor a sufficient condition for the status of any norm as a law. (As will be seen in §3 of this chapter, Exclusive Legal Positivists go further by asserting that moral soundness cannot ever be such a necessary condition or sufficient condition in any jurisdiction.) In reply to Dworkin and other theorists who insist that moral deliberations and judgments are essential in all processes of law-ascertainment, Inclusive Legal Positivists such as Hart have held that the role of moral deliberations and judgments in the processes of law-ascertainment in any particular jurisdiction is a contingent matter that depends on the prevailing Rule of Recognition. The criteria for legal validity in any jurisdiction can include, but need not include, moral standards. Accordingly, the deliberations that occur during the processes of law-ascertainment in some credibly possible jurisdictions do not include moral judgments. In those jurisdictions, the law-ascertaining deliberations are confined to gauging the occurrence or non-occurrence of observable events.

Another area of dispute centered on the moral/empirical dichotomy is a matter of methodology that has surfaced in the opening chapter of this book. Many positivists, including Hart most of the time (though not in the final few pages of the ninth chapter in *The Concept of Law*), have insisted not only on the separability of morality and law but also on the separability of morality and legal philosophy. Notwithstanding that every theory must draw upon evaluative judgments in order to be an intelligible account of its explanandum, the values that inform a philosophical theory of law can be strictly analytical-explanatory rather than moral. In the formation of such a theory, one's evaluations of the relative importance of various phenomena are not perforce moral in their tenor. Instead, a claim about the importance or unimportance of something can derive from one's judgment about the extent to which that thing has to be taken into account by a comprehensive yet parsimonious analysis of the institutions of law and government. Hence, contrary to what Dworkin and many other natural-law philosophers have proclaimed, the inevitably evaluative enterprise of subjecting the nature of law to philosophical investigation is not inevitably oriented toward moral values.

1.6 *A brief peroration*

So ends my laconic survey of the paramount lines of confrontation between legal positivists and their opponents. This survey has not in itself presented any arguments in support of the positivist insistence on the separability of law and morality. Rather, it has simply limned some of the chief points of contention that have led positivists to develop an array of pertinent arguments – arguments such as those which Hart advanced and those which I have advanced elsewhere. Nonetheless, although this compendium has merely described some debates instead of entering into them directly, it should suffice to convey their rich multifariousness. It should therefore suffice to indicate how much is omitted when anyone suggests that the wide-ranging positivist insistence on the separability of law and morality can be encapsulated in one terse thesis. When we keep in view the several aspects or dimensions of morality that have been disentangled here, we can grasp how expansively variegated the tussles between positivists and their opponents have long been.

2 Hart on the minimum content of natural law

Having suggested near the outset of the ninth chapter in *The Concept of Law* that legal positivism is associated above all else with the proposition that the contents of laws do not necessarily reproduce or satisfy any requirements of morality, Hart proceeded to distinguish between two ways in which that proposition can be elaborated. On the one hand, it might be understood as affirming that the inconsistency of various norms with elementary moral obligations does not prevent those norms from being laws in some credibly possible jurisdictions. Insofar as the positivist proposition about the contents of laws is understood in this first way, Hart endorsed it straightforwardly as a rejection of classical natural-law thinking. On the other hand, the positivist proposition might instead be understood as affirming that there can credibly exist a system of governance whose laws do not coincide at all with the correct principles of morality. Insofar as that proposition is understood in this second way, Hart appeared to distance himself from it. We need to examine carefully his reasoning, to judge whether he was retreating at all from his general view that law is not an inherently moral phenomenon.

2.1 *Legal prohibitions and the human condition*

In the second main section of the penultimate chapter in *The Concept of Law* – a portion of the book that has elicited vast amounts of commentary ever since its publication – Hart mulled over the indispensability of some basic legal prohibitions in any viable human society (193–200). Marshaling some ideas propounded by many great political thinkers of the past, such as Thomas Hobbes and John Locke and David Hume, Hart observed that certain elementary facts of the human predicament combine to render the existence of law necessary for the durability of any credibly possible community that is larger than a few families. If a society on even a moderate scale is to stand any chance of lasting, it must be held together in part by a scheme of legal governance that enforces some general restrictions on people's conduct.

The five familiar features of human beings and their environments to which Hart directed the attention of his readers are as follows: (1) the vulnerability of each human being to harms that might be inflicted by other human beings; (2) the approximate equality of most human adults, in that the physical and mental disparities among them are generally not overwhelming; (3) the mixture of selfishness and solicitous benevolence in the make-up of virtually every human being; (4) the moderate scarcity of most resources, and the fact that many resources have to be subjected to considerable labor before they can satisfy human wants directly; and (5) the limitedness of each person's understanding and strength of will, which leads some people to favor their short-term interests at the expense of their long-term interests. Given these characteristics of human beings and of the world in which they live, the sustainability of every credibly possible community beyond a tiny size is dependent on the sway of a system of legal governance. Moreover, among the mandates imposed by any such system, there must be certain fundamental prohibitions. As Hart observed, legal norms forbidding murder, assault, arson, serious fraud, and other grave misdeeds are unforgoable in setting the terms for durable human interaction. If such norms were absent or wholly unenforced, then – given the facts of the human condition which Hart invoked – the security that distinguishes civilization from the frenzy of chaotic anarchy would be gone. The circumstances under which people can live decently and peaceably alongside one another would be missing. Every viable scheme of governance must therefore encompass the basic proscriptions mentioned by Hart, if it is to encompass anything at all. Yet, since the contents of those proscriptions are apparently at one with the substance of key moral precepts, Hart's elementary facts of the human condition appear to make unavoidable a convergence between the demands of law and the demands of morality. The area of that inevitable convergence is what Hart labeled as the "minimum content of natural law."

As Hart's label indicates, his observations about the nature of human beings bear importantly on the debates between legal positivists and natural-law theorists over the separability of law and morality. For one thing, if the system of governance in every viable society must include legal mandates that coincide in content with some key principles of morality, then there is a significant necessary connection between legal requirements and moral requirements. Furthermore, and relatedly, Hart's observations about the human predicament bear far-reachingly on the jurisprudential debates in a way that pertains directly to the matter of political obligation which has preoccupied many political philosophers. That is, in combination with certain other premises that will be specified shortly, Hart's ruminations might appear to imply that everyone in any society is morally obligated to comply with legal mandates simply by dint of their status as legal mandates. A moral obligation of obedience which is borne by everybody in a society, and which is applicable to every one of the society's duty-imposing legal norms, would be another significant necessary connection between morality and law. To probe these issues of legal and political philosophy, this chapter will have to expand upon the implications of Hart's argument. Let us begin by pondering some qualifications that should be attached to the argument straightaway.

2.2 Four qualifications

The first of the qualifications just mentioned was broached by Hart himself. After adumbrating the basic legal prohibitions that are necessary for the durability of any society, and after noting the affinities between those prohibitions and some of the interdictions that are central to morality, he remarked: "The protections and benefits provided by the system of mutual forbearances which underlies both law and morals may, in different societies, be extended to very different ranges of persons" (200). Although the conditions of security that are essential for the sustainment of a society must be extended to quite a few people therein, they might not be extended to everyone. A community can persist as such even if some people residing within it are denied the basic protections that are enjoyed by other people, who belong to relatively privileged groups. "[I]t is plain that neither the law nor the accepted morality of societies need extend their minimal protections and benefits to all within their scope, and often they have not done so. In slave-owning societies the sense that the slaves are human beings, not mere objects to be used, may be lost by the dominant group." As Hart elaborated: "These painful facts of human history are enough to show that, though a society to be viable must offer *some* of its members a system of mutual forbearances, it need not, unfortunately, offer them to all" (200, emphasis in original). People excluded from the protective ambit of the elementary legal prohibitions may very likely be worse off than they would be in a situation of lawlessness. As far as they are concerned, the coercive mechanisms of legal governance are exerted to "subdue and maintain, in a position of permanent inferiority, a subject group whose size, relatively to the master group, may be large or small, depending on the means of coercion, solidarity, and discipline available to the latter, and the helplessness or inability to organize of the former. For those thus oppressed there may be nothing in the system to command their loyalty but only things to fear. They are its victims, not its beneficiaries" (201). In regard to the tribulations of such people, who are less secure within the prevailing system of law than they would be in the absence of any such system, a well-known observation by Locke is pertinent. Replying to the proponents of absolute monarchy such as Robert Filmer, who decried all challenges to the legitimacy of any monarch's brutal oppression, Locke trenchantly declared: "As if when Men quitting the State of Nature entered into Society, they agreed that all of them but one, should be under the restraint of Laws, but that he should still retain all the Liberty of the State of Nature, increased with Power, and made licentious by Impunity. This is to think that Men are so foolish that they take care to avoid what Mischiefs may be done them by *Pole-Cats*, or *Foxes*, but are content, nay think it Safety, to be devoured by *Lions*" (1988, §93, emphases in original).

When thinking about the jurisprudential implications of the ways in which the institutions of legal systems function to provide basic security and to facilitate the coordination of people's activities, one plainly should take account of Hart's point about the credible possibility of societies in which some people are deliberately excluded from the protective reach of prohibitions on very serious misconduct. In such a society, those elementary prohibitions do not coincide in content with any veritable principles of morality. After all, no genuine principle of morality forbids the perpetration of very serious misconduct against white people only (or against non-slaves only); any true principle of morality that forbids the perpetration of such misconduct against white people is also a prohibition on the perpetration of such misconduct against other people. Thus, given that the legal norms which proscribe very serious misconduct in any particular jurisdiction can differ from the correct principles of morality on exactly this point, the "minimum content of natural law" does not constitute any necessary connections between the substance of law and the substance of morality. Hart's meditations on the plight of humanity do not betoken any such connections, despite initial appearances to the contrary.

Three additional qualifications should be attached to those meditations. First, even in societies where the elementary legal prohibitions do coincide in content with genuine principles of morality at an abstract level, they can markedly diverge at more concrete levels. So long as the legal mandates that forbid serious misdeeds in any particular jurisdiction have brought about sufficiently secure conditions to avert a descent into chaos, they can keep a community intact while failing to shield people from numerous harmful modes of conduct that would be legally forbidden in a just society. Merely from the fact that legal norms bestow protection on individuals sufficiently to prevent a community from disintegrating, we cannot infer that those norms provide the degree of protection minimally required by correct principles of morality. Even in a viable society where everyone is protected by the same laws as everyone else, the level of security can fall far short of what it morally ought to be.

Second, the provision of security through well-enforced legal mandates that proscribe serious misconduct is consistent with heavy-handed oppression. Indeed, the engendering of the security can itself be a source of such oppression, when people are protected from one another through the imposition of extremely harsh penalties for minor breaches (as well as major breaches) of laws against theft, vandalism, assault, and the like. Or the security enjoyed by each person against mistreatment at the hands of others in some jurisdiction might be accompanied by stiflingly severe restrictions on the permissibility of any actions that could threaten the dominance of the prevailing regime. In such circumstances, each citizen can live in safety vis-à-vis other citizens and vis-à-vis the regnant government – so long as he or she never utters any open criticisms of the government, never signs any petitions or engages in any protests, never uses a photocopier, and so forth. In short, even in a society where each inhabitant is protected by fundamental legal safeguards to the same extent as every other inhabitant, those safeguards can be situated in an overall matrix of laws that is suffocatingly harsh and restrictive.

Third, the fundamental legal prohibitions themselves can be introduced and maintained by officials for purely prudential reasons. So long as citizens are submissive and productive, they will usually be far more serviceable for the exploitative purposes of evil officials when alive than when dead. Hence, officials who are devoted solely to their own power-hungry ends will have ample reasons for establishing legal prohibitions that protect ordinary citizens from one another. Similarly, in order to foster incentives for compliance with their wicked behests, the officials will have strong reasons for extending to each compliant person a much greater measure of security against the officials' own violence than is extended to any recalcitrant person. In sum, the inclusion of elementary protections (for all or most citizens) among a society's legal mandates does not perforce bespeak any nonprudential concern on the part of the society's legal-governmental officials. The officials might be motivated purely by prudential considerations akin to those which impel a heartless owner of livestock to look after the security of the animals in his herd.

2.3 Hart and the problem of political obligation

Of great importance for political philosophy as well as for legal philosophy is Hart's contemplation of the role of law in furnishing the security and coordination that are essential for the durability of a society. One of the most salient concerns of political philosophers is to pin down the conditions under which people are morally obligated to comply with the legal requirements that are applicable to them.[6] Particularly prominent is the question whether the inhabitants of any society are *always* morally obligated to comply with the prevailing legal requirements. Hart's reasoning about the fundamental circumstances of humankind lends itself to being developed into a line of argument that has been advanced by some philosophers who seek to establish that – at least in liberal-democratic societies – there is always a moral obligation to obey the law. Although a full investigation of this matter is far beyond the scope of the present chapter, a brief account here of the premises and conclusion in the aforementioned line of argument will help to underscore the importance of *The Concept of Law* for political philosophers as well as for legal philosophers.

The first premise in the argument comes directly from Hart's discussion of the minimum content of natural law:

(1) Without a system of law to give effect to certain legal prohibitions on serious misconduct, no community of any substantial size can endure for more than the briefest period.

A second premise articulates a proposition that is accepted by most non-anarchists, though specific understandings of the proposition will naturally vary:

(2) When substantial numbers of people live in proximity to one another over extended periods of time, an organized community with a system of legal governance to give effect to prohibitions on serious misconduct is necessary for the securing of individual freedom and public order and social coordination.

Of course, the necessity invoked in premise 2 is not logical necessity. The existence of an organized community with a system of legal governance is not *logically* necessary for the occurrence of the effects specified in that premise. However, bare logical possibilities are of little or no importance in political and legal philosophy. What matter instead are credible possibilities. The presence of an organized community with a system of legal governance is necessary for the occurrence of the effects specified by premise 2, in that there is no credible possibility of the occurrence of those effects – when large numbers of people are living in proximity over extended periods of time – without the existence of such a community and its system of law.

A third premise is also grounded in Hart's work, though less in *The Concept of Law* than in a famous passage of an article which Hart had published several years earlier. In the relevant portion of the article (1955, 185–6), he maintained that each person who enjoys the benefits of some practice or institution is morally obligated to bear a commensurate share of the burdens of sustaining that practice or institution. More specifically, each person who benefits substantially from the adherence of others to an array of mutual restrictions is in turn morally obligated to abide by those restrictions insofar as they call for him or her to exercise self-restraint. As Hart wrote (1955, 185, emphasis in original):

[W]hen a number of persons conduct any joint enterprise according to rules and thus restrict their liberty, those who have submitted to these restrictions when required have a right to a similar submission from those who have benefited by their submission. ... [T]he moral obligation to obey the rules in such circumstances is *due to* the cooperating members of the society, and they have the correlative moral right to obedience.

Accordingly, a third premise in the argument about each person's obligation to obey the law can be formulated as follows:

(3) If someone benefits substantially from the fact that others in his or her community abide by the mandates of the prevailing system of law with its protections against the perpetration of serious misdeeds, then he or she in turn is morally obligated to abide by those mandates insofar as they apply to his or her conduct.

A fourth premise is closely related to the second and third:

(4) Everyone stands to benefit substantially when others in his or her community help to sustain the prevailing system of legal governance by complying with its mandates, since such compliance upholds a necessary condition for the securing of individual freedom and public order and social coordination.

From these premises, a proponent of this line of argument will then draw the following conclusion:

(5) Everyone in a community is morally obligated to comply with the legal mandates imposed by the prevailing system of governance, provided that all or most other people in the community likewise comply.

Now, as delineated here, the argument is enthymematic. It relies on the premise that, in any jurisdiction, there is no alternative to the regnant system of governance that is both superior and reasonably attainable. Even with reference to any societies about which that suppressed premise is true, however, the soundness of the argument depends on how some of the formulations in its premises and conclusion are to be construed. Although an assessment of the argument's soundness is far beyond the scope of the present chapter,[7] a couple of brief remarks here will help to underscore the fact that Hart's reflections on the rudiments of human nature are of major importance both for philosophers of law and for political philosophers.

First, much will depend on whether the moral obligation to comply with legal mandates – affirmed in the argument's conclusion – is to be understood as universally borne and comprehensively applicable within each jurisdiction. In other words, to gauge the soundness of the argument just outlined, we would need to know whether the specified obligation is supposed to be incumbent on every sane adult and whether it is supposed to comprehend every legal mandate on every occasion to which any such mandate applies. On the one hand, both in the eyes of political philosophers and in the eyes of legal philosophers, the obligation would of course be especially noteworthy if it were indeed universally borne and comprehensively applicable. (Its special significance for legal philosophy would derive from its amounting to a major necessary connection between law and morality – which is why Hart and most other legal positivists have staunchly denied that there is any comprehensively applicable and universally borne moral obligation to obey the law.[8]) On the other hand, however, any noteworthiness is rendered chimerical by the inexistence of such an obligation; at least on this point, the exciting ambitiousness of the argument would entail its unsoundness.

Second, the plausibility of the argument will also hinge on whether its reach is meant to be confined or unconfined (Rawls 1999, 119, 122–3). That is, we have to know whether the argument's conclusion is propounded as a claim about every system of legal governance or instead solely about liberal-democratic systems. Unless the conclusion along with the premises is construed in the latter fashion – as pertaining solely to liberal-democratic systems of governance – it will lack any plausibility. In that respect, the argument built on Hart's discussion of the human condition is markedly different from the general theorizing in *The Concept of Law* (including his discussion of the human condition). Throughout his book, Hart prescinded from the numerous variations among jurisdictions as he expounded the nature and workings of legal institutions. As has been emphasized in my opening chapter, he was aiming to distill the features that are common to all central instances of systems of law; he was therefore not concentrating only on the features of liberal-democratic systems. Hence, when his discussion of the human predicament is seized upon by theorists in their endeavors to underwrite an obligation to obey the law within liberal democracies, their efforts are at variance with the tenor of his jurisprudential project.

3 Inclusive versus Exclusive Positivism

Contemporary legal positivism in the English-speaking world, and in many areas beyond, has largely developed in response to *The Concept of Law* and the criticisms that have been directed against it. During the several decades since the publication of Hart's classic text, positivists have divided into two main camps with numerous variations in each camp: Inclusive Legal Positivism versus Exclusive Legal Positivism. As will be explained shortly, these two camps have emerged chiefly in reaction to some of Dworkin's animadversions on Hart's model of law and adjudication.

3.1 Inclusivism, Incorporationism, and Exclusivism

I will henceforth use the phrase "Inclusive Legal Positivism" for only one of the two principal theses that are embraced by most of the philosophers who classify themselves as Inclusivists. That thesis runs as follows:

> It can be the case, though it need not be the case, that the consistency of any norm N with some or all of the requirements of morality is a precondition for the status of N as a law in this or that jurisdiction.

Though an Inclusivist precondition for legal validity is not inherent in the nature of law, it can be imposed as a threshold test under the Rule of Recognition that prevails in any particular jurisdiction. Such a test, which can be applied by the officials in an Inclusivist system of governance to all of the legal norms therein or to only some subset of those norms, is one of the criteria which the officials use for ascertaining the law. Insofar as a threshold criterion of that kind is operative within some system of law, the moral legitimacy of N is a necessary condition for the validation of N as a law which belongs to the system. Inclusive Legal Positivism, which leaves room for the existence of just such a state of affairs in any given jurisdiction, is inclusive because it affirms that moral precepts can figure among the criteria that guide the ascertainment of legal norms by officials. Inclusivists reject the notion that all the criteria for law-ascertainment in every credibly possible system of governance are focused on empirical matters concerning the procedures or practices – such as voting by legislators or decision-making by adjudicators or the promulgation of regulations by administrators – that are provenances of legal norms. At the same time, the Inclusivists are positivists because they also reject the notion that every credibly possible legal system employs some tests of moral legitimacy among its law-ascertaining criteria. Inclusive Legal Positivists insist that such tests are contingent features, rather than conceptually essential features, of the systems of law in which they are applied. A system of law can credibly exist as such without any tests of moral legitimacy as some of its conditions for legal validity.

Among the philosophers who endorse Inclusive Legal Positivism as it has just been expounded, most additionally endorse a further thesis that is itself also often labeled as "Inclusive Legal Positivism." In line with my previous work on this topic (Kramer 2004, 1–140), however, I will instead adopt the designation of "Incorporationism" for that further thesis:

> It can be the case, though it need not be the case, that the correctness of a norm N as a moral principle is a sufficient condition for the status of N as a law in this or that jurisdiction.

Although the role of moral correctness as a sufficient condition for legal validity is not inherent in the concept of law, it can obtain under the Rule of Recognition that prevails in any particular system of governance. A proponent of Incorporationism maintains that an official practice of treating the moral correctness of principles as sufficient for their legal validity will have incorporated those principles into the law of the jurisdiction where the practice is observed – whether or not any of the principles have ever been set forth in explicit sources such as statutes or administrative regulations or adjudicative justifications. By regularly adhering to that practice of treating the moral soundness of norms as determinative of the norms' legal authoritativeness, the officials of the jurisdiction have brought moral principles into the law of their system of governance even if the applicable principles have not yet been enshrined in any of the aforementioned explicit sources. Advocates of Incorporationism, who unhesitatingly accept the possibility of such a state of affairs, are nonetheless legal positivists because they insist that the incorporation of moral principles into the law of any system of governance is contingent and that it is not a necessary feature of every such system.

Whereas Inclusive Legal Positivism and Incorporationism are smoothly compatible and are typically conjoined, Exclusive Legal

Positivism is opposed to each of them. Exclusive Legal Positivists contend that the very nature of law is inconsistent both with the role of moral principles as laws and with the role of such principles as criteria for the validation of laws. While gladly acknowledging that moral principles do often get invoked and should often get invoked in the adjudicative and administrative activities of legal officials, the Exclusivists declare that those principles are extra-legal standards. Such standards affect the decisions reached by the officials, but only because those decisions are not based solely on legal requirements – or so the Exclusivists affirm.

3.2 The aetiology of the positions

Now, the three positions just adumbrated have scarcely emerged from nowhere. Rather, each of them as a distinctive version of legal positivism has developed chiefly in response to Dworkin's early critiques of Hart. Thus, before we survey the passages in which Hart espoused the theses of Inclusive Legal Positivism and Incorporationism, we should briefly ponder the context in which those theses have developed. Although the details of Dworkin's strictures and of the subsequent rejoinders by positivists to those strictures cannot be recounted here, a few remarks will help to explain why various philosophers of law have adopted the positions which they respectively champion.

Among the many accusations leveled by Dworkin against Hart in the 1960s and 1970s was the claim that legal positivism cannot adequately take account of the role of moral principles as binding bases for decisions by adjudicators and administrators in hard cases (Dworkin 1978, chs. 2–4). Dworkin subsequently extended his anti-positivist account of adjudication beyond hard cases to all cases. Even then, however, he provided the motivation for his discussion by adverting to the operativeness of moral principles in hard cases (1986, 15–30). Retorting to Dworkin's broadsides, some legal positivists have sought to explain how moral principles can enter into the law of a jurisdiction, while other legal positivists have denied that such principles do ever enter into the law of any jurisdiction. In issuing such retorts, the positivists have pursued the routes of Inclusivism and Incorporationism or the route of Exclusivism. The first two of those routes are combinable, of course, whereas the third of them is at odds with the other two.

Inclusive Legal Positivism is the doctrine with the firmest grounding in Hart's writings. Well before Dworkin's onslaughts, Hart had repeatedly accepted that the criteria for law-ascertainment in any particular jurisdiction can include moral principles. He had especially in mind the criteria that lay down restrictions on law-making power. That is, he had especially in mind the role of moral principles as thresholds below which no norm can possess the status of a legal norm; consistency with those principles can be a necessary condition for the validity of any norm as a law within a particular jurisdiction. Having embraced Inclusive Legal Positivism *avant la lettre*, Hart blazed a trail that has been followed by many of his positivist successors.[9] In my next subsection, we shall mull over some of the passages in which he addressed this matter.

However, Dworkin's attacks against legal positivism did not focus primarily on the role of moral principles as law-validating criteria that require consistency with some or all of the demands of morality as a necessary condition for the status of any norm as a law. Instead of concentrating on such Inclusivist matters, Dworkin laid stress on the role of moral principles as laws that are the grounds for judgments by legal-governmental officials in particular cases. According to him, positivists are unable to acknowledge that moral principles do play such a role in certain systems of law. Incorporationism has emerged as a jurisprudential doctrine in response to this throwing down of the gauntlet by Dworkin. Accepting that a Rule of Recognition can direct judges and other officials to draw upon moral principles as binding legal touchstones for assessing the conduct of people, the proponents of Incorporationism have essayed to accommodate Dworkin's queries without implying that *every* credibly possible Rule of Recognition provides that officials are to draw upon moral principles in that fashion. While allowing that such principles can be incorporated into the law of a jurisdiction as determinative bases for decisions by adjudicators and administrators, Incorporationists remain legal positivists by insisting that the presence of those principles in the law of any particular country is a contingency rather than something that follows from the essence of law. As we shall behold in my next subsection, Hart quite straightforwardly subscribed to the Incorporationist position.[10]

Exclusive Legal Positivism has likewise evolved in the context of Dworkin's challenges to positivist theorizing. However, instead of trying to accommodate and defuse those challenges by showing that the positivist model of law is consistent with the role of moral precepts as law-validating criteria or as substantive legal norms, the Exclusivists have denied that moral precepts can play any such role. In other words, they have sought to rebut the Dworkinian onslaughts by arguing that moral principles cannot enter into the law of any jurisdiction; the operativeness of such principles in adjudication is not to be mistaken for their having become laws. Though Raz is the most prominent advocate of this Exclusivist position – which he has adopted in support of his general thesis that systems of law by their nature are capable of being morally authoritative – the position has also been championed by some other notable legal philosophers.[11]

Exclusive Legal Positivism was originally in large part a rejoinder to Dworkin, but more recently it has become at least as much a rejoinder to Inclusive Legal Positivism and Incorporationism. Indeed, the debates over the philosophical merits of Exclusivism have been conducted during the past few decades almost entirely among legal positivists of differing stripes. Although Dworkin occasionally hurled thunderbolts at those debates during the later stages of his career – most vituperatively in Dworkin 2006, ch. 7 – the battles among positivists have been more numerous and persistent than the battles between them and their Dworkinian foes.

3.3 Hart as an Inclusivist and an Incorporationist

In *The Concept of Law* itself and especially in some of his later writings – not least the Postscript to the second edition of *The Concept of Law* – Hart expressed views that are rightly classifiable as Inclusivist or Incorporationist. To be sure, he did not always distinguish clearly between those two doctrines, and he did not use the "Inclusivist" or "Incorporationist" label. When he labeled his relevant views at all, he regrettably opted to designate them as "soft positivism." Even more damaging, as we have seen in my fourth chapter and as we shall observe again here, is that Hart in his Postscript allowed himself to be bullied by Dworkin into suspending his allegiance to Inclusivism and Incorporationism. Still, if the isolated passage containing that capitulation to Dworkin is left aside (as Hart may indeed have left it aside if he had lived long enough to refine his Postscript for publication), Hart made abundantly apparent his alignment with Inclusive Legal Positivism and Incorporationism.

Let us start with the passage from the Postscript in which he explicitly subscribed to Incorporationism. Coming to grips with

Dworkin's complicated interpretive approach to adjudication, Hart declared that "this interpretivist test seems not to be an alternative to a criterion provided by a rule of recognition, but, as some critics have urged, only a complex 'soft-positivist' form of such a criterion identifying principles by their content not by their pedigree" (265, footnote omitted). He added that "to show that the interpretive test criterion was part of a conventional pattern of law-recognition would … be a good theoretical explanation of its legal status. So there is certainly no incompatibility such as Dworkin claims between the admission of principles as part of the law and the doctrine of a rule of recognition" (265–6).

More numerous are the passages in which Hart associated himself with the thesis of Inclusive Legal Positivism. Even in the main text of *The Concept of Law*, written well before the emergence of the Inclusive/Exclusive controversies, he proclaimed that the consistency of any norm N with some or all of the requirements of morality could be prerequisite to the status of N as a law within this or that particular jurisdiction: "In some systems [of law], as in the United States, the ultimate criteria of legal validity explicitly incorporate principles of justice or substantive moral values." Although the tenor of this quoted sentence could be construed either as Inclusivist or as Incorporationist, Hart made clear that the former construal is correct as he indicated that the envisaged criteria of legal validity would impose "restrictions on the competence of the supreme legislature" (204).

In the Postscript to the second edition of *The Concept of Law*, Hart pointed out that he had always accepted that "in some systems of law, as in the United States, the ultimate criteria of legal validity might explicitly incorporate besides pedigree, principles of justice or substantive moral values, and these may form the content of legal constitutional restraints" (247). He was thus retorting to Dworkin, who had baselessly denied that the positivist model of law-ascertainment can allow for standards of legal validity that are not focused on empirical matters of fact. Delivering a riposte to Dworkin's canard, Hart reaffirmed that "the rule of recognition may incorporate as criteria of legal validity conformity with moral principles or substantive values; so my doctrine is what has been called 'soft positivism' and not as in Dworkin's version of it 'plain-fact' positivism" (250).

As I have recounted in §1.1 of my fourth chapter, Dworkin raised two queries about Hart's espousal of Inclusivism and Incorporationism: namely, the Moral Principles Objection and the Aloofness

Objection. Hart did not deal with either of those queries adequately, but he particularly mishandled the Aloofness Objection by succumbing to Dworkin's badgering about the putative aspiration of legal positivists to remain noncommittal on the question whether morality is radically indeterminate or not. As I have remarked in my fourth chapter, legal positivists and other philosophers of law should reject any such preposterous aspiration – whatever Hart may have thought in his brief posthumously published musing on the matter. When legal positivists declare or assume that morality is not radically indeterminate, they have not thereby committed themselves to specific stances on any of the multitude of more concrete moral questions with which philosophers and ordinary citizens must grapple in a variety of settings. In the course of elaborating a positivist account of law that endorses Inclusivism and Incorporationism, they can remain noncommittal on those more concrete matters. That is, they can remain noncommittal on the questions which Dworkin and his followers have regarded as central to any satisfactory theorizing about law. Accordingly, Hart should not have allowed himself to be manipulated by Dworkin into thinking that the methodological austerity which separates positivism from Dworkinianism would require him to suspend his attachment to Inclusive Legal Positivism and Incorporationism.

That attachment antedated Hart's writing of *The Concept of Law*, and it continued thereafter. In a famous essay originally published in 1958, Hart commended Austin and especially Bentham for the insightfulness of their positions on these matters (1983, 54–5, footnote omitted):

> [N]either Bentham nor his followers denied that by explicit legal provisions moral principles might at different points be brought into a legal system and form part of its rules, or that courts might be legally bound to decide in accordance with what they thought just or best. Bentham indeed recognized, as Austin did not, that even the supreme legislative power might be subjected to legal restraints by a constitution and would not have denied that moral principles, like those of the Fifth Amendment [to the American Constitution], might form the content of such legal constitutional restraints.

In a review of Fuller's *The Morality of Law* written several years after the publication of *The Concept of Law*, Hart declared (1983, 361):

> There is, for me, no logical restriction on the content of the rule of recognition: so far as "logic" goes [a Rule of Recognition] could provide

explicitly or implicitly that the criteria determining validity of subordinate laws should cease to be regarded as such if the laws identified in accordance with them proved to be morally objectionable. So a constitution could include in its restrictions on the legislative power even of its supreme legislature not only conformity with due process but a completely general provision that its legal power should lapse if its enactments ever conflicted with principles of morality and justice.

Admittedly, both in the 1958 essay and in the review of Fuller's book, Hart was somewhat imprecise and guarded in his formulations of Inclusivist and Incorporationist ideas. After all, as Leslie Green has observed, "the distinction between Inclusive and Exclusive versions of the positivist thesis was unknown when [Hart wrote *The Concept of Law*] and was therefore not part of the polemical context of the time" (1996, 1706–7). Nonetheless, the roughhewn and excessively cautious statements in those essays, along with the pronouncements in the main text and Postscript of *The Concept of Law*, reveal that Hart throughout his career was a proponent both of Inclusive Legal Positivism and of Incorporationism.

4 Hart as an expressivist?

This final main section of the present chapter could have been located in my third or fourth chapter, since it addresses some issues that relate to the contents of those earlier parts of this book. However, because I will here be impugning an approach to those issues that has been heavily influenced by some of the philosophical literature on the nature of ethical discourse, my reflections are best undertaken in a chapter that has covered Hart's thinking about morality. Specifically, the matter to be addressed in this section is Hart's understanding of the semantics of any legal statements that are uttered from the internal viewpoint of the people who run the institutions of legal governance in this or that jurisdiction.

A number of philosophers in recent years have maintained that Hart in *The Concept of Law* propounded an expressivist account of the semantics of such statements. My discussion of this matter will begin by rehearsing the distinction between the semantics and the pragmatics of utterances – a distinction drawn tersely in §1.4 of my fourth chapter – and will then delineate the doctrine of expressivism which the aforementioned philosophers have in mind when they ascribe that doctrine to Hart. Although I will make reference to a few such philosophers, I will focus chiefly on an article by Kevin Toh that has been the fountainhead of all the subsequent attributions of expressivism to Hart. As will be argued herein, Toh and like-minded philosophers have gone astray in imputing to Hart a semantic version of expressivism. Notwithstanding that Hart's theory of law can aptly be characterized as expressivist, that characterization is appropriate only when expressivism is understood as an account of the pragmatics of legal statements rather than as an account of their semantics.

4.1   The semantics/pragmatics distinction recapitulated

As has been recounted in §1.4 of my fourth chapter, the distinction between semantics and pragmatics can roughly be encapsulated as a contrast between what statements mean and why statements are uttered – a contrast between what a statement is about and what purpose or function is served by the articulation of it. Both the meanings of statements and the purposes served by the utterance of statements are multifarious, of course. Some purposes are operative in nearly all contexts in which statements of certain types are articulated, whereas others are highly context-specific. Some purposes are sweepingly general or abstract, whereas others are more fine-grained and nuanced. Some are consciously and carefully pursued, whereas others are largely taken for granted. Some are quite evident to virtually every competent participant in the modes of communication through which they are fulfilled, whereas others are more subtle. Similarly diverse are the meanings conveyed by statements, of course. Those meanings differ in their degrees of generality and, *mutatis mutandis*, in the sundry other ways in which the purposes or functions of utterances can differ. Partly because the purposes or functions of communicative activity are so heterogeneous, and because the meanings of the statements made in such activity are likewise so heterogeneous, the distinction between semantics and pragmatics is often complicated and elusive. Still, the distinction is quite straightforward in numerous contexts, and it is crucial for any adequate understanding of Hart's philosophy of law.

When I briefly expounded the semantics/pragmatics dichotomy in §1.4 of Chapter 4, I did so to find fault with Hart for his overemphasis on semantic matters in his account of legal interpretation and for his relative inattentiveness there to matters of pragmatics. Here my reason for broaching that distinction afresh is quite different. As I have very readily granted in my earlier exposition, Hart in his overall theorizing about law – rather than in his specific account of legal reasoning and interpretation – was perspicaciously attuned to the intricacies and import of the pragmatics of legal discourse. Indeed, his explorations of the pragmatics of such discourse have profoundly influenced nearly every subsequent theory in the philosophy of law. As will be contended here, those explorations encompass all the aspects of Hart's theorizing which Toh and like-minded exegetes have passed off as an analysis of the semantics of internal legal statements. Hence, far from continuing to reproach Hart for his neglect of pragmatic factors in his ruminations on the interpretation of legal norms, my discussion here will be highlighting the insights into those factors which he advanced throughout his broader model of the workings of legal systems. By reaffirming that the expressivism in Hart's theory of law is focused on the pragmatics of legal discourse rather than on the semantics, I will be commending that very dimension of his theory – since expressivism as an account of the pragmatics of legal or moral discourse is powerfully astute, whereas expressivism as an account of the semantics of such discourse would be badly misguided.

4.2   *Expressivism as non-cognitivism*

What, then, is expressivism? Like many other bits of philosophical parlance, the term "expressivism" is used in more than one way by philosophers. In its most expansive sense, the term denotes any theory that contemplates the ways in which various acts of communication express the aims and attitudes of the people who perform those acts. When expressivism is so expansively understood, it quite plainly cuts across the divide between pragmatics and semantics. So construed, expressivism as an approach to legal or moral discourse can be focused on matters of pragmatics or on matters of semantics or on both. When understood in this capacious fashion, expressivism is furthermore entirely consistent with the notion that beliefs and other cognitive attitudes are given voice through the statements that are characteristically made by the participants in the type of discourse or practice that is under consideration. The contents of beliefs and other cognitive attitudes are propositions, which are evaluable as true or false. Hence, expressivism as an approach to legal or moral discourse can fully uphold the cognitive respectability of such discourse.

However, as Toh rightly observes, the term "expressivism" is usually employed more narrowly. Although expressivism has sometimes been elaborated as a theory of the pragmatics of moral or legal discourse,[12] it has more frequently been elaborated as a theory of the semantics of such discourse. Moreover, it has usually been developed as a theory which holds that only conative or non-cognitive attitudes – such as desires and emotions – are given voice through the statements that are characteristically made by the participants in the discourse or practice that is under consideration. Toh and his fellow philosophers of law have understood expressivism in exactly this fashion. That is, they submit that an expressivist account of internal legal statements will take such statements to be expressive of non-cognitive attitudes such as desires or emotions but not of cognitive attitudes such as beliefs. According to these philosophers, Hart as an expressivist would deny that any internal legal statement is endowed with a semantic content that goes beyond the function of the statement in giving voice to some non-cognitive attitude(s). He would in effect maintain that every such statement is relevantly similar to other utterances whose semantic contents are filled entirely by their non-cognitive pragmatics. In other words, every internal legal statement is relevantly similar to utterances such as "Hurray for the Boston Celtics" or "Boo to the New York Yankees" or "Wow" or "Oh boy" or "Hello" or "Shut the door." No such utterance is appropriately evaluable as true or false, and the meaning of each such utterance is given entirely by its expression of an emotion or a desire or some other non-cognitive attitude. Such is the view of legal semantics which Hart propounded, according to Toh and like-minded exegetes.

Though Toh assures his readers that "expressivists begin with the assumption that [moral and legal] discourses are in good standing, that they are not fundamentally flawed" (2005, 80), his assurances are highly misleading at best. Toh is here submitting that expressivists as non-cognitivists do not contend that the affirmative statements advanced in moral discourse or legal discourse are systematically false. He is contrasting the expressivists with the so-called error theorists in moral philosophy, who do contend that all ascriptions of moral obligations or of other moral properties such as goodness are false.[13] However, the expressivists as non-cognitivists deviate from the error theorists on this matter simply because the expressivists hold that internal legal statements or moral statements are not truth-apt – in other words, not evaluable as true or false – at all. Perhaps such an approach to moral or legal statements is slightly less condescending and dismissive than the error theorists' approach, but it is hardly a very flattering account. As Toh himself observes (2005, 95), early expressivists such as A.J. Ayer were intent on establishing that "ethical statements belong to the category of meaningless 'pseudo-statements.'" Admittedly, expressivists during more recent decades have moved on from the crude heavy-handedness of Ayer's derision. Still, anyone not already enamored of expressivism is unlikely to credit Toh's assertion that expressivism "offers a nondebunking characterization of discursive normative practices" (2005, 81). After all, expressivism as a non-cognitivist analysis of moral or legal discourse holds that no moral judgment or internal legal statement is ever true. It holds that every moral judgment or internal legal statement is relevantly similar to interjections such as "Good-bye" and "Whew" or to imperatives such as "Sit down." Whether or not such a position is properly deemed to be an exercise in debunking, it presents moral or legal discourse as lacking in full solidity.

In short, the version of expressivism imputed to Hart by Toh and others – expressivism as a non-cognitivist semantic doctrine – presents legal discourse in quite a disparaging light. Consequently, we are well advised to examine carefully the considerations adduced by Toh in favor of his classification of Hart as an expressivist. Given how firmly Hart set himself against genuine non-cognitivists like the Scandinavian Legal Realists, we should not readily accept that he in fact shared their general non-cognitivist orientation (while differing with them over the details of that orientation). We should not readily accept that he too assigned a second-class status to legal discourse.

To be sure, Toh himself is more circumspect than some of the other legal philosophers who have classified Hart as an expressivist, and he possesses a wide-ranging knowledge of Hart's writings. Nonetheless, the factors marshaled by him in favor of his reading of Hart as an expressivist are remarkably weak. Let us mull over those factors with wary eyes.

4.3 *Expressivism but neither non-cognitivism nor semantics*

As has been remarked above, expressivism of the kind on which Toh concentrates – namely, expressivism as a non-cognitivist semantic theory – is a variety within a broader class of theories. On the one hand, there is no doubt that Hart was an expressivist of some kind.

As I have already emphasized, and as I will be emphasizing further, Hart incisively charted the attitudes or perspectives that are characteristically associated with the utterance of legal pronouncements. On the other hand, we should be chary of assuming that his expressivism was focused on the semantics of legal pronouncements rather than solely on their pragmatics. *A fortiori*, we should be chary of assuming that his expressivism unfolded as a non-cognitivist account of the semantics of those pronouncements.

Toh therefore moves too quickly near the outset of his article when he writes that "what could be called Hart's 'oblique' analysis of internal legal statements can be characterized as follows: in uttering an internal legal statement, a speaker expresses his acceptance of norms that make up the legal system. What Hart offers then is an expressivist or noncognitivist analysis of internal legal statements" (2005, 76–7, footnote omitted). Toh is here using the phrase "expressivist or noncognitivist" appositionally rather than as a genuine disjunction. That is, he here takes "expressivist" and "noncognitivist" to be interchangeable terms. However, although the first sentence in this quotation is undoubtedly correct, it does not provide any warrant for the conclusion that is inferred by Toh in the second sentence. Hart surely did maintain that internal legal statements are expressive of attitudes of commitment, but the fact that he was an expressivist in that broad sense is per se no basis for concluding that he regarded the aforementioned statements as unexpressive of any cognitive contents.

4.4 *The disavowed early work: a first example*

As has been noted at the end of §1.4 in my fourth chapter, Hart in a few of his very early writings did propound some non-cognitivist analyses of the contents of certain internal legal statements (1949; 1983, ch. 1). Hence, if Toh and his fellow exegetes were training their attention solely on those very early writings, their characterization of Hart as a proponent of non-cognitivism would be largely accurate. However, such a characterization would be peculiarly uninteresting – because Hart explicitly repudiated those writings in his later work. In any event, Toh has decidedly not trained his attention solely on those very early articles. Rather, he knows that Hart disavowed them, and he is concerned mainly with Hart as the author of *The Concept of Law* and subsequent publications. Still, while acknowledging that Hart dissociated himself squarely from his brief non-cognitivist phase, Toh proceeds oddly and unsatisfactorily when coming to grips with Hart's renunciation of that phase.

Particularly strange is the way in which Toh deals with Hart's firm recantation of the non-cognitivist strand of his 1953 article "Definition and Theory in Jurisprudence." When Hart included that article three decades later in his collection *Essays in Jurisprudence and Philosophy*, he used his introductory overview to state unequivocally that he had erred in 1953 by suggesting that ascriptions of legal rights and duties are devoid of any cognitive contents (1983, 2, 4–5). As he aptly indicated, his mistake had lain in his failure to differentiate between the pragmatic aspects and the semantic aspects of utterances – and in his consequent neglect of the semantic aspects. He self-chidingly avowed that "had I commanded at the time of writing ['Definition and Theory in Jurisprudence'] in 1953 the seminal distinction between the 'meaning' and the 'force' of utterances, … I should not have claimed that statements of legal rights and duties were not 'descriptive'" (1983, 2).

While granting that Hart abandoned the specifics of the analysis of internal legal statements which he had furnished in his 1953 essay, Toh quite startlingly asserts that Hart nevertheless continued to adhere to the very element of that essay which Hart in fact resolutely abjured: "But Hart does remain committed to a more general conclusion that he draws in ['Definition and Theory in Jurisprudence']: that the statements that enunciate and apply rules, including legal statements, constitute a special form of nondescriptive speech-acts" (Toh 2005, 99). In a footnote, Toh accepts that his claim about Hart's continued embrace of the non-cognitivist tenor of "Definition and Theory in Jurisprudence" is glaringly inconsistent with Hart's own forthright rejection of that very feature of the 1953 essay. Still, while acknowledging the manifest inconsistency, Toh does nothing to mitigate it (2005, 99 n40, parenthetical citations omitted):

> I must concede that what I say here seems inconsistent with Hart's remarks in the introduction to *Essays in Jurisprudence and Philosophy* disowning his claim in ["Definition and Theory in Jurisprudence"] that conclusions of legal reasoning are nondescriptive. I find Hart's general discussion surrounding these remarks very confusing and the remarks themselves particularly baffling – especially given that Hart says elsewhere in the same introduction that he considers Austin's work on performatives to be of permanent value for analytical jurisprudence.

Toh's bafflement is itself baffling. Hart esteemed the twentieth-century philosopher J.L. Austin not only because of Austin's meticulous charting of the pragmatics of speech-acts but also because of his alertness to the distinction between the pragmatics and the semantics of utterances. That distinction is precisely what Hart in 1983 reproached himself for having neglected three decades earlier; as he said in 1983, he would never have embraced non-cognitivism if he had properly apprehended the contrast between pragmatics and semantics. Had he possessed a command of that contrast in his early years, he would have grasped that the conative pragmatic aspects of attributions of rights and duties – crucial and salient though those aspects are, of course – are perfectly consistent with the fact that the contents of the attributions are propositional. Toh, through his puzzlement over this straightforward insight articulated by the later Hart, is in effect repeating the error of the early Hart. Toh is presuming that someone who perceptively highlights the conative pragmatics of certain types of utterances is committed to the view that utterances of those types are devoid of any cognitive semantic contents.

4.5 The disavowed early work: a second example

Another instance of Hart's disavowal of his very early non-cognitivist phase occurred in his preface to the 1968 collection of his essays on the philosophy of criminal law, *Punishment and Responsibility*. He there explained why he was omitting from the collection his essay "The Ascription of Responsibility and Rights" – an essay published in 1949, near the inception of his non-cognitivist phase. Hart declared: "My reason for excluding it is simply that its main contentions no longer seem to me defensible, and that the main criticisms of it made in recent years are justified" (1968, v). In a footnote, Hart signaled his agreement with the criticisms made by Peter Geach (1960) in a classic article that was directed not only against Hart but also more broadly against the whole non-cognitivist enterprise.

Toh candidly avouches that "I do not believe that the apparent inconsistency between Hart's disowning of his [non-cognitivism] and what I consider his adherence to expressivism can be eliminated" (2005, 102). He somewhat patronizingly adds: "It may be that Hart never realized the full implications of Geach's criticisms" (2005, 102–3). At any rate, after some brief reflections that include a passage by Hart to which I shall turn shortly, Toh again frankly concedes that "I have not explained away the apparent inconsistency between Hart's disowning of [non-cognitivism] and what I consider his continued espousal of an expressivist analysis of internal legal statements" (2005, 105).

Of course, the obvious way of eliminating any inconsistency between Hart's positions is to conclude that Toh has fallen into error by supposing that Hart continued to espouse a non-cognitivist understanding of internal legal statements beyond the early stage of his career. At the very least, the passages in which Hart disowningly looked askance at any such understanding are such as to militate strongly against Toh's reading of *The Concept of Law* (and of Hart's other late-period writings). Given that Hart emphatically rejected the position imputed to him by Toh, we should not accept Toh's reading unless there are cogent considerations in favor of it. So far, the considerations which we have probed are exceedingly feeble. As will become apparent, the remaining factors adduced by Toh or by like-minded exegetes are similarly unavailing.

4.6 Different senses of "non-cognitive"

Toh himself is sufficiently careful to observe that "Hart and Raz, whose characterizations of Hart's position will serve as some of the evidence I will rely on, use the terms 'noncognitive' and 'expressive' to characterize a number of philosophical positions that one or both attribute to Hart. … But only some of these views overlap with my versions of expressivism and noncognitivism" (2005, 78 n6). However, not all of Toh's fellow exegetes are comparably circumspect. Stephen Perry, for example, announces that "Hart explicitly states that he accepts a noncognitivist analysis of legal statements" (2009, 310 n53). In support of his assertion, Perry cites the closing pages of Hart's essay on legal duty and obligation (Hart 1982, 158–61). In fact, the term "noncognitivist" does not appear in Hart's essay at all. Instead, Hart used the term "non-cognitive" – which should alert any readers to the fact that Hart was not there addressing the matters at issue in debates over non-cognitivism as an account of the semantics of legal or moral statements. Rather, he was engaged in a dispute with Raz over the concept of legal duty or obligation. Raz believes that the concept of duty or obligation is the same in legal discourse as in moral discourse, and he therefore believes that all invocations of legal duties by officials in support of their endeavors of law-application imply the existence of moral reasons for people to conform to those duties. Hart disagreed with Raz over the notion that a single concept of obligation is shared between legal discourse and moral discourse, and also over the concomitant thesis about the implications of any assertions in which officials justify their decisions by referring to legal duties. Hart denied that all such assertions imply that the addressees thereof have had moral reasons to fulfill the duties. He labeled Raz's position on that point of contention as "cognitive" and his own position as "non-cognitive." Although those labels may have been unhelpfully misleading, Hart did not adopt them to signal his allegiance to any general non-cognitivist account of the semantics of internal legal statements. He was instead focused on the point of contention that has just been singled out here. That is, he was contesting Raz's view that every official pronouncement which invokes and applies a legal obligation is thereby implying that there are moral reasons for each addressee of the pronouncement to conform to its terms. Someone can endorse and amplify and refine Hart's position on that matter – as I have done elsewhere (Kramer 1999, ch. 4) – while giving a very wide berth to the suggestion that internal legal statements generally are devoid of propositional contents.

4.7 *Naturalistic preoccupations?*

As has been explored in §8 of my opening chapter, the proponents of philosophical naturalism contend that the only real entities and properties are those which are causally efficacious. Although there is no relationship of entailment in either direction between that metaphysical thesis and a non-cognitivist account of the semantics of moral or legal discourse, the two are very often combined. As Toh observes (2005, 80–1), numerous devotees of naturalism have embraced non-cognitivism in order to avoid the conclusion that sundry statements uttered in moral or legal discourse – statements such as ascriptions of duties and rights – are propositional assertions that affirm the existence of numerous unreal entities and properties. Consequently, Toh thinks that his attribution of non-cognitivism to Hart will be strengthened if he can establish that Hart shared the metaphysical convictions of naturalists.

Toh seizes upon the passages in the ninth chapter of *The Concept of Law* where Hart warily expounded the Aristotelian conception of nature – a strongly teleological conception which Hart perceived as underlying the theories of classical natural-law philosophers.

Toh quotes Hart's remark that the Aristotelian "outlook is, in many ways, antithetic to the general conception of nature which constitutes the framework of modern secular thought" (186, quoted in Toh 2005, 84). Let us leave aside here the fact that Hart in his overall discussion of Aristotelian teleology was more sympathetic than might be inferred from the sentence which Toh quotes in isolation. Even if Hart had distanced himself from Aristotelianism more sharply than he did, we could not validly have inferred therefrom that he subscribed to the naturalistic thesis about the unreality of causally inefficacious entities and properties. Aristotelian teleology is scarcely the sole alternative to that naturalistic thesis. Very few of the present-day moral realists who reject naturalism are partisans of any classical teleological conception of nature.

Toh quotes some other sentences from Hart that might seem to bespeak a naturalistic orientation. Toh reports that, after launching an initial salvo of objections to theories which construe invocations of legal norms as predictions that sanctions will be imposed for noncompliance, Hart broached some worries that might be felt by the critics of such theories. Toh (2005, 83) quotes most of the following passage from the opening chapter of *The Concept of Law* (11, emphasis in original):

> Yet among critics who have pressed these objections to the predictive account [of norms and obligations] some confess that there is something obscure here; something which resists analysis in clear, hard, factual terms. What *can* there be in a rule apart from regular and hence predictable punishment or reproof of those who deviate from the usual patterns of conduct, which distinguishes it from a mere group habit? Can there really be something over and above these clear ascertainable facts, some extra element, which guides the judge and justifies or gives him a reason for punishing?

Toh then declares that "Hart says that we may be tempted to 'imagine there is something external, some invisible part of the fabric of the universe guiding and controlling us in these activities'" (2005, 83, quoting Hart 1994, 11–12). Toh tells his readers that "Hart himself resists this temptation. And his resistance is motivated by a desire to have an account of … legal discourse that is congruent with the naturalistic conception of the world that he shares with other expressivists" (2005, 84). Toh proceeds to refer to Hart's doubts about the teleological conception of nature in classical natural-law theories, which I have already discussed near the outset of this subsection.

Toh has badly misrepresented the early portion of *The Concept of Law* from which he quotes. In that portion, Hart was recounting the ideas and concerns of some of the extreme rule-skeptics whom he would go on to criticize in the seventh chapter of his text. The questions included in the relatively long passage quoted just above were not questions posed by Hart; rather, they were questions posed by the extreme rule-skeptics whom Hart was discussing. He was using free indirect discourse – that is, he was writing from the simulative perspective – to give voice to the worries of those rule-skeptics even though he did not share their worries. Moreover, in the sentence that contains the extravagant wording about "some invisible part of the fabric of the universe," Hart was not expressing a temptation felt by himself or likely to be felt by his readers. Instead, he was continuing to articulate the ideas and concerns of some extreme rule-skeptics whose outlook he did not share. According to those rule-skeptics, ordinary people are inclined to think of legal norms in ways that are well captured by the aforementioned extravagant wording. Rule-skeptics respond with equal extravagance by denying the reality or constrainingness of legal norms altogether.

Hart in his own voice replied to the rule-skeptical position not by endorsing any naturalistic dogmas about the unreality of causally inefficacious entities or properties (*pace* Toh), but by indicating that the anxiety of rule-skeptics over the reality of legal norms is something that "calls for further elucidation of the distinction between social rules and mere convergent habits of behaviour. This distinction is crucial for the understanding of law, and much of the early chapters of this book is concerned with it" (12). In sum, Hart replied to the anxiety of the rule-skeptics by underscoring the importance of a refined understanding of the behavioral and attitudinal conditions that are constitutive of legal norms or of other social norms. That reply paralleled his response later in his book to theories which hold that ascriptions of legal obligations are predictions of the levying of legal sanctions for noncompliance. Hart remarked that such theories, associated with Bentham and Austin above all, had been hailed by some legal scholars "as the only alternative to metaphysical conceptions of obligation or duty as invisible objects mysteriously existing 'above' or 'behind' the world of ordinary, observable facts. But there are many reasons for rejecting this interpretation of statements of obligation as predictions, and it is not, in fact, the only alternative to obscure metaphysics" (84). Hart of course maintained that the preferable alternative lies in the careful elucidation of the patterns of behavior and attitudes that constitute the existence of legal obligations. Toh asserts that "[a]n expressivist analysis of internal legal statements is the third alternative Hart has in mind, and that is what he proposes in *The Concept of Law*" (2005, 85). If "expressivist" were being used here in its expansive sense, then Toh's assertion would be unexceptionable. Hart did indeed contend that the conditions for the existence of legal obligations reside in certain social practices through which the officials who run a system of governance express their acceptance of the laws that impose the obligations. However, Toh is quite clearly using "expressivist" not in its capacious sense but in its narrower sense to denote a non-cognitivist analysis of the semantics of internal legal statements. Given as much, his assertion is baseless. Neither when impugning the proclamations of rule-skeptics nor when impugning the predictive theory of obligations did Hart resort to non-cognitivism by suggesting that internal legal statements are devoid of any cognitive contents. Similarly, he did not resort to any naturalistic dogmas about the unreality of causally inefficacious properties and entities. Instead, he accentuated the need for the project in which he was engaged: namely, the project of distilling the patterns of behavior and attitudes that constitute the phenomena (legal norms and legal obligations and so forth) which are invoked in internal legal statements. He regarded that project as the best antidote to the rule-skepticism that has often nihilistically "taken the extreme form of condemning the very notion of a binding rule as confused or fictitious" (12).

To be sure, as I have remarked in my discussion of naturalism in §8 of my opening chapter, Hart wrote *The Concept of Law* and his other works at a time before minimalist accounts of truth and reality had become as prominent and influential as they are today. Consequently, he did not draw overtly on any such account. However, had he written in later decades, he would very likely have been attracted to minimalism because it is so congenial to his project. Faced with skepticism about the reality of legal norms or with efforts to reduce legal obligations to high probabilities of sanctions, Hart retorted by highlighting the salutariness of coming up with precise and illuminating analyses of the social practices in which legal norms and obligations are constituted. Those practices are structured and guided by legal norms and obligations that in turn are constituted by them. Had Hart had at his disposal a minimalist conception of truth and reality – broadly along the lines which I have laconically sketched in §8 of Chapter 1[14] – he could have marshaled it explicitly in the service of his jurisprudential enterprise. Indeed, even though he did not have such a conception readily at his disposal, he can fairly be read as having adopted a minimalist approach *avant la lettre*. Responding as he did to skepticism about the reality or irreducibility of legal norms and obligations, he aligned himself with the central insight of minimalism. In other words, he grasped that the following two questions are equivalent: the question whether there really is a legal prohibition on some mode of conduct MC in a particular jurisdiction J, and the question whether MC is legally prohibited in J. Hart and proponents of minimalism would agree that, if we aim to know whether such a legal prohibition really exists in J, we need to ascertain whether any conditions sufficient to constitute that prohibition are present in J or not. By the reckoning of a positivist such as Hart, of course, those conditions consist fundamentally in certain patterns of behavior and attitudes. Having detected such patterns, we might also need to engage in some moral judgments – if the system of governance in J is Inclusivist or Incorporationist – but no reflections on metaphysical abstrusities will be at all relevant.

4.8 The analysis attributed to Hart

A few pages in the sixth chapter of *The Concept of Law*, on the Rule of Recognition, have been of particular importance for exegetes who attribute to Hart a non-cognitivist analysis of internal legal statements. Those pages are cited frequently by Scott Shapiro in his meditations on the matter (2006, 1168–70), and they are likewise central to Toh's delineation of Hart's position. In that much-scrutinized portion of his text, Hart strove to differentiate between internal statements and moderately external statements. More specifically, he there emphasized that the statements made by the officials in a system of governance as they rely on their Rule of Recognition for the identification of the system's laws are different from the statements made by an observer who reports that the specified Rule of Recognition is operative within the jurisdiction. As Hart wrote in one of the relevant passages (102):

> The use of unstated rules of recognition, by courts and others, in identifying particular rules of the system is characteristic of the internal point of view. Those who use them in this way thereby manifest their own acceptance of them as guiding rules. … This attitude of

shared acceptance of rules is to be contrasted with that of an observer who records *ab extra* the fact that a social group accepts such rules but does not himself accept them.

On the basis of the first two sentences in this quoted passage, Toh attributes to Hart the following account of internal legal statements: "Let R be the norm that a speaker considers the rule of recognition of the legal system in his community. ... The speaker makes a legal statement [if and only if] he: (i) expresses his acceptance of R; and (ii) presupposes that R is generally accepted and complied with by the members of his community" (2005, 88). I henceforth designate this analysis, which Toh imputes to Hart, as "AH."

Though Toh believes that AH is a promising point of departure for an exposition of the semantics of internal legal statements, he allows that it is not satisfactory as it stands. He indicates that he is "only defending it as a reconstruction of Hart's proposal" (2005, 90). However, AH is exegetically and philosophically problematic in ways that go unnoticed by Toh. Furthermore, his discussion of AH is itself defective. I will proceed here to show the following points: AH does not correspond to what Hart wrote in the very passage which Toh quotes as the basis for his imputation of AH to Hart; AH suffers from a profound flaw which Toh does not glimpse; the flaw which Toh does perceive in AH is not in fact present therein; and, even if the attribution of AH to Hart were correct, it would not in itself support the claim that he propounded a non-cognitivist analysis of the semantics of legal discourse.

Whereas the first prong of AH refers simply to expressing one's acceptance of R, Hart in the quoted passage (and elsewhere) referred to manifesting one's acceptance of R by using it to identify other laws of one's system of governance. Even though we should assume that Toh is employing the term "acceptance" in Hart's somewhat technical sense to denote the adoption of all three elements of the critical reflective attitude toward R, many utterances can fulfill the first prong of AH without using R to identify other laws. Here we can behold the major shortcoming in AH which Toh overlooks. Let us suppose that Susan in the jurisdiction of the United States believes that the content of the prevailing Rule of Recognition is equivalent to the content of the American Constitution. Susan's belief is mistakenly simplistic, but for present purposes the correctness or incorrectness of her beliefs about the content of R does not matter. Now suppose that Susan exclaims "Hurray for the American Constitution!" In combination with various other utterances of hers, that exclamation expresses her acceptance of what she takes to be the generally prevailing Rule of Recognition in her jurisdiction. Hence, AH classifies her exclamation "Hurray for the American Constitution" as an internal legal statement. Such a classification reveals not only that AH is inadequate as an account of the nature of internal legal statements, but also that Toh has erred in ascribing AH to Hart. Unlike Toh's formulation of AH, the remarks in the passage which Toh quotes from Hart would not classify "Hurray for the American Constitution" as an internal legal statement.

Notwithstanding the serious shortcomings of AH as an explication of the nature of internal legal statements, it does not suffer from the defect which Toh perceives in it. In response to a posited objection, he concedes that "it is implausible to think, as [AH] implies, that every internal legal statement involves the speaker's appeal to what he considers the rule of recognition of his legal system" (2005, 90). Before we consider why AH is not afflicted by the problem which Toh broaches, we should note that Hart himself – in the passage which Toh quotes from him, and everywhere else – never suggested that all internal legal statements are focused on the identification of laws. Many such statements are indeed so focused, but many others are concerned chiefly instead with the matter of applying various laws to sundry circumstances; utterances of the latter kind frequently take for granted the matter of identifying the laws that are brought to bear on those circumstances. Statements of law-application are internal legal statements, just as are statements of law-ascertainment. Accordingly, if AH implied otherwise, we would have further grounds for denying that AH is an adequate analysis of internal legal statements – and further grounds for denying that AH encapsulates Hart's understanding of such statements.

In fact, however, AH is not marred by the weakness which Toh ascribes to it. Let us first note, in my most recent quotation from Toh, the ambiguity of his wording about "the speaker's appeal to what he considers the rule of recognition." Toh never disambiguates that wording. If it means that the speaker explicitly resorts to the criteria of the perceived Rule of Recognition, then the first prong of AH does not imply that any such appeal is involved in every internal legal statement. Only if the phrase "expresses his acceptance of R" in the first prong of AH were to be construed very narrowly to encompass nothing short of explicit references to the Rule of Recognition, would such an implication follow. Yet, if the first prong of AH were construed so narrowly, it would be flagrantly inaccurate as an encapsulation of Hart's conception of internal legal statements.

Hart repeatedly and emphatically denied that explicit invocations of the prevailing Rule of Recognition are operative in all internal legal statements (101–3). Even in the pronouncements uttered by officials during processes of law-ascertainment, and *a fortiori* in the pronouncements uttered by officials during processes of law-application, most internal legal statements do not involve such explicit invocations of the Rule of Recognition. As Hart wrote: "For the most part the rule of recognition is not stated, but its existence is *shown* in the way in which particular rules are identified, either by courts or other officials or private persons or their advisers" (101, emphasis in original). Thus, if the first prong of AH is to bear any resemblance to Hart's conception of internal legal statements, the phrase "expresses his acceptance of R" therein has to be construed expansively to encompass instances of implicit reliance on R as well as explicit invocations of R. When that phrase is construed in an appropriately expansive fashion, however, AH does not imply that every internal legal statement involves some explicit recourse by officials to the criteria of the perceived Rule of Recognition.

Let us therefore suppose that Toh with his wording about "the speaker's appeal" has in mind not only explicit or conscious references to the criteria of the Rule of Recognition, but also instances of implicit or unreflective reliance on those criteria. In that event, he is correct in thinking that AH implies that every internal legal statement involves some such appeal. He errs, however, in thinking that that implication of AH is implausible. Every internal legal statement does indeed involve reliance by the speaker on the criteria in the perceived Rule of Recognition, whether the reliance be explicit or implicit. This point is especially obvious in connection with statements of law-ascertainment – the sorts of statements with which Hart was concerned in the passage which Toh quotes as the basis for his attribution of AH to Hart – but it also extends to statements of law-application. As has been remarked more than once in my previous chapters, every instance of law-application rests implicitly if not explicitly on the proposition that any norm implemented as a law is endowed with the status of a law under the criteria in the prevailing Rule of Recognition. Either the norm in question is directly validated as a law by those criteria, or else it is directly validated by some other laws that are themselves ultimately validated by the criteria in the Rule of Recognition. Hence, indirect and implicit though the reliance of speakers on the criteria of the Rule of Recognition may be in any number of internal legal statements (especially in statements of law-application but also in statements of law-ascertainment), some such reliance – be it implicit or explicit – is always involved in the utterance of any such statement. Of course, as has been observed in some of my earlier chapters, the fact that the officials in a system of governance are guided by the standards in their Rule of Recognition does not per se mean that they are able to articulate each of those standards with any precision. Still, whether or not the officials can articulate all of those standards with precision, their being guided by the standards is something that explicitly or implicitly underlies every one of their internal legal statements.

Let us finally notice that, even if the failings of AH and the failings of Toh's discussion of AH are put aside, the attribution of AH to Hart does not suffice to vindicate the claim that Hart propounded a non-cognitivist analysis of the semantics of internal legal statements. The two prongs of AH distill the pragmatic aspects of internal legal statements which earmark the internal viewpoint as a perspective that contrasts with the external viewpoint and simulative viewpoint respectively. Whereas the first prong of AH captures an aspect of internal legal statements that distinguishes them from external legal statements and simulative legal statements, the second prong of AH captures an aspect of internal legal statements that distinguishes them from simulative legal statements.[15] A distillation of those pragmatic aspects of internal legal utterances is entirely consistent with the thesis that all or most such utterances are endowed with propositional contents. Consequently, even if Toh had been correct in ascribing AH to Hart, he would not have provided any support for his broader claim that Hart embraced non-cognitivism as an account of the semantics of internal legal statements.

4.9 *An aberrant passage*

There are no passages in *The Concept of Law* that militate in favor of Toh's reading of Hart as a non-cognitivist, but somewhat more problematic is a passage in an encyclopedia entry by Hart that was published in 1967. In the relevant portion of that entry, Hart briefly pondered whether decisions which apply legal norms to particular circumstances can properly be modeled as deductive inferences. According to extreme non-cognitivists, neither any general legal norms nor any concrete conclusions about the legal bearings of particular instances of conduct are ever aptly evaluable as true or false. Because those norms and conclusions are not truth-apt – that is, because they are devoid of propositional contents – they cannot ever serve as the steps in any genuinely deductive arguments. Such was the extreme non-cognitivist view which Hart disdainfully rejected. Justified though he was in dismissing that view brusquely, however, his way of doing so was disconcerting (1983, 100):

> This view depends on a restrictive definition, in terms of truth and falsehood, of the notion of a valid deductive inference and of logical relations such as consistency and contradiction. This would exclude from the scope of deductive inference not only legal rules or statements of law but also commands and many other sentential forms which are commonly regarded as susceptible of logical relations and as constituents of valid deductive arguments. Although considerable technical complexities are involved, several more general definitions of the idea of valid deductive inference that render the notion applicable to inferences the constituents of which are not characterized as either true or false have now been worked out by logicians. In what follows, as in most of contemporary jurisprudential literature, the general acceptability of this more generalized definition of valid inference is assumed.

In other words, Hart reacted to the extreme non-cognitivist view not by affirming that many legal norms and concrete legal conclusions are truth-apt, but by contending that deductive argumentation can be put together with components that are not truth-apt. He appeared to concede that legal norms and concrete legal conclusions are never truth-apt, and – amazingly, in light of his critique of Austin – he grouped together all such norms and conclusions with commands as entities that are not truth-apt. (Commands, qua imperatives such as "Shut the door," are indeed not evaluable as true or false.)

What should be said about this excerpt from an encyclopedia article that was published after *The Concept of Law* and long after Hart's flirtation with non-cognitivism in his very early writings? Should the excerpt lead us to conclude that Hart continued to embrace non-cognitivism in his later jurisprudential writings? One thing to be noted is that, as Toh remarks (2005, 104), the logicians to whom Hart referred in the penultimate sentence of this quoted passage very likely included Georg Henrik von Wright and Richard Hare – each of whom developed a version of deontic logic that excludes the possibility of conflicts between duties. (Each of those philosophers misguidedly effected that exclusion by conflating the conditions under which duty-imposing norms are operative and the conditions under which duty-imposing norms are fulfilled.[16]) In an essay on Kelsen originally published in 1968, Hart wisely recognized that conflicts between legal duties are in fact perfectly possible (1983, 325–7). Given as much, his allegiance to the ideas propounded by von Wright and Hare was obviously very tenuous.

Furthermore, any concession to non-cognitivism in the quoted passage may have been made by Hart purely *arguendo*. After all, his purpose in broaching the matter was to brush aside the extreme non-cognitivist claim that legal norms and concrete legal statements cannot ever serve as premises and conclusions in deductive arguments. For that purpose, he may have elected to grant *arguendo* one of the chief assumptions made by the extreme non-cognitivists – their assumption that legal norms and concrete legal statements are never true or false – even while he assailed the inference which they drew therefrom. By so doing, Hart could keep on board any readers who subscribe to that underlying assumption about truth-inaptitude. Of course, given that the versions of deontic logic to which he adverted are seriously flawed in the way which I have indicated, Hart's invocation of them against the extreme non-cognitivists was unwise. However, my point here is not that Hart was well advised to retort to the extreme non-cognitivists as he did. My point is simply that his acquiescence in their assumption about the truth-inaptitude of legal norms and concrete legal statements may have been purely tactical.

Each of the foregoing two considerations is strengthened by what I have recounted in §4.5 of this chapter. As has been discussed there, Hart in 1968 publicly announced his concurrence with Geach's 1960 critique of non-cognitivist approaches to the semantics of normative discourse. That critique, which took exception to Hart's early work on ascriptions of responsibility, was directed precisely against the non-cognitivist thesis that formulations of ethical judgments or other normative judgments are never evaluable as true or false. It was directed against Hare as much as against Hart. We cannot know exactly when Hart rid himself of his early views (by learning of Geach's objections or perhaps even before learning of those objections), but we can safely presume that that intellectual evolution occurred long before the 1967 publication of his entry in the *Encyclopedia of Philosophy*. Thus, we should be loath to take at face value a passing remark in his entry that might seem to smack of the non-cognitivism which he had abandoned.

Worth noting also are two further points. First, the riposte by Hart to the extreme non-cognitivists was a fleeting preliminary to his discussion of legal reasoning in his encyclopedia entry on problems in the philosophy of law. It hardly stands as a well-considered account of the semantics of internal legal statements. Second, in line with what I have reported in §4.6 of this chapter, Hart maintained that some laws and some concrete legal statements (especially in evil systems of governance) are best analyzed as imperatives. His apparent concession to the non-cognitivists would be appropriate in connection with those exceptional laws and statements, even though it would not be germane to most laws and concrete legal statements.

Admittedly, none of the considerations advanced here is quite sufficient to eliminate completely the dismayingness of the remarks by Hart in the quoted passage. Even so, when that passage is set alongside the numerous passages in his other late-period work where he differentiated clearly between the semantics and the pragmatics of legal statements, the case for classifying him as a non-cognitivist in *The Concept of Law* and in later writings is remarkably weak. Still, to say as much is not to say that he presented a cognitivist account of the semantics of internal legal statements in any sustained and rigorous fashion. Although I have sought to counter Toh's understanding of Hart as a non-cognitivist, I have not suggested that Hart's abandonment of his early non-cognitivism was accompanied by his development of a methodically worked-out alternative to his early views. Nevertheless, there are enough passages in *The Concept of Law* and his other late-period writings to enable a modest reconstruction of his approach to the semantics of internal legal statements. We should now turn to that approach, in a brief conclusion to my discussion of this matter.

4.10 *The semantics of internal legal statements*

As has been noted, the class of internal legal statements comprises both law-ascertaining pronouncements and law-applying pronouncements. Hart supplied some moderately clear indications of the semantics of law-ascertaining assertions. He was particularly expansive in the following passage (103):

> [T]he word "valid" is most frequently, though not always, used in just such internal statements, applying to a particular rule of a legal system, an unstated but accepted rule of recognition. To say that a given rule is valid is to recognize it as passing all the tests provided

Law and Morality 201

by the rule of recognition and so as a rule of the system. We can indeed simply say that the statement that a particular rule is valid means that it satisfies all the criteria provided by the rule of recognition. This is incorrect only to the extent that it might obscure the internal character of such statements; for, like the cricketers' "Out," these statements of validity normally apply to a particular case a rule of recognition accepted by the speaker and others, rather than expressly state that the rule is satisfied.

Several pages later, Hart declared afresh that an affirmation of the existence of a legal norm by an official engaged in an endeavor of law-ascertainment is "an internal statement applying an accepted but unstated rule of recognition and meaning (roughly) no more than 'valid given the system's criteria of validity'" (110).

As is made clear by these remarks, Hart firmly grasped that the semantic contents of any law-ascertaining statements are irreducibly normative. In that respect, his remarks about such statements are at one with his attacks on predictive theories of law. For example, near the end of his rejoinders to the jurisprudential theory propounded by the Danish legal philosopher Alf Ross, Hart submitted (1983, 168, emphases in original):

> The temptation to misrepresent ... internal statements in which use is made of an unstated, accepted rule or criterion of recognition as an external statement of fact predicting the regular operation of the system is due to the fact that the general acceptance of the rules and efficacy of the system is indeed the *normal context* in which such internal normative statements are made. ... But this normal *context* of efficacy presupposed in the making of internal statements must be distinguished from their normative meaning or content.

At this juncture, as elsewhere in his late-period writings, Hart differentiated carefully between the pragmatics of internal legal utterances and their normative semantics.

How, then, should we construe the account of legal semantics that is operative in these passages and in other similar passages? Partisans of the non-cognitivist reading of Hart will doubtless seek to contend that the normative meaning or content to which he referred is a matter of the expression of normative attitudes. Such philosophers might seize upon the following bit of Hart's essay on Ross, which occurs shortly after the portion that I have just quoted: "It is therefore vital if we are to understand social rules and the normative uses of language which are an inseparable part of this complex phenomenon of social life not to accept Ross's dilemma: 'Either construe these as predictions of judicial behaviour and feelings or as metaphysical assertions about unobservable entities above the world of facts'" (1983, 168). Champions of the non-cognitivist interpretation of Hart will be apt to think that he continued to embrace non-cognitivism in his later work as an alternative to the crudities of predictive theories and to obscure metaphysics. Propagators of that interpretation, such as Toh and Shapiro, do indeed insistently presume that Hart cast his lot with naturalism. After all, as has been observed in §4.7 of this chapter, naturalistic worries about the reality of normative entities and properties have always been one of the main factors behind the development of non-cognitivist approaches to the semantics of normative discourses.

However, naturalism is scarcely the lone alternative to obscure metaphysics. As should be evident from my discussions of minimalism in §4.7 of this chapter and in §8 of my opening chapter, a minimalist account of the reality of legal entities and properties – or of the reality of ethical entities and properties – does not confront us with any metaphysical arcana. Instead, it confronts us with the substantive legal matters or substantive ethical matters with which we have begun. By the reckoning of any minimalist account, the following two questions are equivalent: the question whether any legal prohibition on acts of arson in England really exists, and the question whether acts of arson in England are legally prohibited. Metaphysical questions about the reality of substantive legal norms are construed by minimalism as substantive legal questions.

As I have argued in the sections of this book just mentioned, Hart's inclinations in his late-period writings were along the lines of minimalism rather than along the lines of naturalism and reductionism. Though Hart could not avail himself directly of the minimalist approaches to truth and factuality and reality that have been elaborated since his retirement and death, he proceeded very much in accordance with those approaches. Consequently, one of the principal worries that have prompted many philosophers to develop their non-cognitivist accounts of the semantics of moral or legal discourse – the worry of naturalists about the inclusion of causally inefficacious normative entities and properties in a tally of what really exists – was not shared by him.

Proceeding in a minimalist fashion, Hart could avoid any recondite metaphysics while also avoiding the severe problems that afflict expressivism as a non-cognitivist semantic doctrine. In his later work he was certainly aware of one of the most formidable such problems, for attention was drawn to it by Geach's critique of non-cognitivism which I have noted in §4.5 of this chapter – a critique that Hart endorsed in his repudiation of his own early work – and by a further article that Geach published in 1965.[17] Because the difficulty exposed by Geach is discussed by Toh (2005, 102–4), and because my primary concern throughout this section of the chapter has been to contest the classification of Hart as a non-cognitivist rather than to establish the untenability of non-cognitivism as a semantic doctrine, I shall not expound the aforementioned difficulty here. Suffice it to say that the efforts by non-cognitivists to resolve that difficulty have run afoul of the conflation which I have condemnatorily touched upon in §4.9 of this chapter: the conflation of the existence-conditions and the fulfillment-conditions of duty-imposing norms.[18] Hart in his later writings could escape such cruxes by eschewing the non-cognitivist semantics which he had espoused in some of his very early publications. In those later writings, he grasped that the semantic contents of any number of internal legal statements are normative propositions which refer to normative entities and properties that are to be construed minimalistically. (Again, I am not suggesting that Hart himself presented his theorizing overtly in these terms. My claim, rather, is that we can best make sense of the analyses in *The Concept of Law* and in his other late-period writings if we construe them in these terms.)

In short, although Hart can accurately be classified as an expressivist in the broad sense of that label, his expressivism in his later work was an account of the pragmatics of legal discourse rather than an account of the semantics thereof. He subtly analyzed the sundry purposes that are characteristically pursued through the articulation of internal legal statements, and he adverted to those purposes in order to differentiate between such statements and the statements that are articulated from an external perspective or from the simulative perspective. His attending to those intricate aspects of the pragmatics of legal discourse was entirely consistent with his recognizing that myriads of internal legal statements are endowed with propositional contents. Contrary to what has been proclaimed by quite a few present-day legal philosophers, Hart advanced a theory of law in which the propositional form of any ordinary internal legal statement is matched by its propositional substance.

6

Conclusion

Although this book has at several junctures made clear my enormous esteem for Hart, it has not shrunk from criticizing him quite sharply on occasions when such criticism is due. Profoundly incisive though he was in his theorizing about the nature of law, he went astray on many important points. Especially because some of his errors have been nearly as influential as some of his abundant insights, the correction of those errors is integral to any responsible engagement with his work. One mark of the richness and depth of Hart's account of law is the susceptibility of that account to improvement through successive waves of objections directed against it. Quite a few of those objections over the years have been misguided, of course – sometimes badly misguided – but Hart himself acknowledged in the Postscript to *The Concept of Law* that "in more instances than I care to contemplate my critics [other than Ronald Dworkin] have been right" (239).

Ever since the publication of *The Concept of Law*, indeed, the greatness of Hart's jurisprudential ruminations has lain as much in their eliciting of disagreement as in their power to persuade doubters and to rectify misapprehensions. Most natural-law theories propounded since the early 1960s, as well as virtually all legal-positivist theories from that time forward, have emerged partly in response to Hart's ideas. Moreover, his account of legal governance has stimulated the development of new lines of thought and new foci of debate for which *The Concept of Law* has been a key point of reference. We have seen in my fifth chapter, for example, how the disputation between Inclusive Legal Positivists and Exclusive Legal

Positivists has sprouted from Hart's reflections on the relationships between law and morality. Similarly, we have seen how philosophers sympathetic to present-day minimalist conceptions of truth and reality and factuality can find inspiration in the method which Hart adopted throughout *The Concept of Law* (and in his other late-period jurisprudential writings). When Hart's texts are reconstrued in light of the concerns and innovations of philosophers in later periods, they are strengthened far more often than they are weakened.

Of course, as has been observed at the outset of this book, the contributions by Hart to legal and political and moral philosophy went well beyond his analyses of the structure and functioning of legal institutions. Within the confines of the present volume, we have not been able to examine any of the following matters: Hart's championing of the values of the liberal tradition in political philosophy; his immensely influential exploration of the nature of legal causation; his elucidation of the intricacies of agency and responsibility in the philosophy of criminal law; and his efforts to specify the fundamental characteristics of legal rights. Those endeavors and achievements, most of which I have discussed at length elsewhere,[1] are deserving of a separate book-length study.

Indeed, I have had to be somewhat selective even in connection with *The Concept of Law*. Though most parts of that book have been covered herein, I have said very little about its eighth chapter – on justice and the general character of morality[2] – and I have commented on only one portion of its final chapter (on international law). Still, every main component of Hart's theory of law has been carefully scrutinized in the present volume. Most of the components have stood up pretty well under the scrutiny, but often my investigations of them have revealed that a considerable amount of work remains to be done by philosophers of law who hope to sustain a model of legal systems that is broadly in line with the model which Hart propounded.

Let us summarily note five examples of the tasks that remain to be carried out. First, Hart's tendency to neglect power-conferring laws and immunity-conferring laws at crucial junctures in his theorizing has to be rectified through efforts to delineate the internal point of view that is adopted by officials and citizens with reference to such laws. In Chapter 2 of this book, I have sought to begin the fulfillment of that first task. Second, a satisfactory theory of law has to include a much better account of legal reasoning and interpretation than the account offered by Hart in *The Concept of Law*. Such an explication will draw on insights from the philosophy of language while being attentive to the variability of modes of legal reasoning and interpretation across jurisdictions and even within jurisdictions. Third, Hart's tendency to neglect the sundry roles of administrators who give effect to legal norms is likewise badly in need of rectification. Law-application is an enterprise conducted by the executive branch as well as by the judicial branch of any system of governance. Fourth, hugely valuable though Hart's analyses of the pragmatics of legal discourse are, they should be amplified with some more fine-grained analyses. That endeavor of amplification will involve not only the fleshing out of the internal point of view for laws other than duty-imposing laws, but also the distilling of pragmatic aspects of legal discourse that constitute the distinctiveness of such discourse in relation to other social practices (Etchemendy 2016, 17–19). Fifth, the more detailed expositions of the pragmatics of legal discourse should be accompanied by expositions of the semantics of internal legal statements – where the latter expositions are both cognitivist and minimalist. Along with my discussions of minimalist accounts of truth in a couple of my previous books (Kramer 2007, 71–82; 2009a, 200–7, 261–88), Chapters 1 and 5 of the present volume have provided some suggestions on how the requisite analyses of the semantics of internal legal statements should proceed; nonetheless, much remains to be done in the elaboration and defense of those analyses.

Obviously, the five tasks just listed are hardly exhaustive of the challenges that have to be met by legal positivists who aim to bolster the tradition of jurisprudential theorizing in which Hart played such an invigorating role. Many other tasks, which are comparably difficult and stimulating, also loom. By rising to those numerous challenges, positivists will naturally supplant some elements of Hart's philosophy of law with more sophisticated lines of analysis. Overall, however, they will be continuing and refining his project. Hart bequeathed to his intellectual heirs a general jurisprudential approach and a bevy of arresting ideas, but most of all he bequeathed to them an aspiration to come up with a clear and precise account of the nature of law through rigorous philosophical reflection. That aspiration is furthered rather than thwarted when his intellectual descendants strive to improve upon his theory of law through just such reflection.

Notes

Chapter 1 A Discourse on Method

1. For an excellent biography of Hart, see Lacey 2004. For some lovely recollections of Hart as a person, see Waluchow 2011.
2. Hart 1994, 17. In light of this passage and the many other passages in which Hart forswore any definitional ambitions, readers should feel baffled and dismayed by Ronald Dworkin's labeling of Hart's theory as "semantic" and by Dworkin's suggestion that Hart fell prey to the fallacy of the "semantic sting." See Dworkin 1986, 33–5, 45–6.
3. I should note that I do not concur with Hart on this point. In Kramer 2007, ch. 2, I have argued that a suitably revised and amplified exposition of Lon Fuller's eight principles of legality can arrive at a set of individually necessary and jointly sufficient conditions for the existence of the rule of law.
4. In philosophical parlance, the extension of a concept is the range of things to which the concept is applicable.
5. Though Mark Greenberg generally writes in the tradition of Dworkin, some of his recent work is astutely supportive of Hart's position on this matter. See especially Greenberg 2011.
6. See Kramer 1999, 233–9. For another retort to Finnis, see Leiter 2007, 166–70. Finnis's moralized methodology is endorsed in Endicott 2013, 35–6; Gardner 2012, 228; and Perry 2009, 302.
7. For a relatively sophisticated example of this line of thought, see Cotterrell 2003, 94–5.

8   When I say that the actions and dispositions are oriented toward the rules and guided by them, I am not implying that all or most of the competent users of the relevant language would be able to articulate the rules in any precise fashion. Without being able to formulate the rules in such a fashion, people can be guided by them through steady adherence to them. One adheres to the rules not only through one's implicit applications of them in one's own utterances, but also through one's tendency to recognize when they have been contravened by others.
9   Insofar as Hart took such a position on this matter, I firmly dissent from his view. See Kramer 2009a, ch. 2.
10 For my principal expositions of minimalism, see Kramer 2007, 71–82; 2009a, 200–7, 261–88. I there draw quite heavily, though not uncritically, on Horwich 1998 as well as on other sources.

Chapter 2   Hart on Legal Powers and Law's Normativity

1   Hart was wary of saying that laws are *addressed* to classes of people (21–2). I do not share his reservations about using the term "addressed" and its cognates in connection with laws. A duty-imposing law is addressed to everyone on whom it imposes a duty and to everyone on whom it confers a correlative claim-right.
2   See Hohfeld 1923, 50–1. For a full exploration of Hohfeld's analysis of legal positions, see Kramer 1998, 7–60, 101–11.
3   For a different (though compatible) construal of Hart's conception of legal powers in *The Concept of Law*, see MacCormick 2008, 97–8. Of course, I am not suggesting that Hart assumed that the *justification* for a power-conferring law will always reside in the fact that the power conferred is typically beneficial for the people who hold it. Any such justificatory assumption would be particularly outlandish in connection with laws that confer public powers.
4   To be sure, as I have discussed elsewhere (1999, 45–8; 2007, 113–15), there could exist *in extremis* a legal system wherein the promulgation of laws to citizens is effected solely by adjudicative and administrative decisions. As the decisions and the concomitant rationales accumulate, the patterns of those decisions and the contents of those rationales will serve as indicators through which ordinary citizens and their lawyers can become

apprised of the norms under which the legal consequences of their conduct are being assessed. A legal system operating with only this indirect method of promulgation would be untenable in any credibly possible large society, but something approximating it could obtain in a very small and simple society. (Also to be noted here is that – as my fifth chapter will emphasize – the paramount functions which I ascribe to law are not inherently moral.)

5   One of the very few commentators to notice this point is Stephen Perry (2009, 308–9). However, Perry interweaves this point with some badly mistaken claims about Hart's legal philosophy.
6   Although Jeremy Waldron (2013) includes a lot of supercilious criticism in his discussion of Hart's ruminations on international law, he oddly makes no mention of the line of reasoning by Hart to which I shall take exception here.

Chapter 3   The Components of Hart's Jurisprudential Theory

1   See Hart 1994, 89–91. In this paragraph and the next paragraph, I draw intermittently upon Kramer 1999, 165–6.
2   Hart did fleetingly broach the moderate external perspective anew in the sixth chapter of *The Concept of Law* (102–3), and he invoked it much more conspicuously and sustainedly in the Postscript to the second edition.
3   Though Hart never expounded the notion of presuppositions with any precision, his understanding of it was closely similar to Robert Stalnaker's broad pragmatic conception: "A person's presuppositions are the propositions whose truth he takes for granted, often unconsciously, in a conversation, an inquiry, or a deliberation. They are the background assumptions that may be used without being spoken – sometimes without being noticed – for example as suppressed premises in an enthymematic argument, or as implicit directions about how a request should be fulfilled or a piece of advice taken" (1973, 447). See also Toh 2005, 87 n21.
4   I have elsewhere discussed psychopathy at some length. See Kramer 2009a, 277–80; 2011a, 242, 244–5; 2017a, 164, 166; 2017b.
5   Hart 1994, 109, 110, emphases added. These final quoted statements are dubious in a further respect, for they wrongly characterize the Rule of Recognition as a practice of

law-ascertainment. Rather, as Hart usually discerned, the Rule of Recognition is an array of norms immanent in a practice of law-ascertainment. I have elsewhere shown that Hart did indeed have a firm grasp of this point despite the occasional slight carelessness in his wording. See Kramer 2013b, 31–3.

6   I have elsewhere staunchly resisted his reading. See Kramer 1999, 134. For some other commentators who have observed that Hart confined the addressees of the Rule of Recognition to legal-governmental officials, see Gardner 2012, 283; Green 2012b, xxviii–xxx; Lamond 2013, 108–12.

7   For the most notable expression of the view that the Rule of Recognition is solely power-conferring, see Fuller 1969, 137. For some examples of the view that the Rule of Recognition is solely duty-imposing, see Gardner 2012, 103–5; Lamond 2013, 101, 114, 115; MacCormick 2008, 32–3; Perry 2009, 296; Raz 1979, 93; Raz 1980, 199; Shapiro 2009a, 239–40; Shapiro 2011, 85.

8   In a federal system of governance such as that of the United States, there are indeed multiple Rules of Recognition that are comprehended in an overarching national Rule of Recognition. Hart said virtually nothing about federal systems of governance in *The Concept of Law*, but he contemplated them at several junctures in an essay about Bentham's account of legal limitations on sovereignty (1982, ch. 9).

9   This formulation takes account of an astute observation in Lamond 2013, 113 n85. Note, incidentally, that the domain of correct moral principles can be one of the fundamental sources of laws under this or that Rule of Recognition.

10 This formulation prescinds from various complexities. For example, whereas certain enactments by Parliament are addressed to the whole of the United Kingdom, other such enactments are addressed to only some of the four main components of the United Kingdom (England, Wales, Scotland, and Northern Ireland). Providing a full and precise account of any of the strands in a real-world Rule of Recognition is no easy task, as is evident in the classic essay by Kent Greenawalt on the Rule of Recognition in the United States (1987).

11 Hart himself conflated the Rule of Recognition with norms of law-application when he wrote that "[r]ules of recognition accepted in the practice of the judges require them to apply the laws identified by the criteria which they provide" (1982, 156). For some similar missteps, see Gardner 2012, 103–4; Green 2012b, xxiii; Lamond 2013, 115; Perry 2009, 296, 297–8, *et passim*.

Chapter 4 Hart on Legal Interpretation and Legal Reasoning

1. For Dworkin's main objections to Hart's account of law, see especially Dworkin 1978, chs. 2–4; 1986, chs. 1–4. However, versions of those objections also surfaced in some of Dworkin's later books and articles. See, for example, Dworkin 2006, ch. 6; 2017. For my most sustained defense of legal positivism against Dworkin's animadversions, see Kramer 1999, ch. 6.
2. See especially Dworkin 1996; 2011, chs. 2–5. On the proposition that the matter of the objectivity of morality is fundamentally a moral matter, I am in full agreement with Dworkin. See especially Kramer 2009a; 2013c; 2017c. See also Kramer 1999, 152–8.
3. I am assuming here that the objectivity of morality consists in the existence of determinately correct answers to moral questions. That aspect of moral objectivity is what is relevant to my present discussion, but it is only one of many dimensions of moral objectivity. For an exposition of all those dimensions, see Kramer 2009a.
4. In this paragraph and the next paragraph, I draw – with some modifications – on Kramer 2007, 20–1.
5. In several of the paragraphs in this subsection, I draw quite heavily – albeit with many significant modifications – on Kramer 2007, 3–12.
6. Of course, the views held in common by the people who undertake some collective enterprise are often not merely held in common but are also complicatedly interlocked. Very frequently, a key reason for the harboring of such views by each participant in a collaborative endeavor is his recognition that virtually every other participant harbors them and expects him to harbor them.
7. For some recent writings that have aptly emphasized this point, see Marmor 2008; Marmor 2011; Soames 2009. Though I agree with the incisive critique of those writings (and similar writings) in Greenberg 2011, that critique is fully consistent with the point which I have stated here.
8. Hart 1994, 126–7. For an entertaining discussion, see Schauer 2008.
9. As will be made clear in my next chapter, I am talking here about Hart as the author of *The Concept of Law*. In his very early writings, Hart did embrace non-cognitivism in his analyses of

certain types of legal statements. He later disavowed those analyses explicitly.
10 For Wittgenstein's ruminations on the following of rules, see especially Wittgenstein 1958, §§143–242. Some commentators on Hart have underscored the degree to which his general conception of language was influenced by Wittgenstein. See, for example, Bix 1993, ch. 1.
11 For some of my previous discussions of vagueness, see Kramer 2007, 36–7, 70; 2009a, 109–13, 260–1; 2011a, 120–4, 194–5, 202–3, 226–7, 252–6. For the most sustained exploration of the problem of vagueness in the workings of legal systems, see Endicott 2000. For an impressive recent collection of essays on the topic, see Keil and Poscher 2016.
12 Hart 1994, 139. For a rigorous analysis that is supportive of Hart's position, see Holton 2010. Worth noting here is that Hart inappositely sought to illustrate his point with a scenario involving a promisor who breaches an undertaking for the purpose of going to the aid of a seriously ill person. Such a scenario recounts a moral conflict – a conflict between the promisor's moral duty to do x and her simultaneous moral duty to do y, where doing x entails not doing y and where doing y entails not doing x – rather than an exception. For a full exposition of the nature of moral conflicts, see Kramer 2014a, 1–19.

Chapter 5 Law and Morality

1 Hart touched on Kelsen's work intermittently in *The Concept of Law*, but his main engagements with Kelsen are in Hart 1983, chs. 14–15. There are also some interesting reflections on Kelsen in Hart 2013, 287–92.
2 Though David Plunkett does not use the phrase "the separability thesis," he speaks of "the debate between legal positivists and antipositivists" – as if there were only one major line of controversy between positivists and their opponents. Plunkett (2016, 206) writes: "What exactly is at issue in the debate between positivists and antipositivists? … [A]t its core, it is a debate about what kinds of facts ultimately determine the existence and content of legal systems. In short: Is it social facts alone? Or is it a combination of social facts and moral facts?" Plunkett

here implies that the stance taken by positivists on a key point of contention between themselves and Dworkinians is the whole, or the core, of legal positivism.

3   I have previously differentiated among these aspects or dimensions of morality at several junctures in Kramer 1999. I have also invoked them prominently in Kramer 2004, ch. 7. I here develop and occasionally modify some of the strands in my past discussions of this matter.

4   See especially Kramer 1999, chs. 3–8; 2004, chs. 5–7. Of particular relevance are the articles that I published from 2004 to 2011 in response to the arguments propounded by the natural-law theorist Nigel Simmonds. For the final installment in that series of articles, which includes citations to the earlier installments, see Kramer 2011b.

5   Coleman 2001, 151. Elsewhere, Coleman (2001, 193 n21; 2007) has adopted a somewhat more capacious view of legal positivism's insistence on the separability of law and morality.

6   For two valuable introductions to this topic, see Horton 1992 and Knowles 2010.

7   For a full assessment, with many relevant citations, see Kramer 1999, ch. 9.

8   For Hart's clearest statement on the matter, see Hart 1987, 40–2. For my own denial of the existence of such an obligation, see Kramer 1999, ch. 9.

9   For some of the relevant works of those successors, see Himma 2001; 2002; Kramer 2004, 1–140; 2009b; Lyons 1977, 423–6; Waluchow 1994; 2000; 2009.

10 For some other articulations of the Incorporationist doctrine, see Coleman 2001, chs. 6–10; Kramer 2004, 1–140; Soper 1977, 509–15.

11 For some of Raz's relevant discussions, see Raz 1979, ch. 3; 1994, ch. 10. For some discussions by several other notable legal philosophers, who have been influenced to varying degrees by Raz, see Giudice 2002; 2008; Leiter 2007, ch. 4; Marmor 2001, ch. 3; Shapiro 1998; 2009b; 2011, ch. 9.

12 For an expressivist account of the pragmatics of moral discourse – an account which I take to be largely a distillation of some elements of Simon Blackburn's expressivism – see Kramer 2017c, 198–206. For a recent article that appears to be advocating an expressivist approach to the pragmatics of legal discourse, see Etchemendy 2016.

13 For the *locus classicus* of the error theory of morality, see Mackie 1977, ch. 1. For a sustained critique of the error theory, see Kramer 2017c, 186–96.
14 As I note in Chapter 1, I have elsewhere expounded and defended a minimalist conception of truth and reality and factuality at much greater length (Kramer 2007, 71–82; 2009a, 200–7, 261–88).
15 Admittedly, as has been noted in §2 of my third chapter, some simulative legal statements do presuppose the general efficacy of R. However, whereas every internal legal statement is endowed with such a presupposition, some simulative legal statements are not.
16 That disastrous conflation was also characteristic of Bentham's so-called logic of the will; see Hart 1982, 111–17. For a full exposition of the possibility of moral conflicts, with ripostes to the likes of von Wright and Hare, see Kramer 2014a, 1–19.
17 For a good discussion of the problem highlighted by Geach, see Kalderon 2005, ch. 2. For my own discussion of various related matters, see Kramer 2009a, ch. 8.
18 That conflation is palpable, for example, in Blackburn 1993, ch. 10. In his later writings, Blackburn has given a wide berth to expressivism as a semantic doctrine and has subscribed instead to expressivism as an account of the pragmatics of ethical discourse. See Kramer 2017c, 202–8.

Chapter 6 Conclusion

1 In Kramer 2014b, I discuss Hart's conception of responsibility and his endeavors to uphold the values of Millian liberalism. In Kramer 2003, ch. 4, I seek to build on Hart's analysis of causation. In Kramer 1998, I intermittently take exception to various aspects of Hart's account of legal rights.
2 For a lengthy attack on an argument prominently advanced by Hart in the eighth chapter of *The Concept of Law*, see Kramer 2004, 249–94.

References

Bix, Brian. 1993. *Law, Language, and Legal Determinacy*. Oxford: Oxford University Press.
Blackburn, Simon. 1993. *Essays in Quasi-Realism*. Oxford: Oxford University Press.
Coleman, Jules. 2001. *The Practice of Principle*. Oxford: Oxford University Press.
Coleman, Jules. 2007. "Beyond the Separability Thesis: Moral Semantics and the Methodology of Jurisprudence." *Oxford Journal of Legal Studies* 27: 581–608.
Cotterrell, Roger. 2003. *The Politics of Jurisprudence*, 2nd edn. London: LexisNexis Butterworths.
Dworkin, Ronald. 1978. *Taking Rights Seriously*. Cambridge, MA: Harvard University Press.
Dworkin, Ronald. 1984. "A Reply by Ronald Dworkin." In Marshall Cohen (ed.), *Ronald Dworkin and Contemporary Jurisprudence*. London: Duckworth, pp. 247–300.
Dworkin, Ronald. 1986. *Law's Empire*. London: Fontana Press.
Dworkin, Ronald. 1996. "Objectivity and Truth: You'd Better Believe It." *Philosophy and Public Affairs* 25: 87–139.
Dworkin, Ronald. 2006. *Justice in Robes*. Cambridge, MA: Harvard University Press.
Dworkin, Ronald. 2011. *Justice for Hedgehogs*. Cambridge, MA: Harvard University Press.
Dworkin, Ronald. 2017. "Hart's Posthumous Reply." *Harvard Law Review* 130: 2096–2130.

Endicott, Timothy. 2000. *Vagueness in Law*. Oxford: Oxford University Press.
Endicott, Timothy. 2013. "The Generality of Law." In Luis Duarte d'Almeida, James Edwards, and Andrea Dolcetti (eds.), *Reading HLA Hart's* The Concept of Law. Oxford: Hart Publishing, pp. 15–36.
Etchemendy, Matthew. 2016. "New Directions in Legal Expressivism." *Legal Theory* 22: 1–21.
Finnis, John. 1980. *Natural Law and Natural Rights*. Oxford: Oxford University Press.
Finnis, John. 2013. "How Persistent are Hart's 'Persistent Questions'?" In Luis Duarte d'Almeida, James Edwards, and Andrea Dolcetti (eds.), *Reading HLA Hart's* The Concept of Law. Oxford: Hart Publishing, pp. 227–236.
Fuller, Lon. 1969. *The Morality of Law*, rev. edn. New Haven, CT: Yale University Press.
Gardner, John. 2012. *Law as a Leap of Faith*. Oxford: Oxford University Press.
Geach, Peter. 1960. "Ascriptivism." *Philosophical Review* 69: 221–225.
Geach, Peter. 1965. "Assertion." *Philosophical Review* 74: 449–465.
Giudice, Michael. 2002. "Unconstitutionality, Invalidity, and Charter Challenges." *Canadian Journal of Law and Jurisprudence* 15: 69–83.
Giudice, Michael. 2008. "The Regular Practice of Morality in Law." *Ratio Juris* 21: 94–106.
Green, Leslie. 1996. "The Concept of Law Revisited." *Michigan Law Review* 94: 1687–1757.
Green, Leslie. 2012a. "Notes to the Third Edition." In H.L.A. Hart, *The Concept of Law*, 3rd edn. Oxford: Oxford University Press, pp. 309–25.
Green, Leslie. 2012b. "Introduction." In H.L.A. Hart, *The Concept of Law*, 3rd edn. Oxford: Oxford University Press, pp. xv–lv.
Green, Leslie. 2013. "The Morality in Law." In Luis Duarte d'Almeida, James Edwards, and Andrea Dolcetti (eds.), *Reading HLA Hart's* The Concept of Law. Oxford: Hart Publishing, pp. 177–207.
Greenawalt, Kent. 1987. "The Rule of Recognition and the Constitution." *Michigan Law Review* 85: 621–671.
Greenberg, Mark. 2011. "Legislation as Communication? Legal Interpretation and the Study of Linguistic Communication." In Andrei Marmor and Scott Soames (eds.), *Philosophical Foundations of Language in the Law*. Oxford: Oxford University Press, pp. 217–256.

Hacker, Peter. 1977. "Hart's Philosophy of Law." In Peter Hacker and Joseph Raz (eds.), *Law, Morality, and Society*. Oxford: Oxford University Press, pp. 1–26.

Hart, H.L.A. 1949. "The Ascription of Responsibility and Rights." *Proceedings of the Aristotelian Society* 49: 171–194.

Hart, H.L.A. 1955. "Are There Any Natural Rights?" *Philosophical Review* 64: 175–191.

Hart, H.L.A. 1968. *Punishment and Responsibility*. Oxford: Oxford University Press.

Hart, H.L.A. 1982. *Essays on Bentham*. Oxford: Oxford University Press.

Hart, H.L.A. 1983. *Essays in Jurisprudence and Philosophy*. Oxford: Oxford University Press.

Hart, H.L.A. 1987. "Comment." In Ruth Gavison (ed.), *Issues in Contemporary Legal Philosophy*. Oxford: Oxford University Press, pp. 35–42.

Hart, H.L.A. 1994. *The Concept of Law*, 2nd edn. Oxford: Oxford University Press.

Hart, H.L.A. 2013. "Answers to Eight Questions." In Luis Duarte d'Almeida, James Edwards, and Andrea Dolcetti (eds.), *Reading HLA Hart's* The Concept of Law. Oxford: Hart Publishing, pp. 279–297.

Himma, Kenneth. 2001. "The Instantiation Thesis and Raz's Critique of Inclusive Positivism." *Law and Philosophy* 20: 61–79.

Himma, Kenneth. 2002. "Inclusive Legal Positivism." In Jules Coleman and Scott Shapiro (eds.), *The Oxford Handbook of Jurisprudence and Philosophy of Law*. Oxford: Oxford University Press, pp. 125–165.

Hohfeld, Wesley. 1923. *Fundamental Legal Conceptions as Applied in Judicial Reasoning*, ed. Walter Wheeler Cook. New Haven, CT: Yale University Press.

Holton, Richard. 2010. "The Exception Proves the Rule." *Journal of Political Philosophy* 18: 369–388.

Horton, John. 1992. *Political Obligation*. London: Macmillan.

Horwich, Paul. 1998. *Truth*, 2nd edn. Oxford: Oxford University Press.

Kalderon, Mark. 2005. *Moral Fictionalism*. Oxford: Oxford University Press.

Keil, Geert and Poscher, Ralf (eds.). 2016. *Vagueness and Law*. Oxford: Oxford University Press.

Knowles, Dudley. 2010. *Political Obligation*. New York: Routledge.

Kramer, Matthew. 1991. *Legal Theory, Political Theory, and Deconstruction*. Bloomington: Indiana University Press.

Kramer, Matthew. 1998. "Rights without Trimmings." In Matthew Kramer, N.E. Simmonds, and Hillel Steiner, *A Debate over Rights*. Oxford: Oxford University Press, pp. 7–111.

Kramer, Matthew. 1999. *In Defense of Legal Positivism*. Oxford: Oxford University Press.

Kramer, Matthew. 2001. "Getting Rights Right." In Matthew Kramer (ed.), *Rights, Wrongs, and Responsibilities*. Basingstoke: Palgrave Macmillan, pp. 28–95.

Kramer, Matthew. 2003. *The Quality of Freedom*. Oxford: Oxford University Press.

Kramer, Matthew. 2004. *Where Law and Morality Meet*. Oxford: Oxford University Press.

Kramer, Matthew. 2007. *Objectivity and the Rule of Law*. Cambridge: Cambridge University Press.

Kramer, Matthew. 2009a. *Moral Realism as a Moral Doctrine*. Oxford: Wiley-Blackwell.

Kramer, Matthew. 2009b. "Moral Principles and Legal Validity." *Ratio Juris* 22: 44–61.

Kramer, Matthew. 2011a. *The Ethics of Capital Punishment*. Oxford: Oxford University Press.

Kramer, Matthew. 2011b. "For the Record: A Final Reply to N.E. Simmonds." *American Journal of Jurisprudence* 56: 115–133.

Kramer, Matthew. 2013a. "John Austin on Punishment." *Oxford Studies in Philosophy of Law* 2: 103–121.

Kramer, Matthew. 2013b. "In Defense of Hart." In Wil Waluchow and Stefan Sciaraffa (eds.), *Philosophical Foundations of the Nature of Law*. Oxford: Oxford University Press, pp. 22–50.

Kramer, Matthew. 2013c. "Working on the Inside: Ronald Dworkin's Moral Philosophy." *Analysis* 73: 118–129.

Kramer, Matthew. 2014a. *Torture and Moral Integrity*. Oxford: Oxford University Press.

Kramer, Matthew. 2014b. "Legal Responses to Consensual Sexuality between Adults: Through and Beyond the Harm Principle." In Christopher Pulman (ed.), *Hart on Responsibility*. Basingstoke: Palgrave Macmillan, pp. 109–128.

Kramer, Matthew. 2017a. *Liberalism with Excellence*. Oxford: Oxford University Press.

Kramer, Matthew. 2017b. "Shakespeare, Moral Judgments, and Moral Realism." In Craig Bourne and Emily Caddick Bourne (eds.), *Shakespeare and Philosophy*. London: Routledge.

Kramer, Matthew. 2017c. "There's Nothing Quasi about Quasi-Realism: Moral Realism as a Moral Doctrine." *Journal of Ethics* 21: 185–212.
Lacey, Nicola. 2004. *A Life of H.L.A. Hart: The Nightmare and the Noble Dream*. Oxford: Oxford University Press.
Lamond, Grant. 2013. "The Rule of Recognition and the Foundations of a Legal System." In Luis Duarte d'Almeida, James Edwards, and Andrea Dolcetti (eds.), *Reading HLA Hart's* The Concept of Law. Oxford: Hart Publishing, pp. 97–122.
Leiter, Brian. 2007. *Naturalizing Jurisprudence*. Oxford: Oxford University Press.
Leiter, Brian. 2011. "The Demarcation Problem in Jurisprudence: A New Case for Scepticism." *Oxford Journal of Legal Studies* 31: 663–677.
Locke, John. 1988. *Two Treatises of Government*, ed. Peter Laslett. Cambridge: Cambridge University Press. Original edition published in 1689.
Lyons, David. 1973. "On Formal Justice." *Cornell Law Review* 58: 833–861.
Lyons, David. 1977. "Principles, Positivism, and Legal Theory." *Yale Law Journal* 87: 415–435.
MacCormick, Neil. 2008. *H.L.A. Hart*, 2nd edn. Stanford, CA: Stanford University Press.
Mackie, John. 1977. *Ethics: Inventing Right and Wrong*. London: Penguin Books.
Marmor, Andrei. 2001. *Positive Law and Objective Values*. Oxford: Oxford University Press.
Marmor, Andrei. 2008. "The Pragmatics of Legal Language." *Ratio Juris* 21: 423–452.
Marmor, Andrei. 2011. "Can the Law Imply More Than It Says? On Some Pragmatic Aspects of Strategic Speech." In Andrei Marmor and Scott Soames (eds.), *Philosophical Foundations of Language in the Law*. Oxford: Oxford University Press, pp. 83–104.
Marmor, Andrei. 2013. "Farewell to Conceptual Analysis (in Jurisprudence)." In Wil Waluchow and Stefan Sciaraffa (eds.), *Philosophical Foundations of the Nature of Law*. Oxford: Oxford University Press, pp. 209–229.
Perry, Stephen. 2009. "Where Have All the Powers Gone? Hartian Rules of Recognition, Noncognitivism, and the Constitutional and Jurisprudential Foundations of Law." In Matthew Adler and Kenneth Himma (eds.), *The Rule of Recognition and the U.S. Constitution*. Oxford: Oxford University Press, pp. 295–326.

Plunkett, David. 2016. "Negotiating the Meaning of 'Law': The Metalinguistic Dimension of the Dispute over Legal Positivism." *Legal Theory* 22: 205–275.

Rawls, John. 1999. "Legal Obligation and the Duty of Fair Play." In *Collected Papers*, ed. Samuel Freeman. Cambridge, MA: Harvard University Press, pp. 117–129. Originally published in 1964.

Raz, Joseph. 1979. *The Authority of Law*. Oxford: Oxford University Press.

Raz, Joseph. 1980. *The Concept of a Legal System*, 2nd edn. Oxford: Oxford University Press.

Raz, Joseph. 1994. *Ethics in the Public Domain*. Oxford: Oxford University Press.

Schauer, Frederick. 2008. "A Critical Guide to Vehicles in the Park." *New York University Law Review* 83: 1109–1134.

Shapiro, Scott. 1998. "On Hart's Way Out." *Legal Theory* 4: 469–507.

Shapiro, Scott. 2006. "What is the Internal Point of View?" *Fordham Law Review* 75: 1157–1170.

Shapiro, Scott. 2009a. "What is the Rule of Recognition (and Does It Exist)?" In Matthew Adler and Kenneth Himma (eds.), *The Rule of Recognition and the U.S. Constitution*. Oxford: Oxford University Press, pp. 235–268.

Shapiro, Scott. 2009b. "Was Inclusive Legal Positivism Founded on a Mistake?" *Ratio Juris* 22: 326–338.

Shapiro, Scott. 2011. *Legality*. Cambridge, MA: Harvard University Press.

Soames, Scott. 2009. "Interpreting Legal Texts: What is, and What is Not, Special about the Law." In *Philosophical Essays: Volume I*. Princeton, NJ: Princeton University Press, pp. 403–423.

Soper, Philip. 1977. "Legal Theory and the Obligation of a Judge: The Hart/Dworkin Dispute." *Michigan Law Review* 75: 473–519.

Stalnaker, Robert. 1973. "Presuppositions." *Journal of Philosophical Logic* 2: 447–457.

Tapper, Colin. 1973. "Powers and Secondary Rules of Change." In A.W.B. Simpson (ed.), *Oxford Essays in Jurisprudence: Second Series*. Oxford: Oxford University Press, pp. 242–277.

Toh, Kevin. 2005. "Hart's Expressivism and His Benthamite Project." *Legal Theory* 11: 75–123.

Waldron, Jeremy. 2009. "Who Needs Rules of Recognition?" In Matthew Adler and Kenneth Himma (eds.), *The Rule of Recognition and the U.S. Constitution*. Oxford: Oxford University Press, pp. 327–349.

Waldron, Jeremy. 2013. "A 'Relatively Small and Unimportant' Part of Jurisprudence?" In Luis Duarte d'Almeida, James Edwards, and Andrea Dolcetti (eds.), *Reading HLA Hart's* The Concept of Law. Oxford: Hart Publishing, pp. 209–223.

Waluchow, W.J. 1994. *Inclusive Legal Positivism*. Oxford: Oxford University Press.

Waluchow, W.J. 2000. "Authority and the Practical Difference Thesis: A Defense of Inclusive Legal Positivism." *Legal Theory* 6: 45–81.

Waluchow, W.J. 2009. "Four Concepts of Validity: Reflections on Inclusive and Exclusive Positivism." In Matthew Adler and Kenneth Himma (eds.), *The Rule of Recognition and the U.S. Constitution*. Oxford: Oxford University Press, pp. 123–144.

Waluchow, W.J. 2011. "H.L.A. Hart: Supervisor, Mentor, Friend, Inspiration." *Problema: Anuario de Filosofía y Teoría del Derecho* 5: 3–10.

Wittgenstein, Ludwig. 1958. *Philosophical Investigations*, trans. G.E.M. Anscombe. Oxford: Basil Blackwell.

Index

acceptance of norms
    as critical reflective attitude 61, 63, 89–91, 102, 108–9, 141, 185, 194, 208 n8
    mere obedience contrasted with 108–9
adequacy 13–14, 55
    Hart on 14, 16–17
adjudication, Hart's inordinate focus on 76, 83, 112, 206
administration, Hart's neglect of 76, 83, 112, 206
administrative regulations
    Hart on 136–7
    validity of 91–2
"ain't" 121–2
Aloofness Objection 115–16, 177–9
    dubiousness of 115, 179
    Hart's capitulation to 115–16, 177–9
anthropology from an armchair 10–11, 17–18, 71, 75
Aristotelian conception of nature 189–90
Austin, J.L. 186–7
Austin, John 72, 76, 108, 198
    and command theory of law 32–46, 52–61

    customary laws distorted by 14, 36, 53–6
    on electorate as sovereign 57–9
    on generality and durability of legal norms 34–5
    Hart's critique of 36–46, 52–61
    immunity-conferring laws neglected by 38
    inadequacy of theory propounded by 14
    on liberty-conferring laws 37–8
    and limits on sovereignty 56–9
    model of law propounded by 33–6
    on moral assessability of law 155
    normativity neglected by 3, 16–17, 28, 36–9, 52–60
    power-conferring norms neglected by 14, 36–46, 53, 57–9
    as predecessor of Hart 148, 157
    and predictive theory of obligations 191
    as proto-Inclusivist 179
    on sovereignty 33–7, 52–9
    strengths of 33

on tacit approval 54–5
and vagueness in account of sovereignty 35
Ayer, A.J. 184

basic legal prohibitions 164–70
  convergence with contents of moral principles 165–9
  not necessarily protective of everyone 166–8
  potential heavy-handedness of 168–9
  potential meagerness of 168
  potentially underlain by moral considerations 169
Bentham, Jeremy
  and command theory of law 32–3
  Hart's editing of works by 2
  and liberty-conferring laws 37–8
  and limits on sovereignty 56, 210 n8
  on "logic" of the will 214 n16
  on moral assessability of law 155
  normativity neglected by 3
  as predecessor of Hart 32, 148, 157
  on predictive theory of obligations 191
  as proto-Inclusivist 179
  and Subsumability Thesis 43
Bix, Brian 212 n10
Blackburn, Simon 213 n12, 214 n18
borderline legal systems 6–10
breadth, as theoretical virtue 11–13

Canadian English 121
causation
  constitutive relationships contrasted with 25
  Hart on 1, 205, 214 n1
  Marmor on 24–5

central-instance method 5–8
  Finnis's approval of 15–16
central instances of legal systems
  contrast between officials and citizens in 80
  necessary and sufficient conditions for 7–8
chess 141–2
circularity seemingly in Hart's theory 78, 99, 105–7
  Shapiro on 105–7
"citizens," definition of viii
clarity, as theoretical virtue 13–14
codified Rule of Recognition
  dependent on foundational level 93–7
  dictionaries analogous to 93–7
  foundational level influenced by 94–7
coercion, law as 2–3, 33–46, 52–61
Coleman, Jules
  on Incorporationism 213 n10
  on separability of law and morality 162, 213 n5
command theory of law
  Bentham's version of 32–3
  Hart's critique of 32–46, 52–61, 110, 148
communicative activities
  and disagreements among speakers 75, 85
  semantic and syntactic rules immanent in 26–7, 92, 93, 208 n8
  semantics and pragmatics of 130–2
  unreflective adherence to rules in 141–2, 208 n8
Communist regimes 45, 149, 152
concepts shared between law and morality 3
conceptual analysis 4–18
conditional duties
  as liabilities 42–3
  MacCormick on 41–3
consilience 13–14

constitutional amendments in USA 88–9
constitutive relationships
 causation contrasted with 25
 and reductionism 24–8
Cotterrell, Roger 207 n7
credible possibilities 170
critical reflective attitude
 acceptance as 61, 63, 89–91, 102, 108–9, 141, 185, 194, 208 n8
 applicable only to duty-imposing laws 46–8
 of officials toward Rule of Recognition 82–3
customary laws
 distorted by Austin 14, 36, 53–6
 Hart on 53–6
 validated by Rule of Recognition 99–100

deductive inferences, law-application as 197–200
definitional method 4–8
deontic logic 198–9
depth, as theoretical virtue 13
descriptive-explanatory method 12–23
determinate correctness, moral objectivity as 211 n3
Detmold, Michael 156
dictionaries
 codified Rule of Recognition analogous to 93–7
 language influenced by 94–7
disaffected citizens 64
disagreements over Rule of Recognition 75, 84–5, 86, 89
durability of legal norms 34–5
Durkheim, Emile 9
duties 3
duty-imposing laws
 power-conferring laws comprised by 43–6
 power-conferring laws contrasted with 36–46, 70–3, 77–8, 81–4

power-conferring laws portrayed as 39–43
 unconditional requirements imposed by 38
Dworkin, Ronald 204
 and addressees of Rule of Recognition 79
 Aloofness Objection raised by 115–16, 177–9
 Greenberg influenced by 207 n5
 Hart on 17
 Hart's account of legal reasoning criticized by 111, 114–17, 173, 175–9, 211 n1
 on Inclusive/Exclusive debates 177
 indeterminacy/indemonstrability distinction grasped by 116–17
 and internal point of view 63
 on law-ascertainment as inherently moral 163
 and misrepresentation of Hart's theory as "semantic" 207 n2
 and moralized methodology 12–13, 15, 17, 163
 on objectivity of morality 211 n2
 parochialism of 8, 11–12
 on rules/principles distinction vii, 175–6
 and superfluous insistence that law is morally assessable 156
Dworkinians 212–13 n2

efficacy, presupposition of 66–9, 132, 201, 214 n15
Egg Principle 105–7
electorate as sovereign 57–9
elementary facts of human condition 165–72
empirical conjectures 19–22
empirical falsification 8–10
empirical matters, contrasted with morality 153, 162–3, 173–4, 178

Endicott, Timothy 207 n6, 212 n11
error theory of morality 183–4, 214 n13
errors by officials 126–8
Etchemendy, Matthew 206, 213 n12
evaluative judgments 15–16, 18, 163
evil laws 20, 21
exceptions
    conflated with moral conflicts 212 n12
    Hart on 139–40, 212 n12
    and rule-skepticism 139–40
Exclusive Legal Positivism 114, 162–3, 173–7
existential mind-independence 29–30, 122–30
explanatory reductionism 23–4
expressivism
    attributed to Hart 180–203
    broad conception of 182–5, 192, 203
    narrow conception of as noncognitivism 183–203
    as pragmatic doctrine 181–3, 192, 197, 203, 213 n12, 214 n18
    as semantic doctrine 181–203
extensions of concepts 72, 207 n4
external viewpoint 46, 197
    extreme version of 62–5
    moderate version of 62–5
extreme external viewpoint 62–5
    not usually adopted by disaffected citizens 64

fascism 149, 152
federal systems of governance 210 n8
Filmer, Robert 167
finality
    infallibility contrasted with 129–30, 142–5
    and rule-skepticism 142–5
    of rulings by US Supreme Court 142–3, 144–5

Finnis, John 2, 21
    on central-instance method 15–16
    on internal viewpoint 15–16
    and moralized methodology 15–16, 18, 207 n6
First Amendment to American Constitution 38, 57
first-order and second-order beliefs 125–30
formalism 133–4, 139–40, 146–7
foundational Rule of Recognition 92–7
    influenced by codified level 94–7
free indirect discourse 191
Frege–Geach problem 202–3, 214 n17
Fuller, Lon 155–6, 159, 179
    on principles of legality 207 n3
    on Rule of Recognition as solely power-conferring 210 n7
functions of law 44–5, 158
    not inherently moral 209 n4

games, laws analogized to rules of 40–1, 44–5, 141–2, 143–4
Gardner, John
    on addressees of Rule of Recognition 210 n6
    and conflation of Rule of Recognition with norms of law-application 210 n11
    Finnis's moralized method endorsed by 207 n6
    on intertwining of secondary norms 100–1
    on philosophy and social science 9
    on Rule of Recognition as solely duty-imposing 210 n7
Geach, Peter 187, 199, 202–3, 214 n17
general laws, weak existential mind-independence of 123–4, 126–8

generality
  of address 34–5
  of application 34–5
Giudice, Michael 213 n11
Green, Leslie
  on addressees of Rule of
    Recognition 210 n6
  and conflation of Rule of
    Recognition with norms of
    law-application 210 n11
  on Hart's moralized
    method 22–3
  on Inclusive/Exclusive
    debates 180
  on primary/secondary
    contrast 71
Greenawalt, Kent 88–91, 210 n10
Greenberg, Mark 207 n5, 211 n7
gunman writ large, Austinian
  sovereign as 34

habitual behavior, contrasted with
  norm-guided behavior 46, 191
habitual obedience 35
Hacker, Peter 71
Hare, Richard 198–9, 214 n16
Hart, H.L.A.
  accused of armchair
    anthropology 10–11
  on addressees of Rule of
    Recognition 78–81
  on adequacy as theoretical
    virtue 14, 16–17
  adjudication overemphasized
    by 76, 83, 112, 206
  administration neglected by 76,
    83, 112, 206
  on administrative
    regulations 136–7
  and Aloofness Objection,
    capitulation to 115–16, 177–9
  on Aristotelian conception of
    nature 189–90
  on Austin 3, 14, 16–17, 28,
    32–46, 52–61, 179
  on basic legal
    prohibitions 164–70
  on Bentham 2, 3, 179
  biographical sketch of 2
  on borderline legal
    systems 6–10
  on causation 1, 205, 214 n1
  on central-instance method 5–8,
    15–16
  on chess 141–2
  on clarity as theoretical
    virtue 14
  closer to formalism than to
    rule-skepticism 133, 146–7
  on coercion 2–3
  command theory rejected
    by 32–46, 52–61, 110
  on conceptual analysis 4–18
  on conflicts between legal
    duties 199
  on critical reflective attitude 46–
    7, 61–3, 102, 108–9, 141
  on customary laws 53–6
  definitional method eschewed
    by 4–8, 207 n2
  descriptive-explanatory
    methodology of 12–23
  on disagreements over Rule of
    Recognition 85, 86
  on duty-imposing and power-
    conferring nature of Rule of
    Recognition 81–3
  Dworkin's criticisms of 111,
    114–17, 173, 175–9, 211 n1
  Dworkin's moralized
    methodology rejected
    by 12–13
  on Dworkin's parochialism 8
  on elementary facts of human
    condition 165–72
  on evil laws 20, 21
  on exceptions 139–40,
    212 n12
  exceptions conflated with moral
    conflicts by 212 n12

Index 227

expressivism attributed to 132–3, 180–203
on external viewpoint 46, 62–5
on federal systems of governance 210 n8
on finality in contrast with infallibility 129–30, 142–5
Finnis's objections to 15–16
on formalism versus rule-skepticism 133–4, 136–7, 139–47
on foundational Rule of Recognition 93
on Fuller 155–6
on functions of law 44–5
on Holmes 14
on hunches or instincts 140–2
on ignorance of fact and indeterminacy of aim 136
immunity-conferring laws neglected by 205
and Inclusive Legal Positivism 114–16, 163, 175–80, 204–5
Inclusive/Exclusive debates stimulated by 204–5
Incorporationism embraced by 176–8
on indeterminacy 114–17, 118–19, 133–47
on indeterminacy in Rule of Recognition 87–8, 145–7
indeterminacy/indemonstrability distinction neglected by 112–17, 130, 134, 137, 145
indeterminacy/uncertainty distinction neglected by 117–20, 130, 134, 137, 145, 146
influence of on legal philosophy 204–5
on internal point of view 15–16, 46–8, 61–3, 102, 108–9, 132–3, 141, 193–7

on internal viewpoint of power-holders 45
on international law 50–2, 205, 209 n6
on intertwining of secondary norms 97–8
jurisdiction-transcendence of theorizing by 8–12, 172
on Kelsen 43–5, 212 n1
on laws that bind supreme legislators 52–3
on legal positivism 1, 148–80
on legal powers, nature of 36–7, 106, 208 n3
on legal reasoning and interpretation 110–47, 205–6
on legal validity 91
on legislation in contrast with judicial rulings 136
on legislative powers 39, 40
Leiter on 28–31
on liabilities 42
on liberal democracy 1, 205
and limits on sovereignty 56–9
on marginal legal systems 15–16
Marmor on 23–8
on methodology 2–31
minimalism embraced by, *avant la lettre* 192–3, 202–3, 205
on minimum content of natural law 12, 158, 164–70
on moderate external viewpoint 62–5, 209 n2
and moral arguments for legal positivism 19–23
on moral assessability of law 155
as a moral skeptic 117
moralized methodology, limited embrace of 19–23, 157, 163
moralized methodology rejected by 12–18
on motivations for adoption of internal viewpoint 61–3, 160

Hart, H.L.A. (cont.)
  on multiple points of contention for legal positivists 149–64
  naturalism attributed to 18–31, 189–92
  natural-law theories opposed by 148–64
  on nature of norms 3–4
  on necessary and sufficient conditions for central instance of legal system 107–9
  on neglect of normativity by Austin 16–17, 28
  noncognitivism aberrantly acquiesced in 197–200
  noncognitivism attributed to 132–3, 180–203
  noncognitivism in very early work 185–8, 211–12 n9
  normativity emphasized by 110
  on norms of law-application 76–7, 97–8
  on nullity as a sanction 39–41
  on open texture of legal norms 114, 138
  on parasitic relationships 72–3, 77–8
  Perry on 29, 188–9
  Perry's attribution of noncognitivism to 188–9
  philosophical scope of theorizing by 8–11
  on philosophy in contrast with history 1–2
  on power-conferring aspect of Rule of Recognition 81–3
  on power-conferring laws 36–53, 56–9
  power-conferring laws neglected by 46–52, 108–9, 205
  pragmatics highlighted by 132–3, 182, 184–5, 192, 197, 201, 203, 206
  pragmatics neglected by in account of interpretation 131–2, 181–2
  on precedents in English law 111, 136–7
  on predictive theories of law 190–2, 201–2
  on presupposition of efficacy 66–9
  on pre-theoretical knowledge 4–5
  on primary/secondary distinction 70–8
  on principle of fair play 170–1
  on private legal powers 45
  on procedural justice 159
  on promissory norms 41–2, 52
  on public legal powers 45–6
  Raz's concept of duty contested by 188–9
  and receptivity to criticisms 204
  reductionism attributed to 23–8
  on responsibility and punishment 1, 205, 214 n1
  on rights 1, 205, 214 n1
  on roller skates 131
  "rule" as misleading term used by vii
  on Rule of Recognition vii, 75–6, 78–107, 193–7
  Rule of Recognition conflated with norms of law-application by 210 n11
  on Rule of Recognition as implicit fundaments of law-ascertainment 193–7
  on Rule of Recognition as legal or pre-legal 107
  on scorer's discretion 143–4
  on secondary norms 10–11, 18
  semantics overemphasized by in account of interpretation 131–2, 181–2

Index

semantics/pragmatics distinction neglected by 130–2, 186–7
on separability of law and morality 148–80
Shapiro's attribution of naturalism to 29, 202
Shapiro's attribution of noncognitivism to 193
on simulative viewpoint 66–9, 132
"soft positivism" label used by 177, 178
on stagnancy 74–6
on theoretical-explanatory virtues 14–18
Toh on 29, 181–203
on ultimacy of Rule of Recognition 91–2
on uncertainty 74–6
on variations among legal systems 11–12
on vehicles in park 131
on voluntarist theories of international obligations 50–2
and wariness of speaking of laws as "addressed" to people 208 n1
on Wittgenstein 134, 212 n10
helium atoms 153
Himma, Kenneth 213 n9
history of ideas 1–2
Hobbes, Thomas 165
Hohfeld, Wesley 208 n2
on immunities 38
on legal powers 36–7
Holmes, Oliver Wendell 14
Holton, Richard 212 n12
Horton, John 213 n6
Horwich, Paul 208 n10
Hume, David 165
Hume's Law 153

Iago 66
ignorance of fact 136

immorality, contrasted with morality 151–3, 156–9
immunities 3, 38
immunity-conferring laws
Austin's neglect of 38
Hart's neglect of 205
imperatives 184, 198, 200
importance, as theoretical consideration 15–16, 18
Inclusive/Exclusive debates 173–7, 204–5
chiefly among positivists 177
Dworkin on 177
Green on 180
Inclusive Legal Positivism 157–8, 162–3, 173–80, 193, 204–5
Dworkin's critiques of Hart as stimulus for 173, 175–6
Hart's adherence to 114–16, 163, 175–80
Hart's suspension of his adherence to 115–16, 177–9
radical indeterminacy inconsistent with 114–17, 179
incommensurability 117–18
Incorporationism 174–6, 193
Dworkin's critiques of Hart as stimulus for 173, 175–6
Hart's embrace of 176–8
indemonstrability, contrasted with indeterminacy 112–17, 120, 128–30, 134, 137, 145
indeterminacy
of aim 136
Hart on 114–19, 133–47
Inclusive Legal Positivism inconsistent with 114–17, 179
indemonstrability contrasted with 112–17, 120, 128–30, 134, 137, 145
in Rule of Recognition 87–8, 145–7
uncertainty compatible with 119

indeterminacy (cont.)
  uncertainty conflated with by Hart 118–20, 130, 134, 137, 145, 146
  uncertainty contrasted with 117–20, 128–30, 134, 137, 145, 146
  unforeseeability as source of 136–7
  vagueness as source of 137–9, 212 n11
  Wittgenstein's critique of rule-following unrelated to 134–6
indexicals 34
individualized legal directives, strong existential mind-dependence of 123–4
infallibility, in contrast with finality 129–30, 142–5
instincts and rule-skepticism 140–2
interjections 183, 184
interlocked expectations 211 n6
internal legal statements
  arising both in law-ascertainment and in law-application 195–7, 200
  semantics of as irreducibly normative 200–3, 206
  semantics of 180–203, 206
  simulative statements contrasted with 214 n15
internal point of view
  blurring of distinctness from simulative viewpoint 68–70
  Finnis on 15–16
  Hart on 46–8, 61–3, 102, 108–9, 132–3, 141, 193–7
  of power-holders 45–50, 61, 101–3, 108–9, 141, 205, 206
international law, Hart on 7, 50–2, 205, 209 n6
interpretation, focused both on semantics and on pragmatics 211 n7
intertwining of secondary norms 77, 83, 97–101, 103–5, 107, 196–7
  Gardner on 100–1
  Hart on 97–8

jaywalking ordinances 124
jigsaw puzzles 154
judicial precedents 136–7
judicial review 56
jurisdiction-transcendence of Hart's theorizing 8–12, 111–12, 172

Kalderon, Mark 214 n17
Keil, Geert 212 n11
Kelsen, Hans 28, 148, 212 n1
  and conflicts between legal duties 199
  on presupposition of efficacy 67
  and Subsumability Thesis 43–5
Kennedy, John 113
Knowles, Dudley 213 n6

Lacey, Nicola 207 n1
Lamond, Grant 210 n6, n7, n9, n11
language
  influenced by dictionaries 94–7
  semantic and syntactic rules immanent in 26–7, 92, 93, 208 n8
  unreflective adherence to rules in 141–2, 208 n8
law
  and coercion 2–3, 33–46, 52–61
  formal homologies with morality 161–2
  and morality 3, 11, 148–80
  rules of games analogous to 40–1, 44–5, 141–4
  terminological affinities with morality 161–2
law-application, as deductive inferences 197–200
law-ascertainment
  Dworkin on 163

Index

moral considerations only contingently a basis of 162–3, 173–6
Law of Noncontradiction 135
laws that bind supreme legislators 52–3
legal norms
  reality of 25–31
  weak existential mind-independence of 29–30
legal positivism 11
  Austin and Bentham as Hart's predecessors in 32
  and broad concept of law 19–23
  command theory severed from 60
  and distrust of government 149
  diversity of clashes with natural-law theories 149–64
  Hart on 148–80
  Hart's moral arguments for 19–23
  and moral assessability of law 154–6
  and variability of laws 12
  varying degrees of adherence to 156–7
legal powers
  Hart's conception of 36–7, 106, 208 n3
  Hohfeld on 36–7
  liabilities correlated with 37, 42–3
  private 37, 38–9, 45, 76, 108
  public 37, 39, 45–6, 76
  two senses of 78, 99, 105–7
legal reasoning and interpretation 11–12
  Dworkin's critique of Hart on 111, 114–17, 173, 175–9, 211 n1
  Hart on 110–47, 205–6
  semantics overemphasized in by Hart 131–2, 181–2
  variable across jurisdictions 11–12, 111–12, 131–2, 205–6

legal validity
  Hart's conception of viii, 200–1
  inapplicable to Rule of Recognition 91
  moral tests for 157–8, 164, 173–4
legislation
  contrasted with judicial rulings 136
  norms that confer powers of 76, 82, 98
legislative powers 39, 40, 76, 82, 98
"legitimacy," definition of viii
"legitimate," equivalent to "permissible" viii
Leiter, Brian
  Exclusive Legal Positivism espoused by 213 n11
  Finnis's moralized methodology criticized by 207 n6
  naturalism attributed to Hart by 28–31
liabilities 37, 42–3
liberal democracies 80–1
  Hart on principles of 1, 205, 214 n1
  and problem of political obligation 169, 172
  Rule of Law instantiated by viii
liberties 3
liberty-conferring laws 37–8
limits on sovereignty
  Austin's denial of possibility of 56–9
  Bentham's acknowledgment of possibility of 56
  supreme governmental power consistent with 57
  as withheld powers 56–7
Locke, John 165, 167
logical necessity 170
logical possibilities, contrasted with credible possibilities 170
logical validity, contrasted with legal validity viii
Lyons, David 159, 213 n9

MacCormick, Neil 2
  on conditional duties 41–3
  on Hart's conception of legal powers 208 n3
  on power-conferring laws as duty-imposing laws 41–3
  on primary/secondary contrast 71
  on promissory norms 41–3
  on Rule of Recognition 103–5, 210 n7
Mackie, John 214 n13
marginal legal systems, Finnis on 15–16
Marmor, Andrei
  on Exclusive Legal Positivism 213 n11
  incoherence of position on observational mind-independence 126
  on interpretation 211 n7
  on metaphysical reductionism 23–4
  on observational mind-independence of laws 125–8, 130
  reductionism attributed to Hart by 23–8
  on semantic reductionism 24
methodology of legal philosophy 2–31, 163
mind-independence
  chart of types of 123
  of legal norms 120–30
  observational contrasted with existential 122–30
  strong contrasted with weak 121–30
minimalism about truth and reality 30–1, 192–3, 206, 208 n10, 214 n14
  Hart's inclination toward 202–3, 205
  and moral objectivity 115
  obscure metaphysics averted by 202–3
minimum content of natural law 12, 158, 164–70
  four qualifications to 166–9
minimum wage 117–18
moderate external viewpoint 62–5, 209 n2
  on Rule of Recognition 193
  typically adopted by disaffected citizens 64
moral conflicts 214 n16
  exceptions conflated with by Hart 212 n12
  von Wright and Hare on 198–9, 214 n16
moral duties, existence-conditions versus fulfillment-conditions 198–9, 203, 214 n16
moral/empirical contrast, jurisprudential debates centered on 162–3, 173–4, 178
morality
  basic legal prohibitions convergent in content with 165–9
  Dworkin on objectivity of 211 n2
  empirical matters contrasted with 153, 162–3, 173–4, 178
  and formal homologies with law 161–2
  immorality contrasted with 151–3, 156–9
  and law 3, 11, 148–80
  multiple aspects or dimensions of 150–64
  non-moral phenomena contrasted with 153–6
  prudence contrasted with 17, 151–3, 159–62, 169
  as source of laws 210 n9
  strong mind-independence of 208 n9

terminological affinities with law 161–2
morality/immorality contrast 151–3
  jurisprudential debates centered on 156–9
  morality/prudence contrast different from 152–3
morality/prudence contrast 151–3
  jurisprudential debates centered on 159–62
moralized methodology
  of Dworkin 12–13, 15, 17, 163
  of Finnis 15–16, 18
  Hart's limited embrace of 19–23, 157, 163
  Hart's rejection of 12–18
moral legitimacy
  asserted or implied in officials' pronouncements 158–9
  as precondition for legal validity 157–8, 164, 173–4
moral/non-moral contrast, no jurisprudential debates centered on 154–6
moral objectivity
  as determinate correctness 211 n3
  Dworkin on 211 n2
  as moral matter 115, 211 n2
  Moral Principles Objection 115–17, 178–9
moral skepticism 117
Morris, Herbert 2
motivations for adoption of internal viewpoint 61–3, 159–60

naturalism
  attributed to Hart 28–31, 189–92
  noncognitivism often combined with 189–92, 202
  and rule-skepticism 191–2
natural-law theories
  functions of law perceived as inherently benign by 158
  Hart's opposition to 148–64
  with moral tests for legal validity 157–8, 164
  multifariousness of 149–64
  narrow concept of law in 19–23
necessary and sufficient conditions for central instance of legal system 107–9
noncognitivism
  attributed to Hart 132–3, 180–203
  and conflation of duties' existence-conditions and fulfillment-conditions 203, 214 n18
  Hart's aberrant alignment with 197–200
  naturalism often combined with 189–92, 202
non-moral phenomena 153–6
non-natural entities 30
"norm," definition of vii
normativity
  Hart's highlighting of 36, 52, 53, 55–6, 59, 60, 110
  moral versus prudential 17, 151–3, 159–62, 169
  neglected by Austin 3, 16–17, 28, 36–9, 52–60
  neglected by Bentham 3
norm-guided behavior, contrasted with merely habitual behavior 46, 191
norms
  of change 76
  Hart on nature of 3–4
  of law-application 76–7, 97–8
norms of change
  Hart on 76
  Rule of Recognition not reducible to 99–103
norms of law-application
  both duty-imposing and power-conferring 78, 103–4, 109

norms of law-application (cont.)
  Hart on 76–7, 97–8
  Rule of Recognition intertwined with 77, 83, 97–8, 100–1, 103–4, 196–7
  Rule of Recognition not reducible to 103–5, 210 n11
Not Counted Thesis 26
nullity as a sanction 39–41

objectivity, as strong existential mind-independence 29–30
obligation to obey law 3, 166, 169–72
  comprehensively applicable and universally borne, or not 166, 169, 172
  positivists' denials of 213 n8
observational mind-independence 122–30
officials
  as addressees of Rule of Recognition 79–81, 210 n6
  distinguished from private citizens viii, 79–81
open texture
  of legal norms 114, 138
  of Rule of Recognition 86
origins of legal systems 10–11, 17–18, 71, 75, 77
  and problem of apparent circularity 105–7
Oswald, Lee Harvey 113–14
Othello 66
Oxford 2

parasitic relationships between norms 72–3, 77–8
parliamentary enactments 210 n10
parsimony, as theoretical virtue 13
peripheral legal systems 6–10
permissibility viii, 154
"permissible," equivalent to "legitimate" viii

Perry, Stephen
  Finnis's moralized methodology endorsed by 207 n6
  on Hart's neglect of power-conferring laws 209 n5
  naturalism attributed to Hart by 29
  noncognitivism attributed to Hart by 188–9
  Rule of Recognition conflated with norms of law-application by 210 n11
  on Rule of Recognition as solely duty-imposing 210 n7
philosophy, contrasted with social science 8–11
Plunkett, David 212–13 n2
political obligation, problem of 166, 169–72
  in liberal democracies 169, 172
Poscher, Ralf 212 n11
Possibility Puzzle 105–7
power-conferring norms
  Austin's neglect of 14, 36–46, 53, 57–9
  duty-imposing norms contrasted with 36–46, 70–3, 76, 77–8, 81–4
  Hart on 36–53, 56–9
  Hart's neglect of 46–52, 108–9, 205
  MacCormick on 41–3
  not reducible to duty-imposing norms 39–43
  stagnancy averted or alleviated by 76
  subsumption into duty-imposing norms 43–6
  unconditional requirements not established by 38
power-holders, internal viewpoint of 45–50, 61, 101–3, 108–9, 141, 205, 206
power of sentencing 72–3
powers of law-alteration 100–3

powers of law-ascertainment 100–5
powers in law and morality 3
pragmatics
  expressivist account of 213 n12, 214 n18
  Hart's attentiveness to 132–3, 182, 184–5, 192, 197, 201, 203, 206
  Hart's neglect of in his account of interpretation 131–2, 181–2
  semantics contrasted with 130–3, 180–203, 206
precedential force 98, 126
precedents in English law 111
precision, as theoretical virtue 13
predictive theories of law 190–2, 201–2
presupposition of efficacy 66–9, 132, 201, 214 n15
presuppositions, general nature of 209 n3
pre-theoretical knowledge 4–5
primary/secondary distinction 70–8
  duty-imposing/power-conferring contrast different from 72–3, 77–8
principle of fair play 170–1
principles/rules distinction vii, 175–6
priority rules 86–7
private/public distinction, unavailable to Austin 53
procedural justice 159
promissory norms 41–3, 52
promulgation of laws 208–9 n4
prudence
  contrasted with morality 17, 151–3, 159–62, 169
  as underpinning of basic legal prohibitions 169
psychopaths 70, 209 n4
punishment 1, 205

punishment-centered reasons for compliance with law 161, 162

Rawls, John 172
Raz, Joseph 2
  on concept of duty 188–9
  on Exclusive Legal Positivism 177, 213 n11
  on multiple Rules of Recognition 85–91
  on primary/secondary contrast 71
  on reasons invoked or implied by official pronouncements 160–1
  on Rule of Recognition and official hierarchies 88–91
  on Rule of Recognition as solely duty-imposing 210 n7
reality
  of causally inefficacious entities 27–31
  of legal norms 25–31
  minimalist accounts of 30–1, 192–3, 206, 208 n10, 214 n14
  of semantic/syntactic rules 26–7
reasonableness, vagueness of 138–9
reasons
  for adherence to rule of law 159–60
  invoked or implied by official pronouncements 160–1
reductionism 23–8
  attributed to Hart 23–8
  and constitutive relationships 24–8
"resolved," ambiguity of 119
responsibility 1, 205, 214 n1
rights in law and morality 3
  Hart on 1, 205, 214 n1
roller skates 131
Roman Law 67, 68, 132
Ross, Alf 201–2

"rule," potential misleadingness
   of vii
rule of law
   necessary and sufficient
      conditions for 207 n3
   reasons for adherence to 159–60
   Rule of Law contrasted
      with viii, 160
Rule of Law, contrasted with rule
   of law viii, 160
Rule of Recognition vii, 75–6,
   78–107, 193–7
   addressees of 78–81, 210 n6
   complexities of 210 n10
   critical reflective attitude of
      officials toward 82–3, 89–90
   customary laws validated
      by 99–100
   disagreements over 75, 84–5, 86,
      89
   duty-imposing and power-
      conferring 75, 78, 81–4,
      99–104, 109, 210 n7
   duty-imposing dimension
      of 102–3
   foundational level and codified
      level 92–7
   foundational level influenced by
      codified level 94–7
   and hierarchies among
      officials 88–91
   as implicit fundaments of
      processes of law-
      ascertainment 92–7, 107, 142,
      193–7
   indeterminacy in 87–8, 145–7
   integratedness of 87–91
   intertwined with other
      secondary norms 77, 83,
      97–101, 103–5, 107, 196–7
   legal or pre-legal 107
   MacCormick on 103–5
   multiplicity and ranking of
      criteria in 85–8
   neither valid nor invalid 91
   norms of change not equivalent
      to 99–103
   norms of law-application not
      equivalent to 103–5, 210 n11
   as norms rather than
      practices 209–10 n5
   power-conferring dimension
      of 99–101
   plurality of in federal system of
      governance 210 n8
   Raz on 85–91
   Shapiro on 99–101
   ultimacy of 91–2
   uncertainty alleviated by 75–6
   unreflective adherence to criteria
      in 142
   Waldron on 101–3
"Rule of Recognition," aptness of
   phrase 87
rule-skepticism 133–4, 136–7,
   139–47
   exceptions invoked by 139–40,
      212 n12
   finality invoked by 142–5
   hunches or instincts invoked
      by 140–2
   and indeterminacy in Rule of
      Recognition 145–7
   and infallibility 142–5
   and naturalism 191–2
rules/principles distinction vii,
   175–6

sanctions, authoritative
   administration of 74, 77
Scandinavian Legal Realism 184
Schauer, Frederick 211 n8
scorer's discretion 143–4
secondary norms 10–11, 18
   not inherently benign 75
   intertwining of 77, 83, 97–101,
      103–5, 107, 196–7
   primary norms contrasted
      with 70–8
self-help remedies 74, 77

self-presentation of law 158–9
semantic reductionism 24
semantic and syntactic rules
  reality of 26–7
  unreflective adherence to 141–2
semantic sting 207 n2
semantics
  Hart's overemphasis on in his account of interpretation 131–2, 181–2
  of internal legal statements 180–203, 206
  pragmatics combined with in interpretation 211 n7
  pragmatics contrasted with 130–3, 180–203, 206
sentencing, power of 72–3
separability of law and morality 148–80
separability thesis 162, 164
  inexistence of 149–50, 164
"settled," ambiguity of 119
Shakespeare, William 66
Shapiro, Scott
  on circularity in origins of legal system 105–7
  on Exclusive Legal Positivism 213 n11
  naturalism attributed to Hart by 29, 202
  noncognitivism attributed to Hart by 193
  on Rule of Recognition 99–101, 210 n7
Simmonds, Nigel 213 n4
simulative statements, contrasted with internal statements 214 n15
simulative viewpoint 65–70, 191, 197
  contrast with internal viewpoint blurred 68–70
  Hart on 66–9, 132
slavery 75, 167

small and simple legal systems 7, 80
smoking 152
Soames, Scott 211 n7
social science, contrasted with philosophy 8–11
"soft positivism" 177, 178
solitaire 154
Soper, Philip 213 n10
"sorites paradox" 138
sovereignty
  Austin's understanding of 33–7, 52–9
  limits on 56–9
  relocated in the electorate 57–9
stagnancy 74–6
Stalnaker, Robert 209 n3
strong existential mind-independence 29–30
strong mind-independence 121–30
  of morality 208 n9
strong observational mind-independence
  of laws 124–30
  Marmor's denial of 125–8
Subsumability Thesis 43–6
  Bentham on 43
  extreme version of 43–5
  moderate version of 43, 45–6
supernatural entities 30

tacit approval 54–5
Tapper, Colin 71
terminological affinities between law and morality 161–2
theoretical-explanatory virtues 13–18
  Hart on 14–18
theorizing, evaluative judgments in 15–16, 18
Toh, Kevin 209 n3
  naturalism attributed to Hart by 29
  noncognitivism attributed to Hart by 181–203

Tolkien, J.R.R. 94
truth, minimalist accounts of 30–1
truth-aptitude 182, 183, 198, 199

ultimacy of Rule of
  Recognition 91–2
unanimity 121–2
uncertainty 74–6
  alleviated by norms of
    law-application 76–7
  alleviated by Rule of
    Recognition 75–6
  indeterminacy compatible
    with 119
  indeterminacy contrasted
    with 117–20, 128–30, 134, 137,
    145, 146
unconditional requirements 38
unenforceable legal
  mandates 40–1
unenforced legal mandates 124
unforeseeability 136–7
unreasonableness, vagueness
  of 138–9
"unresolved," ambiguity of 119
"unsettled," ambiguity of 119
utilitarianism 155

vagueness
  in Austin's conception of
    sovereignty 35
  indeterminacy due to 137–9, 212
    n11
  of reasonableness and
    unreasonableness 138–9
validity, legal versus logical viii
variations among legal
  systems 11–12
  in legal reasoning and
    interpretation 111–12, 131–2,
    205–6
vehicles in the park, ban on 131
voluntarist theories of
  international obligations
  50–2
von Wright, G.H. 198–9, 214 n16

Waldron, Jeremy 101–3, 209 n6
Waluchow, Wilfrid 2, 207 n1, 213
  n9
weak existential
  mind-independence
  of general legal norms 29–30,
    123–4, 126–8
  unanimity not usually required
    by 121–2
weak mind-independence
  120–30
Weber, Max 9
White Russians 67, 68–9, 132
Wittgenstein, Ludwig 134–6, 212
  n10